THE

CULTURE

OF

DISBELIEF

How American Law
and Politics
Trivialize Religious Devotion

STEPHEN L. CARTER

BasicBooks
A Division of HarperCollins*Publishers*

Designed by Ellen Levine

93 94 95 96 ◆/HC 9 8 7 6 5

Library of Congress Cataloging-in-Publication Data

Carter, Stephen L., 1954–
  The culture of disbelief : how American law and politics
trivialize religious devotion / by Stephen L. Carter.
     p.   cm.
  Includes bibliographical references and index.
  ISBN 0–465–02647–8
    1. United States—Religion. 2. Law—United States—Religious
aspects. 3. Religion and politics—United States. I. Title.
BL2525.C367   1993
291.1'7'097—dc20   92-56168
                                                                  CIP

For Leah Cristina
and Andrew David,
who should be able to live in a world
that respects your choices
instead of tolerating them.
God bless.

CONTENTS

ACKNOWLEDGMENTS

THE intellectual odyssey that generated this book has been underway for a number of years, often in fits and starts. An earlier and much shorter version of chapter 9 appeared in the *Duke Law Journal* in 1987, under the title "Evolutionism, Creationism, and Treating Religion as a Hobby." A quite different version of chapter 11 appeared in the *Oregon Law Review* in 1990 under the title "Scientific Liberalism, Scientistic Law." Both articles were based on lectures that I delivered. Also, a small part of chapter 10 previously appeared in *Constitution* magazine.

As to the rest, some of the arguments, or the ideas underlying them, were previously presented as lectures or workshops at New York Law School, Williams College, Yale College, and the law schools of the following institutions: Boston University, University of Chicago, University of Cincinnati, Cornell University, University of Dayton, George Washington University, New York University, Northwestern University, University of Notre Dame, University of Oklahoma, Southern Methodist University, University of Virginia, College of William and Mary, and Yale University. I am very grateful in each instance to my hosts and to the many listeners who aided me with keen and thoughtful questions. Some of the lectures were published in the law reviews of the host institutions. Several of the underlying themes were also the bases of presentations on panels organized by the Episcopal Church at Yale, the Law and Religion Section of the Association of American Law Schools, and the American Society for Political and Legal Philosophy.

For their comments on all or part of the manuscript, I am particularly indebted to Bruce Ackerman, Akhil Amar, Boris Bittker, Guido Calabresi, Lisle Carter, Jesse Choper, Kent Greenawalt, Martin Guggenheim, Emily Fowler Hartigan, Stanley Ingber, George Jones, Dean M. Kelley, Douglas Laycock, Paul Marshall, Michael McConnell, Michael Perry, and Philip Turner. I am also grateful to those whose pointed questions at lectures or workshops over the past several years caused me to rethink substantial portions of what I wrote, including Lea Brilmayer, Walter Dellinger, Rochelle Dreyfuss, Stanley Fish, Michael Graetz, Anita Hill, Ira Lupu, Tom Nagel, John Robinson, and Carol Rose, along with many others whose names, I fear, I never learned or have forgotten. I have also had the benefit of extensive comments from my literary agent, Lynn Nesbit, and my editors, Martin Kessler, Jane Judge, and Adrienne Mayor. Over the past several years, I have also had the benefit of splendid research assistance from Yasmin Cader, Riel Faulkner, Dina Friedman, Phyllis Griffin, Carla Jones, J. Donald Moorehead, Denise Morgan, Lewis Peterson, Sushma Soni, and Christopher Wray.

Finally, as always, my greatest reliance, for intellectual critique as well as for spiritual and emotional support, has been upon my wife, Enola Aird. Her love, and the love of our children, Leah Cristina Aird Carter and Andrew David Aird Carter, and the opportunity to love them all, are a blessing from God that I do not deserve.

Hamden, Connecticut
June 1993

AUTHOR'S NOTE

All scriptural quotations in this book
are taken from the
New Revised Standard Version of the Holy Bible.

I

THE
SEPARATION
OF
FAITH AND SELF

1

The Culture of Disbelief

CONTEMPORARY American politics faces few greater dilemmas than deciding how to deal with the resurgence of religious belief. On the one hand, American ideology cherishes religion, as it does all matters of private conscience, which is why we justly celebrate a strong tradition against state interference with private religious choice. At the same time, many political leaders, commentators, scholars, and voters are coming to view any religious element in public moral discourse as a tool of the radical right for reshaping American society. But the effort to banish religion for politics' sake has led us astray: In our sensible zeal to keep religion from dominating our politics, we have created a political and legal culture that presses the religiously faithful to be other than themselves, to act publicly, and sometimes privately as well, as though their faith does not matter to them.

Recently, a national magazine devoted its cover story to an investigation of prayer: how many people pray, how often, why, how, and for what. A few weeks later came the inevitable letter from a disgruntled reader, wanting to know why so much space had been dedicated to such nonsense.[1]

Statistically, the letter writer was in the minority: by the magazine's figures, better than nine out of ten Americans believe in God and some four out of five pray regularly.[2] Politically and culturally, however, the writer was in the American mainstream, for those who do pray regularly—indeed, those who believe in God—are encouraged to keep it a secret, and often a shameful one at that. Aside from the ritual appeals to God that are expected of our politicians, for Americans to take their religions seriously, to treat them as ordained rather than chosen, is to risk assignment to the lunatic fringe.

Yet religion matters to people, and matters a lot. Surveys indicate that Americans are far more likely to believe in God and to attend worship services regularly than any other people in the Western world. True, nobody prays on prime-time television unless religion is a part of the plot, but strong majorities of citizens tell pollsters that their religious beliefs are of great importance to them in their daily lives. Even though some popular histories wrongly assert the contrary, the best evidence is that this deep religiosity has always been a facet of the American character and that it has grown consistently through the nation's history.[3] And today, to the frustration of many opinion leaders in both the legal and political cultures, religion, as a moral force and perhaps a political one too, is surging. Unfortunately, in our public life, we prefer to pretend that it is not.

Consider the following events:

- When Hillary Rodham Clinton was seen wearing a cross around her neck at some of the public events surrounding her husband's inauguration as President of the United States, many observers were aghast, and one television commentator asked whether it was appropriate for the First Lady to display so openly a religious symbol. But if the First Lady can't do it, then certainly the President can't do it, which would bar from ever holding the office an Orthodox Jew under a religious compulsion to wear a yarmulke.

- Back in the mid-1980s, the magazine *Sojourners*—published by politically liberal Christian evangelicals—found itself in the unaccustomed position of defending the conservative evangelist Pat Robertson against secular liberals who, a writer in the magazine sighed, "see[m] to consider Robertson a dangerous neanderthal because he happens to believe that God can heal diseases."[4] The point is that the editors of *Sojourners,* who are no great admirers of Robertson, also believe that God can heal diseases. So do tens of millions of Americans. But they are not supposed to say so.

- In the early 1980s, the state of New York adopted legislation that, in effect, requires an Orthodox Jewish husband seeking a civil divorce to give his wife a *get*—a religious divorce—without which she cannot remarry under Jewish law. Civil libertarians attacked the statute as unconstitutional. Said one critic, the "barriers to remarriage erected by religious law . . . only exist in the minds of those who believe in the religion."[5] If the barriers are religious, it seems, then they are not real barriers, they are "only" in the woman's mind—perhaps even a figment of the imagination.

- When the Supreme Court of the United States, ostensibly the final refuge of religious freedom, struck down a Connecticut statute requiring employers to make efforts to allow their employees to observe the sabbath, one Justice observed that the sabbath should not be singled out because all employees would like to have "the right to select the day of the week in which to refrain from labor."[6] Sounds good, except that, as one scholar has noted, "It would come as some surprise to a devout Jew to find that he has 'selected the day of the week in which to refrain from labor,' since the Jewish people have been under the impression for some 3,000 years that this choice was made by God."[7] If the sabbath is just another day off, then religious choice is essentially arbitrary and unimportant; so if one sabbath day is inconvenient, the religiously devout employee can just choose another.

- When President Ronald Reagan told religious broadcasters in 1983 that all the laws passed since biblical times "have not improved on the Ten Commandments one bit," which might once have been considered a pardonable piece of rhetorical license, he was excoriated by political pundits, including one who charged angrily that Reagan was giving "short shrift to the secular laws and institutions that a president is charged with protecting."[8] And as for the millions of Americans who consider the Ten Commandments the fundaments on which they build their lives, well, they are no doubt subversive of these same institutions.

These examples share a common rhetoric that refuses to accept the notion that rational, public-spirited people can take religion seriously. It might be argued that such cases as these involve threats to the separation of church and state, the durable and vital doctrine that shields our public institutions from religious domination and our religious institutions from government domination. I am a great supporter of the separation of church and state, and I will have more to say about the doctrine later in the book (chapter 6)—but that is not what these examples are about.

What matters about these examples is the *language* chosen to make the points. In each example, as in many more that I shall discuss, one sees a trend in our political and legal cultures toward treating religious beliefs as arbitrary and unimportant, a trend supported by a rhetoric that implies that there is something wrong with religious devotion. More and more, our culture seems to take the position that believing deeply in the tenets of one's faith represents a kind of mystical irrationality, something that thoughtful, public-spirited American citizens would do better to avoid. If you must worship your God, the lesson runs, at least have the courtesy to disbelieve in the power of prayer; if you must observe your sabbath, have the good sense to understand that it is just like any other day off from work.

The rhetoric matters. A few years ago, my wife and I were startled by a teaser for a story on a network news program, which asked what was meant to be a provocative question: "When is a church more than just a place of worship?" For those to whom worship is significant, the subtle arrangement of words is arresting: *more than* suggests that what follows ("just a place of worship") is somewhere well down the scale of interesting or useful human activities, and certainly that whatever the story is about is *more than* worship; and *just*—suggests that what follows ("place of worship") is rather small potatoes.

A friend tells the story of how he showed his résumé to an executive search consultant—in the jargon, a corporate head-hunter—who told him crisply that if he was serious about moving ahead in the business world, he should remove from the résumé any mention of his involvement with a social welfare organization that was connected with a church, but not one of the genteel mainstream denominations. Otherwise, she explained, a potential employer might think him a religious fanatic.

How did we reach this disturbing pass, when our culture teaches that religion is not to be taken seriously, even by those who profess to believe in it? Some observers suggest that the key moment was the Enlightenment, when the Western tradition sought to sever the link between religion and authority. One of the playwright Tom Stoppard's characters observes that there came "a calendar date—*a moment*—when the onus of proof passed from the atheist to the believer, when, quite suddenly, the noes had it."[9] To which the philosopher Jeffrey Stout appends the following comment: "If so, it was not a matter of majority rule."[10] Maybe not—but a strong undercurrent of contemporary American politics holds that religion must be kept in its proper place and, still more, in proper perspective. There are, we are taught by our opinion leaders, religious matters and important matters, and disaster arises when we confuse the two. Rationality, it seems, consists in getting one's priorities straight. (Ignore your religious law and marry at leisure.) Small wonder, then, that we have recently been treated to a book, coauthored by two therapists, one of them an ordained minister, arguing that those who would put aside, say, the needs of their families in order to serve their religions are suffering from a malady the authors call "toxic faith"—for no normal person, evidently, would sacrifice the things that most of us hold dear just because of a belief that God so intended it.[11] (One wonders how the authors would have judged the toxicity of the faith of Jesus, Moses, or Mohammed.)

We are trying, here in America, to strike an awkward but necessary balance, one that seems more and more difficult with each passing year. On the one hand, a magnificent respect for freedom of conscience, including the freedom of religious belief, runs deep in our political ideology. On the other hand, our understandable fear of religious domination of politics presses us, in our public personas, to be wary of those who take their religion too seriously. This public balance reflects our private selves. We are one of the most religious nations on earth, in the sense that we have a deeply religious citizenry; but we are also perhaps the most zealous in guarding our public institutions against explicit religious influences. One result is that we often ask our citizens to split their public and private selves, telling them in effect that it is fine to be religious in private, but there is something askew when those private beliefs become the basis for public action.

We teach college freshmen that the Protestant Reformation began the process of freeing the church from the state, thus creating the possibility of a powerful independent moral force in society. As defenders of the separation of church and state have argued for centuries, autonomous religions play a vital role as free critics of the institutions of secular society. But our public culture more and more prefers religion as something without political significance, less an independent moral force than a quietly irrelevant moralizer, never heard, rarely seen. "[T]he public sphere," writes the theologian Martin Marty, "does not welcome explicit Reformed witness—or any other particularized Christian witness."[12] Or, for that matter, any religious witness at all.

Religions that most need protection seem to receive it least. Contemporary America is not likely to enact legislation aimed at curbing the mainstream Protestant, Roman Catholic, or Jewish faiths. But Native Americans, having once been hounded from their lands, are now hounded from their religions, with the complicity of a Supreme Court untroubled when sacred lands are taken for road building or when Native Americans under a bona fide religious compulsion to use peyote in their rituals are punished under state antidrug regulations.[13] (Imagine the brouhaha if New York City were to try to take St. Patrick's Cathedral by eminent domain to build a new convention center, or if Kansas, a dry state, were to outlaw the religious use of wine.) And airports, backed by the Supreme Court, are happy to restrict solicitation by devotees of Krishna Consciousness, which travelers, including this one, find irritating.[14] (Picture the response should the airports try to regulate the wearing of crucifixes or yarmulkes on similar grounds of irritation.)

The problem goes well beyond our society's treatment of those who simply want freedom to worship in ways that most Americans find troubling. An analagous difficulty is posed by those whose religious convictions move them to action in the public arena. Too often, our rhetoric treats the religious impulse to public action as presumptively wicked—indeed, as necessarily oppressive. But this is historically bizarre. Every time people whose vision of God's will moves them to oppose abortion rights are excoriated for purportedly trying to impose their religious views on others, equal calumny is implicitly heaped upon the mass protest wing of the civil rights movement, which was openly and unashamedly religious in its appeals as it worked to impose its moral vision on, for example, those who would rather segregate their restaurants.

One result of this rhetoric is that we often end up fighting the wrong battles. Consider what must in our present day serve as the ultimate example of religion in the service of politics: the 1989 death sentence pronounced by the late Ayatollah Ruhollah Khomeini upon the writer Salman Rushdie for his authorship of *The Satanic Verses,* which was said to blaspheme against Islam. The death sentence is both terrifying and outrageous, and the Ayatollah deserved all the fury lavished upon him for imposing it. Unfortunately, for some critics the facts that the Ayatollah was a religious leader and that the "crime" was a religious one lends the sentence a particular monstrousness; evidently they are under the impression that writers who are murdered for their ideas are choosy about the motivations of their murderers, and that those whose writings led to their executions under, say, Stalin, thanked their lucky stars at the last instant of their lives that Communism was at least godless.

To do battle against the death sentence for Salman Rushdie—to battle against the Ayatollah—one should properly fight against official censorship and intimidation, not against religion. We err when we presume that religious motives are likely to be illiberal, and we compound the error when we insist that the devout should keep their religious ideas—whether good or bad—to themselves. We do no credit to the ideal of religious freedom when we talk as though religious belief is something of which public-spirited adults should be ashamed.

The First Amendment to the Constitution, often cited as the place where this difficulty is resolved, merely restates it. The First Amendment guarantees the "free exercise" of religion but also prohibits its "establishment" by the government. There may have been times in our history when we as a nation have tilted too far in one direction, allowing too much religious sway over politics.

But in late-twentieth-century America, despite some loud fears about the influence of the weak and divided Christian right, we are upsetting the balance afresh by tilting too far in the other direction—and the courts are assisting in the effort. For example, when a group of Native Americans objected to the Forest Service's plans to allow logging and road building in a national forest area traditionally used by the tribes for sacred rituals, the Supreme Court offered the back of its hand. True, said the Justices, the logging "could have devastating effects on traditional Indian religious practices." But that was just too bad: "government simply could not operate if it were required to satisfy every citizen's religious needs and desires."[15]

A good point: but what, exactly, are the protesting Indians left to do? Presumably, now that their government has decided to destroy the land they use for their sacred rituals, they are free to choose new rituals. Evidently, a small matter like the potential destruction of a religion is no reason to hault a logging project. Moreover, had the government decided instead to prohibit logging in order to preserve the threatened rituals, it is entirely possible that the decision would be challenged as a forbidden entanglement of church and state. Far better for everyone, it seems, for the Native Americans to simply allow their rituals to go quietly into oblivion. Otherwise, they run the risk that somebody will think they actually take their rituals seriously.

THE PRICE OF FAITH

When citizens do act in their public selves as though their faith matters, they risk not only ridicule, but actual punishment. In Colorado, a public school teacher was ordered by his superiors, on pain of disciplinary action, to remove his personal Bible from his desk where students might see it. He was forbidden to read it silently when his students were involved in other activities. He was also told to take away books on Christianity he had added to the classroom library, although books on Native American religious traditions, as well as on the occult, were allowed to remain. A federal appeals court upheld the instruction, explaining that the teacher could not be allowed to create a religious atmosphere in the classroom, which, it seems, might happen if the students knew he was a Christian.[16] One wonders what the school, and the courts, might do if, as many Christians do, the teacher came to school on Ash Wednesday with ashes in the shape of a cross imposed on his forehead—would he be required to wash them off? He just might. Early in 1993, a judge required a prosecutor arguing a case on Ash Wednesday to clean the ashes from his forehead, lest the jury be influenced by its knowledge of the prosecutor's religiosity.

Or suppose a Jewish teacher were to wear a yarmulke in the classroom. If the school district tried to stop him, it would apparently be acting within its authority. In 1986, after a Jewish Air Force officer was disciplined for wearing a yarmulke while on duty, in violation of a military rule against wearing headgear indoors, the Supreme Court shrugged: "The desirability of dress regulations in the military is decided by the appropriate military officials," the Justices explained, "and they are under no constitutional mandate to abandon their considered professional judgment."[17] The Congress quickly enacted legislation permitting the wearing of religious apparel while in uniform as long as "the wearing of the item would [not] interfere with the performance of the member's military duties," and—interesting caveat!—as long as the item is "neat and conservative."[18] Those whose faiths require them to wear dreadlocks and turbans, one supposes, need not apply to serve their country, unless they are prepared to change religions.

Consider the matter of religious holidays. One Connecticut town recently warned Jewish students in its public schools that they would be charged with *six* absences if they missed two days instead of the officially allocated one for Yom Kippur, the holiest observance in the Jewish calendar. And Alan Dershowitz of Harvard Law School, in his controversial book *Chutzpah,* castigates Harry Edwards, a Berkeley sociologist, for scheduling an examination on Yom Kippur, when most Jewish students would be absent. According to Dershowitz's account, Edwards answered criticism by saying: "That's how I'm going to operate. If the students don't like it, they can drop the class." For Dershowitz, this was evidence that "Jewish students [are] second-class citizens in Professor Edwards's classes."[19] Edwards has heatedly denied Dershowitz's description of events, but even if it is accurate, it is possible that Dershowitz has identified the right crime and the wrong villain. The attitude that Dershowitz describes, if it exists, might reflect less a personal prejudice against Jewish students than the society's broader prejudice against religious devotion, a prejudice that masquerades as "neutrality." If Edwards really dared his students to choose between their religion and their grade, and if that meant that he was treating them as second-class citizens, he was still doing no more than the courts have allowed all levels of government to do to one religious group after another—Jews, Christians, Muslims, Sikhs, it matters not at all. The consistent message of modern American society is that whenever the demands of one's religion conflict with what one has to do to get ahead, one is expected to ignore the religious demands and act . . . well . . . *rationally.*

Consider Jehovah's Witnesses, who believe that a blood transfusion from one human being to another violates the biblical prohibition on ingesting blood. To accept the transfusion, many Witnesses believe, is to lose, perhaps forever, the possibility of salvation. As the Witnesses understand God's law, moreover, the issue is not whether the blood transfusion is given against the recipient's will, but whether the recipient is, at the time of the transfusion, actively protesting. This is the reason that Jehovah's Witnesses sometimes try to impede the physical access of medical personnel to an unconscious Witness: lack of consciousness is no defense. This is also the reason that Witnesses try to make the decisions on behalf of their children: a child cannot be trusted to protest adequately.

The machinery of law has not been particularly impressed with these arguments. There are many cases in which the courts have allowed or ordered transfusions to save the lives of unconscious Witnesses, even though the patient might have indicated a desire while conscious not to be transfused.* The machinery of modern medicine has not been impressed, either, except with the possibility that the Witnesses have gone off the deep end; at least one hospital's protocol apparently requires doctors to refer protesting Witnesses to psychiatrists.[20] Although the formal text of this requirement states as the reason the need to be sure that the Witness knows what he or she is doing, the subtext is a suspicion that the patient was not acting rationally in rejecting medical advice for religious reasons. After all, there is no protocol for packing *consenting* patients off to see the psychiatrist. But then, patients who consent to blood transfusions are presumably acting rationally. Perhaps, with a bit of gentle persuasion, the dissenting Witness can be made to act rationally too—even if it means giving up an important tenet of the religion.

And therein lies the trouble. In contemporary American culture, the religions are more and more treated as just passing beliefs—almost as fads, older, stuffier, less liberal versions of so-called New Age—rather than as the fundaments upon which the devout build their lives. (The noes have it!) And if religions *are* fundamental, well, too bad—at least if they're the *wrong* fundaments—if they're inconvenient, give them up! If you can't remarry because you have the wrong religious belief, well, hey, believe something else! If you can't take your exam because of a Holy Day, get a new Holy Day! If the government decides to

---

* In every decided case that I have discovered involving efforts by Jehovah's Witness parents to prevent their children from receiving blood transfusions, the court has allowed the transfusion to proceed in the face of parental objection. I say more about transfusions of children of Witnesses, and about the rights of parents over their children's religious lives, in chapter 11.

destroy your sacred lands, just make some other lands sacred! If
you must go to work on your sabbath, it's no big deal! It's just a
day off! Pick a different one! If you can't have a blood transfusion because you think God forbids it, no problem! Get a new
God! And through all of this trivializing rhetoric runs the subtle
but unmistakable message: pray if you like, worship if you must,
but whatever you do, do not on any account take your religion
seriously.

That rhetoric, and that message, are the subjects of this
book. This book is not about law, but about attitudes—the attitude that we as a political society hold toward religion. It is not a
call to tear down the wall between church and state or to impose
oppressive religious regimes on each other willy-nilly. It is an
effort to understand our instincts and our rules and our rhetoric,
to figure out why it is that religion is seen as worse than other
forces that mold people's minds, and to try to discover whether
there might be a way to preserve the separation of church and
state without trivializing faith as we do today.

In the pages to follow, I will present the case for taking religion seriously as an aspect of the lives and personas of the tens
of millions of Americans who insist that religion is for them of
first importance. I will, in the process, take up a number of social
issues that often generate fierce religious debate. On many issues,
I defend outcomes that are the same ones that our secular culture
reaches. For example, I support the ban on organized public
school prayer and the refusal to teach scientific creationism in the
biology classroom. But I hope to defend these positions without
resort to the antireligious fervor that often characterizes the liberal
case. In other situations, I defend positions that liberals tend to
reject—for example, broad parental rights to exempt children
from educational programs on religious grounds and participation
by parochial schools in private school voucher programs—but I
hope to do so without resort to the sort of liberal-bashing that
often characterizes the rhetoric of the religious right.

In the first part of the book, chapters 2 through 5, I assess and seek to understand some of the many ways in which our culture has come to belittle religious devotion, to humiliate believers, and, even if indirectly, to discourage religion as a serious activity. I explain how democracy is best served when the religions are able to act as independent moral voices interposed between the citizen and the state, and how our tendency to try to wall religion out of public debate makes that role a harder one to play. At the outset, I argue that we should stop the steady drumbeat, especially in our popular culture, for the proposition that the religiously devout are less rational than more "normal" folks and that we should avoid the pat assumption, all too common in our rhetoric, that religion is more dangerous than other forces in American society and must therefore be more carefully reined in (chapter 2). I point out how politicians on both right and left, by trying to turn God into a supporter, and with the connivance of religious leaders, have contributed to this trivialization (chapters 3 and 4). I also assess the risk that the more powerful religions might try to oppress the less powerful, a legitimate fear too often ignored by those who complain that secularism is growing too dominant, but sometimes exaggerated by those who insist that religions are inherently dangerous (chapter 5).

The second part of the book, chapters 6 through 10, discusses the constitutional status of American religion. I strongly defend the separation of church and state, but insist that it is possible to maintain that crucial separation while treating religious beliefs with respect, and treating religious believers as something other than irrational (chapter 6). My principal solution is for the courts and the society they serve to ensure that legislation does not infringe on religious freedom unless the burden is absolutely essential (chapter 7)—a tricky problem that I pursue by examining the treatment of religious objections to laws against discrimination and other regulations of the welfare state (chapter 8). I further investigate the constitutional issues by entering the quagmire of the role of religion in public education. The battle over the teaching of scientific creationism is a backdrop for a discussion of whether, as critics charge, the classroom has become hostile to religion (chapter 9), and whether we can find better ways to deal with the religious concerns of parents (chapter 10).

The third part of the book offers a criticism of liberal political theory for its treatment of religion and offers a brief sketch of a more sensitive alternative (chapter 11). I use this alternative to consider the way religion should figure in policy debates over issues that require us to define and place value on life—euthanasia, abortion, and the death penalty (chapter 12). The concluding chapter (chapter 13) warns of the dangers of religious dominance and also sketches a series of possible futures for our law and politics, depending on what attitudes toward religious belief we as a society choose to adopt.

SOME DEFINITIONS

It will be useful before proceeding to pause for some definitions and clarifications. When I refer to religion, I will have in mind a tradition of group worship (as against individual metaphysic) that presupposes the existence of a sentience beyond the human and capable of acting outside of the observed principles and limits of natural science, and, further, a tradition that makes demands of some kind on its adherents. I emphasize the group because, as will become clear, the most difficult problems in the relationship of religion to our political and legal cultures arise because of conflicts that will often develop between the understanding of reality conveyed by the state and the very different understanding developed by a religious community struggling together toward the ultimate.[21] It makes no difference whether the tradition in question believes that supernatural events actually occur or that this sentience cares about, or even pays attention to, the human realm, as long as, in the words of William James, it involves human beings "as they apprehend themselves to stand in relation to whatever they consider divine," and as long as, as Emile Durkheim put it, the people involved "share beliefs and practices relative to sacred things," which combine to unite them "into a single moral community."[22]

Some scholars object to efforts at defining religion, and their words tend to be firm. "[A]ny definition of religion would seem to violate religious freedom in that it would dictate to religions, past and future, what they must be," writes one.[23] Another worries that "the very act of defining religion may impermissibly dictate the terms of a religion's form and existence."[24] The trouble is that it is not possible to have a conversation about religion unless I first make sure that the reader knows what I mean. I understand that the definition I have proffered excludes any number of competing traditions and thus represents a monstrous presumption—a federal court once bought itself serious scholarly criticism by choosing a definition similar to mine—but it is important to be clear.[25]

When I make reference to people who live faith-guided lives, I have in mind individuals who look to their religious traditions for instruction, or at least influence, not only about how they should behave, but about moral truth. Certainly there are religious traditions that do not make demands in the conventional sense, but adherents to those traditions rarely suffer the trivialization and abuse that I describe in this book. Also, when I refer to the religious mainstream, I have in mind the definition adopted by Wade Clark Roof and William McKinney in their classic study of America's mainline religions: "the dominant, culturally established faiths held by the majority of Americans."[26]

GOD-TALK

The reader might have perceived that many of the political examples I have discussed so far (although not the judicial ones) are situations in which the right is "using" religion and the left is fearful of its use. There are, as I note in chapter 4, just as many examples of the shoe on the other foot. However, there is a point here that serves as a subtext for much of what follows. In recent decades, religious argument has seemed largely a captive of the right, whereas the left, which once gloried in the idea that God stands for social progress, has more and more shied away from it. This imbalance may be less a result than a cause of the fact that more and more religiously devout people have come to see their natural home as the Republican party.

American liberals have made a grievous error in their flight from religious dialogue. Many observers attribute the Democrats' electoral difficulties during the 1980s to the relentlessly materialistic character of their campaign rhetoric. (Bill Clinton appears to represent change in this respect.) Of Michael Dukakis's devastating defeat by George Bush in 1988, Garry Wills observes: "For many Americans, the coldly technological 'Massachusetts miracle' was not only godless but the enemy of God."[27] Michael Lerner argues that liberals have "framed their intellectual commitments around a belief that the only things that *really* move people are economic entitlements and political rights"; they miss the fact that "human beings have a deep need to have their lives make sense, to transcend the dynamics of individualism and selfishness that predominate in a competitive market society and to find a way to place their lives in a context of meaning and purpose."[28]

Still, although the Democrats have generally ceded "God-talk" to the Republicans, one must be wary of attributing too much influence to the emergent religious right. The Reverend Pat Robertson's effort to gain the 1988 Republican presidential nomination was of interest mainly to the mass media, which continue to regard deep religious devotion as a troubling curiosity. With minor exceptions, the evidence that the much-feared Moral Majority, Inc., (now defunct) and other similar groups ever had much influence on actual government policy is thin (see chapters 3 and 13).[29] The journalist Mark Silk reports the reason for the group's demise: "By the time the elections of 1986 returned the Senate to the Democrats, Jerry Falwell had put the Moral Majority on hold and largely withdrawn from secular politics; his public backing now did candidates more harm than good."[30] As one observer has noted, "Clearly, the upsurge of fundamentalism in this country has not put the fear of God into General Motors."[31]

To be sure, Robertson's Christian Coalition, an umbrella group for conservative Christians that is far better organized than Moral Majority, has become a political force to be reckoned with, less because of the scary religious rhetoric of the 1992 Republican Convention than because of the success of many of the Coalition's candidates in local elections. (See chapters 5 and 13.) But ideological religious organizations, like other interest groups, ultimately will have impact only insofar as the issues that form the core of their political passions are issues about which millions of other citizens are also concerned. In other words, even if one thinks that the Christian Coalition's positions are a threat, no problem arises unless millions of voters share them. Given the general public revulsion at the calls for a jeremiad emanating from Houston during the 1992 Republican Convention, that is not currently a serious prospect.

Still, religious belief is resurgent in America, especially within religions that offer clear rules of right and wrong, such as those described as conservative and fundamentalist (which are not the same thing).[32] Despite repeated proclamations that religion has lost its importance, most Americans insist that their religious faith is a compelling force in making moral decisions. Thus liberalism, if it is to retain substantial political influence and demonstrate that the 1992 presidential election was no fluke, will have to find a better way to cope than simply saying to religious people, in effect, that they are superstitious primitives for believing that prayer can work.

It must be added, of course, that many of the examples I discuss in this book will square with a widely shared intuition—

that is, many readers will not immediately find them problematic. To the extent that the intuition is a suspicion of what might appear to be moves toward religious domination of our public institutions, it is one that I essentially share. If it is an intuition that is concerned about the world's, and the nation's, woeful history of oppression of disfavored religious groups, then it is an intuition to be celebrated, for religious pluralism and equality—*never* mere "toleration"—should be essential parts of what makes American democracy special.

At the same time, the intuition is worth considering in more detail, for it can press too far. In holding, as we must, that religion is part of the purely private arena that the state must never disrupt, we run the risk of disabling the religiously devout from working seriously in the realm of policy. I speak here not simply of arguments for or against the adoption of any *government* policy, although that will, of necessity, be part of my subject. My concern, more broadly, is with the question of what religiously devout people should do when they confront state policies that require them to act counter to what they believe is the will of God, or to acquiesce in conduct by others that they believe God forbids. The intuition of our contemporary political and legal culture is that they should do nothing. Sometimes, as with the Native Americans whose rituals were threatened by logging, the message seems to be that they should, if necessary, change their religion; but if they protest on religious grounds, they are somehow acting in an illiberal manner.

Thus, in some of its aspects, this intuition is what I mean most fundamentally to challenge, for it encourages a tendency to say of religious belief, "Yes, we cherish you—now go away and leave us alone." It is an intuition that makes religion something that should be believed in privacy, not something that should be paraded; and if religion *is* paraded, it is this same intuition that assures that it likely will be dismissed. This intuition says that anyone who believes that God can heal diseases is stupid or fanatical, and the same intuition makes sure that everyone understands that this belief is a kind of mystic flight from hard truths—it has nothing to do with the real world. The same intuition tells the religious that those things that they know to be true are wrong or irrelevant, as with the Jehovah's Witnesses who fear that they will be denied salvation if forced to accept blood transfusions. At its most extreme, it is an intuition that holds not only that religious beliefs cannot serve as the basis of policy; they cannot even be debated in the forum of public dialogue on which a liberal politics crucially depends.

The intuition says, in short, that religion is like building model airplanes, just another hobby: something quiet, something private, something trivial—and not really a fit activity for intelligent, public-spirited adults. This intuition, then, is one that in the end must destroy either religion or the ideal of liberal democracy. That is a prospect that can please only those who hate one or the other or both.

2

God as a Hobby

ONE good way to end a conversation—or start an argument—is to tell a group of well-educated professionals that you hold a political position (preferably a controversial one, such as being against abortion or pornography) because it is required by your understanding of God's will. In the unlikely event that anyone hangs around to talk with you about it, the chances are that you will be challenged on the ground that you are intent on imposing your religious beliefs on other people. And in contemporary political and legal culture, nothing is worse.

That awful phrase—"imposing religious beliefs"—conjures up images of the religious right, the Reverend Jerry Falwell's Moral Majority, the Reverend Pat Robertson's presidential campaign, the 1992 Republican Convention, and the rest comes out in a jumble of post-Enlightenment angst: We live in a *secular* culture, devoted to sweet reason. We separate church and state. We believe in tolerance. We aren't superstitious. Taking religion seriously is something that only those wild-eyed zealots do: Operation Rescue, blocking the entrances to abortion clinics . . . you know who we mean, those Christian fundamentalists . . . the evangelicals . . . the folks who want classroom prayer in public schools, but think that God doesn't hear the prayers of Jews . . . you know, those television preachers . . . those snake-charming faith healers . . . and John Cardinal O'Connor . . . and the "scientific" creationists . . . *Southern Baptists,* for goodness sake! The labels often seem to run together this way with no particular logic to them, and, to be sure, without any context either. (Trying to explain, for example, that Christian fundamentalists and Christian evangelicals are not the same usually just confuses matters more.) But there is a message in this miasma, and the message is that people who take their religion seriously, who rely on their understanding of God for motive force in their public and political personalities—well, they're scary people.

Not only scary, but maybe irrational too. After the 1992 Republican Convention, which filled the air with the kind of cruel and divisive rhetoric that gives religion a bad name, Tom Wicker of the *New York Times* was led to draw an analogy between the antics of the religious right and the Salem witch trials of three centuries past.[1] The comparison was apt, for the Salem trials, most historians now agree, rested on a societal distaste for those who were different, particularly when those who were different were women.[2]

Still, lurking beneath the surface of rhetoric of this kind is the sense that nobody in our technological century would be so irrational as to believe in witches as supernatural beings. (I should make clear that I don't believe in them either). But the jump from disbelief in the supernatural aspects of witchcraft to disbelief in the supernatural aspects of mainstream religion is a very small one. Back in the early 1980s, when Oral Roberts warned that God planned to call him home, as he put it, unless he raised the money he needed for his university, the media had a good laugh. Garry Trudeau drew a clever series of cartoon strips for *Doonesbury* wondering whether God, by threatening Roberts with death unless enough cash was forthcoming, now qualified as a terrorist.

Perhaps God did not in fact plan to call Oral Roberts home; as a Christian, I certainly had my doubts. What bothered me about the media response, however, was the thinly veiled suggestion that it was somehow *impossible* that Roberts had it right. He might be a charlatan, he might be a dupe, but one thing he was not—and this was quite clear—he could not be in actual touch with God. Newspapers sent reporters to Tulsa, Oklahoma, where the university is located, doubtless hoping for a good laugh, then seemed surprised when students shrugged. "Almost everything that happens around here is at some level supernatural," one explained. "They call it the miracle campus for a reason."[3]

Why should anybody have been surprised? To be devoutly religious, after all, is to believe in some aspect of the supernatural, whether the belief involves a certainty that God parted the Red Sea so that the Israelites could escape, a conviction that Jesus Christ is the Son of God and rules the universe as part of the Holy Trinity, or a sense that a powerful sentience beyond human ken is prepared, for whatever reason, to intervene in human affairs. Although many thoughtful sociologists and historians have defined religion in other ways, the belief in supernatural intervention in human affairs is a useful divider for our present purposes, because that is where the culture seems to draw the line between that which is suspect and that which is not.

The message of contemporary culture seems to be that it is perfectly all right to *believe* that stuff—we have freedom of conscience, folks can believe what they like—but you really ought to keep it to yourself, especially if your beliefs are the sort that cause you to act in ways that are . . . well . . . a bit unorthodox. Consider our general cultural amusement each time the Reverend Sun Myung Moon of the Unification Church holds one of his joint marriage ceremonies in which he weds thousands of couples simultaneously—always including some who have never met before, but were chosen for each other by the church. In Korea in the summer of 1992, some 12,000 couples were joined. Television commentators poked eager fun, and even the usually dead-pan *Wall Street Journal* found the occasion deserving of a bit of wry humor.[4] The idea seems to be that taking one's religion seriously is one thing, but letting one's church control the choice of a mate—a life companion—well, there a hint of irrationality creeps in. It is fine to be pious and observant in the small things, but marriage is serious! No normal person, evidently, would allow a religious leader to make so important a decision; and anyone who does so is worthy of ridicule. And therein hang two tales.

THE DEPROGRAMMING OF MARIA AUGUSTA TRAPP

The first tale involves our children. One of their favorite films is that much-beloved family classic, *The Sound of Music*. They have watched the videotape so often that my wife and I sometimes wonder whether there is a single line of dialogue that they have not committed to memory. We are glad they like the film, because it tells a clear, clean, spiritually uplifting story, in which the protagonists rely on wits and faith for their survival, instead of the ruthless destruction of the opposition that is today a staple of "children's" programming. Because the kids so enjoy the story and the music, we decided one fine June weekend to take them to visit the Trapp Family Lodge, nestled in the rolling green hills above Waterbury, Vermont. There, we thought, the children might learn about the connection—or, perhaps, the disconnection—between art and life. So off we went on a grand family outing. The children got a kick out of seeing the place where the *real* Maria and the *real* Baron Von Trapp once lived and walked and presumably even sang—and so, to top it off, we gave in to their pleas and bought Maria's autobiography (the story, so the cover proclaims, that inspired the musical).

What we learned from the autobiography was that Maria's religion was even more important to her than the film lets on. Because (she says this, right in the book) after she fell in love with Captain Von Trapp, she didn't just visit Mother Superior for a bit of sung advice about climbing every mountain and then make up her own mind, the way it happens in the musical. Oh, no. She went to visit Mother Superior and *asked her permission*. Not her advice, mind you, but her permission; Maria needed a yes or no.

The answer Maria received from Mother Superior took the following form: "We prayed to the Holy Ghost, and we held council, and it became clear to us . . . that it is the Will of God that you marry the Captain and be a good mother to his children." Did I say "permission"? This was virtually a command. Maria quotes her own nervous answer to the captain: "Th-they s-s-said I have to m-m-m-marry you-u!"[5] Not *I can if I want to*—but *I have to*. And had Mother Superior refused permission, so Maria suggests, she would never have married the Captain, which would have meant no spine-tingling escape from Austria following the *Anschluss,* no best-selling book, no singing career, no lodge in Vermont, no musical play, no Hollywood film. She would have had a different life altogether, all because of the decision (dare we say the whim?) of one individual, a religious leader, her Mother Superior.

Let us for a moment take Maria out of the mainstream and place her not in Roman Catholicism but in, say, the Unification Church; now imagine that the decision on whether she may marry the Captain rests in the hands not of Mother Superior but of the Reverend Sun Myung Moon. All at once her decision to consult with her religious superior before marrying takes on a cast either sinister or amusing, depending on one's preferences.

At that point, Maria Trapp believes *too* deeply; she becomes a weirdo.

Freud believed that deep religiosity was neurotic in nature, and many psychiatrists still do.[6] Robert Coles, in his fine book *The Spiritual Life of Children,* relates his frustration during his training in psychiatry when a troubled young girl who was tormented by "bad habits" that could be controlled only through prayer never got around to doing what his teachers said she inevitably would—she never admitted that she was really talking about sex, not religion.[7] Coles came to understand that religious commitments, whatever their characteristics, tend to be genuine expressions of human personality. Other therapists have not. That is why Stephen Arterburn and Jack Felton, in their 1991 book *Toxic Faith: Understanding and Overcoming Religious Addiction,* probably thought they were being progressive when they decided that some religious commitments were dysfunctional and others were just fine.

What would Arterburn and Felton have thought of Maria's decision to seek the permission of her religious leader before marrying the Captain? They do not tell us, exactly, but they do give us this account of some of the goings-on in one church's "toxic faith system": "The pastor, or shepard as he was called, had final say in everything in the lives of his flock: whether to buy a house, take a vacation, get married, and even whom to marry."[8] *Even whom to marry.* So if Maria really thought she could not marry without the approval of her Mother Superior, does that make the Catholic Church a kind of toxic faith itself, at least if people take it seriously?

America's discomfort, never slight, with religions that lie outside the mainstream seems to be at its zenith in matters touching procreation in general and marriage in particular. When the Supreme Court in 1879 sustained the authority of the state to prosecute Mormons for polygamy—which their religious doctrines allowed—one might suppose that the Justices were simply weighing the demands of religious freedom against the general regulatory power of the state. In fact, the Justices were reflecting the anti-Mormon fervor of the age, a fervor with religious roots and repressive results. Mormons, seen as blasphemers, were beaten and sometimes killed, their homes destroyed, their property stolen. Going off to Utah was of little help to the widely persecuted Mormons: "The West was no sanctuary," notes the historian Cushing Strout, "so long as Mormons persisted in their peculiarity."[9] The Supreme Court understood perfectly well that the Mormons could not be permitted to be different. Even if it was required by religious belief, the Court wrote, the practice of polygamy was "subversive of good order."[10] In other words, hatred of Mormons caused other people to act disorderly.

It has long been the American habit to be more suspicious of—and more repressive toward—religions that stand outside of the mainline Protestant–Roman Catholic–Jewish troika that dominates America's spiritual life.[11] Even within the acceptable mainline, we often seem most comfortable with people whose religions consist of nothing but a few private sessions of worship and prayer, but who are too secularized to let their faiths influence the rest of the week. This attitude exerts pressure to treat religion as a hobby: one does not talk about one's faith and one does not follow the rules of one's faith if they cause behavior that the society considers immoral, such as polygamy, or actually dangerous, such as handling poisonous snakes. At that point, what has already been reduced to the level of hobby becomes even worse: "subversive of good order."

So, what does one do about the Mormons, Maria Trapp, and other people intoxicated by faith—people who not only refuse to keep quiet about their beliefs, but actually place the demands of their religions above the secular society's demands of "good order"? When mocking them doesn't work, we have another way to deal with them. In most of the world, it would be called kidnapping. In our media-dominated secular society, however, it is dressed up with the fancy name of "deprogramming." The tales are luridly familiar: child X is drawn into a religious cult, pressured, coerced, and brainwashed, loses the power of independent judgment, turns over all of her worldly possessions to the church, and works to draw in and brainwash others. What, other than a similar effort by those who love her, could possibly pull her free of the cult's influence?[12]

For parents who watch in helpless pain as their children surrender free will to the regulation of some eccentric or repressive cult, the option of deprogramming must be attractive indeed. It takes a brainwashing, one might say, to undo a brainwashing. But just what is a cult? After all, Maria Trapp, well-known religious maniac who needed permission to marry, might be described as someone who has been drawn into a cult, even if her cult is a big and old and powerful one that does business under the name of the Roman Catholic Church. Roger Finke and Rodney Stark, in their 1992 book *The Churching of America, 1776–1990,* suggest defining a cult as a minority religion that is not a spinoff from a major religion. (The spinoffs, they say, are sects.) This definition carries no normative judgment. In popular usage, however, the term "cult" is used derisively. We envision something like the Branch Davidians, led by David Koresh, whose Waco, Texas, compound was the scene of a disastrous confrontation with law enforcement personnel early in 1993.

The psychiatrist Robert Jay Lifton, an expert on the problem of brainwashing and a critic of many cults but of deprogramming as well, argues that the cult problem "is best addressed educationally." According to Lifton, as public knowledge of cult tactics grows, "the elements of deception are less easy to maintain" and the decision on whether to enter a purported cult or not can therefore be a more informed one.[13] And no matter how evil outsiders may think a cult to be, the more informed the choice to enter it, the less justification for interfering with that choice later. To Lifton's evident frustration, many deprogrammers have cited his work on brainwashing to justify the tactics that he deplores.[14]

However, many of the people whose families wanted to deprogram them have a different view of matters. True, some of them recant after lengthy sessions with the deprogrammers (some have written sentimental accounts of the experience)[15] but many others have refused to give up their new beliefs. Of those, some have sworn out criminal or civil complaints against those to whom they refer as kidnappers. Although a number of jurisdictions have prosecuted deprogrammers for kidnapping their subjects, nearly all trials have ended in acquittals. (Several actions for civil damages against deprogrammers have apparently been successful.)[16]

Obviously, there are psychologically damaging cults and, just as obviously, there are people whose religious piety is a cloak for some neurosis. The trouble is telling which are which. We seem too ready to assume that people who surrender to their religious leaders authority over matters that most of us prefer to decide for ourselves must be on the edge of at least temporary insanity, especially when the religious leaders are outside of the mainstream religions. When people begin to sign over wages and property, when they leave family and community behind, we too often judge them as not just religiously eccentric (which is problematic enough) but as members of a cult.

Moreover, there remains that nettlesome question of just who defines the mainstream. One might conclude that the distinction between cults and bona fide religions should be left to the experts, but it is not clear who the experts are. Mainstream denominations understandably have a bias in the matter, and they often support anticult literature and organizations. At the other extreme, it is not clear that psychiatrists, given the profession's historical antipathy toward religious devotion, are in the best position to judge.

But the distinction matters if one is to take seriously the problem of cults. In Margaret Atwood's powerful novel *The Handmaid's Tale,* some of the techniques practiced by today's deprogrammers are used to get Roman Catholic nuns to recant. Within the fiction, this is entirely consistent, for Atwood sketches a society in which holding to Catholicism in the face of secular punishment is seen by others as more than eccentric—even a bit maniacal. (They compare the nuns to witches.) The novel, of course, is only fiction, but Atwood intended it as a warning, insisting that every oppressive practice she describes has been used by some society. And one cannot help concluding that the society that tries to make members of unpopular religious groups renounce their views is, unhappily, our own.

Even if (as is certainly true) some cults are every bit as evil as the culture paints them, our mainstream antipathy toward the religions we call cults has gone a bit too far. Our tolerance for the practice of deprogramming supplies the evidence. We must not make the error of approving illegitimate means—kidnapping, psychological battering—because of the importance we attach to the end. Perhaps more imperative, we must resist the pressure to define what is outside of the mainstream, what is eccentric, as necessarily "subversive of good order." For unless one views the purpose of religion as making the mainstream comfortable, there will always be religious people—one hopes, lots of them—who are guided more by their faith than by the standards and demands of others, and who will therefore seem eccentric.

This brings us back to Maria Trapp. Had she grown up in today's America instead of Europe between the world wars, and had her religion not been Catholicism, perhaps she would never have gone to Mother Superior seeking permission to marry; more to the point, she might never have been a person of the sort who would go to Mother Superior for permission to marry. But if she had been the type to ask, and if she had done it, she would likely have been ridiculed for letting some religious leader control her personal life, much like the Western press poked fun at the 25,000 people who were married by the Reverend Sun Myung Moon. And if the ridicule did not persuade Maria to change, perhaps some well-meaning deprogrammer, hired by her worried parents, would have snatched her up and subjected her to psychological battering until she renounced her devotion to the eccentric, domineering Catholic cult. And this would have been sad, because it would have meant no book, no play, no film for our kids to enjoy.

And, incidentally, no religious freedom either.

RELIGIOUS AUTONOMY: THE PARADE PROBLEM

But what does religious freedom really mean? The answer may best be found by pursuing a concrete example, which is our second tale.

Early in 1992, the Ancient Order of Hibernians, the organizer of New York's traditional St. Patrick's Day Parade, created a stir when it refused to allow a group of gays and lesbians of Irish descent to join the march. The City of New York took legal action against the Hibernians, arguing that because the parade was on public property—Fifth Avenue, no less—it represented a form of public accommodation and was therefore subject to the city's human rights law, which prohibits discrimination on the basis of sexual orientation. Many in the city's thick community of civil libertarians, who in other circumstances favor gay and lesbian rights, rushed to the aid of the Hibernians, and with good reason. The Hibernians, by their charter, follow the dictates of the Roman Catholic Church, which considers homosexuality sinful, as it does nearly all forms of sexual activity for purposes other than procreation. Consequently, the decision to exclude the homosexual organization was defended as a religious choice by what is in effect a religious organization. After a flurry of litigation, the parade organizers prevailed, and so the parade was held the way they wanted it to be, which is for the best if one believes in religious freedom as a bedrock principle of our democracy.

Then in 1993, the City of New York took a different route, denying the Ancient Order of Hibernians the required parade permit and awarding it to another group that promised to hold a more inclusive celebration. The Hibernians sued, claiming that denial of the permit violated their First Amendment rights, and, in an opinion by Federal District Judge Kevin Duffy, won hands down. "Every parade is designed to convey a message," Judge Duffy wrote. "[A] parade organized by a private sponsor is the quintessential exercise of the First Amendment right of freedom of expression." The message that the Hibernians wished to convey was "to honor the patron saint of Ireland and to proclaim their allegiance to the Roman Catholic Church and its teachings." That the city found these teachings objectionable was no defense. On the contrary: "The First Amendment protects the right of individuals to hold a point of view different from the majority and to refuse to foster, in the way [the State] commands, an idea they find morally objectionable."[17] The end result, in fact, was a celebration of the First Amendment: the Ancient Order of Hibernians held the parade they wanted to hold, conveying the message they wanted to send; opponents protested, conveying the message *they* wanted to send, and 200 who blocked Fifth Avenue were arrested.[18]

Although the surface issue was discrimination, the underlying issue was autonomy: the religions, to be truly free, must be able to engage in practices that the larger society condemns. The state has a perfect right to send a message that it is wrong to discriminate on the basis of sexual orientation—a message with which I agree—but government must not be allowed to conscript private organizations, least of all religions, to assist. The fact that the litigation arose at all—and that the outcome was in question—signals how far the religions have come from the autonomous and independent role that the First Amendment tradition contemplates and democracy desperately needs.

What does it mean to say that religious groups should be autonomous? It means, foremost, that they should not be beholden to the secular world, that they should exist neither by the forbearance of, nor to do the bidding of, the society outside of themselves. It means, moreover, that they should be unfettered in preaching resistance to (or support of or indifference toward) the existing order.

Autonomy is often the missing element in America's confused relationships with its religions. Our tendency is to speak not of autonomy but of freedom: we talk about the freedom of people to worship, which is not quite the same as the freedom of religions, of corporate worship, to be left alone. We think of the rights of people to be religious, as though religion is simply another belief, a part of conscience; but the autonomy of the religions involves a recognition that what is most special about religious life is the melding of the individual and the faith community in which, for the devout, much of reality is defined.

Religions are in effect independent centers of power, with bona fide claims on the allegiance of their members, claims that exist alongside, are not identical to, and will sometimes trump the claims to obedience that the state makes. A religion speaks to its members in a voice different from that of the state, and when the voice moves the faithful to action, a religion may act as a counterweight to the authority of the state. This point is surely what John Courtney Murray had in mind when he wrote that rather than asking "whether Catholicism is compatible with American democracy," a Catholic must ask "whether American democracy is compatible with Catholicism."[19] That is why the Supreme Court was ironically right in 1879 to call the Mormons "subversive," and why segregationists were right in the 1960s to apply the same epithet to the Southern Christian Leadership Conference—for a religion, in its corporate self, will often thumb its nose at what the rest of the society believes is right.

Democracy needs its nose-thumbers, and to speak of the religions as intermediaries is to insist that they play important roles in the proper function of the republic. When Alexis de Tocqueville visited the United States early in the nineteenth century, he wrote, in *Democracy in America,* that the young nation's "religious atmosphere was the first thing that struck me on arrival in the United States." Indeed, Tocqueville claimed, America was "the place where the Christian religion has kept the greatest power over men's souls."[20] In Tocqueville's view, this meant that liberty was tempered by a common morality: "Thus, while the law allows the American people to do everything, there are things which religion prevents them from imagining and forbids them to dare."[21] Put simply, as political scientist Rogers M. Smith has noted, Tocqueville "believed that the support given by religious to virtuous standards of behavior was indispensable for the preservation of liberty."[22]

For Tocqueville, religions provided Americans with the strong moral character without which democracy cannot function; but, perhaps equally important, they helped to fill the vast space between the people and the government created in their name—a space, Tocqueville recognized, that the government might otherwise fill by itself. In many countries, Tocqueville noted, people relied upon the state to solve all problems, and concomitantly lost their liberty. But in America, things were otherwise. He was pleased to see that America had found in its plentitude of private associations, "associations in civil life which have no political object," a replacement for the aristocracy that once stood, in theory, as a bulwark against government tyranny: "The morals and intelligence of a democratic people would be in as much danger as its commerce and industry if ever a government wholly usurped the place of private associations," Tocqueville wrote. "Among democratic peoples associations must take the place of the powerful private persons whom equality of conditions has eliminated."[23]

Translating Tocqueville's observations to the present day (and removing his pro-Christian bias), one therefore sees two chief functions that religions can serve in a democracy. First, they can serve as the sources of moral understanding without which any majoritarian system can deteriorate into simple tyranny, and, second, they can mediate between the citizen and the apparatus of government, providing an independent moral voice. Indeed, from Tocqueville's day to contemporary theories of pluralism, the need for independent mediating institutions has been a staple of political science.

Although the influence of many intermediate institutions (particularly political parties, civic clubs, and state governments) has weakened over time, the continued vitality of intermediaries is crucial to preventing the reduction of democracy to simple and tyrannical majoritarianism, in which every aspect of society is ordered as 51 percent of the citizens prefer. Like other intermediate institutions, religions that command the devotion of their members actually promote freedom and reduce the likelihood of democratic tyranny by splitting the allegiance of citizens and pressing on their members points of view that are often radically different from the preferences of the state. As the theologian David Tracy has observed, "Despite their own sin and ignorance, the religions, at their best, always bear extraordinary powers of resistance. When not domesticated as sacred canopies for the status quo nor wasted by their own self-contradictory grasps at power, the religions live by resisting."[24]

Thus the very aspect of religions that many of their critics most fear—that the religiously devout, in the name of their faith, take positions that differ from approved state policy—is one of their strengths. Naturally the religiously devout see many things differently from the way their fellow citizens do. Taking an independent path—exercising what Tracy calls the power of resistance—is part of what religions are *for*. This is not only because of the belief, as one Christian evangelical has put it, that "a society succumbing to secularism demand[s] a comprehensive local and national witness."[25] It is also because, in the words of Harold Kushner, even if religion "can't change the facts about the world we live in . . . it can change the way we see those facts, and that in itself can often make a real difference."[26]

But religions can make a difference in how their adherents see the world only if they remain independent from the world. Thus, there is nothing wrong, and much right, when a religion refuses to accommodate itself to the policies that the state prefers. To insist that the state's secular moral judgments should guide the practices of all religions is to trivialize the idea that faith matters to people. When Martin Luther King, Jr., declared in his "Letter from Birmingham City Jail" that a "just law is a man-made code that squares with the moral law or the law of God," he was not bandying words; he was stating a bedrock commitment to the authority of God as *superior to* the authority of the state, a commitment on which much of the civil rights movement explicitly and enthusiastically rested.[27] Nowadays, such commitments are evidently suspect, the mark of the fanatic, especially when urged in service of positions often described as right wing; consider the popular image of the pro-life movement. But our culture cannot be so hypocritical in its protection of religious freedom as to endorse the intervention of the church against the state only in pursuit of expressly liberal ends.

At times, the Supreme Court has been the great protector of the autonomy of religions as faith communities, as, for example, when it sustained the right of Old Order Amish parents to take their children out of school after the eighth grade.[28] More often (as related in chapter 7), the Court has failed badly, allowing the state to run roughshod over religions in the interest of regulating for the general welfare, as, for example, when it allowed the state of Oregon to punish Native Americans for using peyote in a ritual that existed long before the antidrug laws.[29]

But American society should not depend on its courts as the sole or even the most important protectors of religious autonomy. Judicial authority extends to the bounds of, but not beyond, the Constitution. The nation's need for autonomous religions stands outside of that document; it is a need that flows from the nature (and the dangers) of popular democracy as a form of governance. To try to make the religions, in their internal organization, conform to the state's vision of a properly ordered society is not simply a corruption of the constitutional tradition of religious freedom; it is also an assault on the autonomy of religions as bulwarks against state authority.

The idea of religion as independent moral force is crucial both to the self-definition of faith and to the role of the religions as intermediate institutions to which citizens owe a separate allegiance. As autonomous intermediate institutions, the religions can work against the state; as partners with the state, they cannot. Writes Garry Wills, "That is one of the American paradoxes we can be most proud of—that our churches have influence because they are independent of any government."[30] And influence (which is not at all the same thing as authority) is precisely what we should want our churches to have, for that is how they serve democracy. It is for that reason—not an endorsement of discrimination—that the state would be wrong were it to seek to pressure the Roman Catholic Church to change its positions on abortion or homosexuality, just as it would have been wrong, back in the days of legally mandated racial segregation, for the state to press racially integrated congregations to "reform." The state would be wrong not because the positions of the Roman Catholic Church are necessarily the right ones in a secular moral analysis, but rather because the integrity of religious freedom should be inviolate; we too often forget that the principal purpose of the metaphorical wall of separation between church and state was always to prevent governmental interference with a religion's decisions about what its own theology requires.

Of course, this ideal of religious autonomy disables only the state—not the faithful. There is no threat to religious freedom when adherents to a faith press for change from within, whether on issues regarding the clergy or on anything else, which very often happens. In my own church, the Episcopal Church, the end to the long-standing bar on the ordination of women was accomplished because of pressure from the laity. Even if, as opponents have bitterly charged, the change came about through methods that are constitutionally suspect (I here refer to the constitution of the church),[31] it was, for many of us, a necessary change to move us as a church a tiny step closer to what we

hope and pray that God would want us to be. (See chapter 4.)
There was no other compelling justification. To be sure, the decision to allow women to respond to God's call by becoming
priests also was one that resonated with the nation's secular
moral position. But that is not by itself reason enough to change.

As a nation, we indulge the critical impulse of looking past
the wall that separates church from state and trying to describe
what happens inside a faith community in the terms that would
be appropriate were it to happen outside. Consequently, we
make a habit of referring to such religions as Catholicism and
Orthodox Judaism as relegating women to "inferior" positions
because they cannot be clergy.[32] (I admit I often share the
impulse and the habit.) But criticisms of this kind miss the point
of the religions as alternative sources of meaning for their adherents: the truth is that outsiders have no standpoint from which to
judge what counts as a "superior" or "inferior" position or,
indeed, whether the words have any meaning within the faith
community.[33] That is what it means to treat the religions as
autonomous communities of resistance and as independent
sources of meaning. That is why, had the organized Episcopal
Church not responded to pressure for the ordination of women,
the result might have seemed illiberal in secular political terms,
but it would not have been any of the government's business.

The same need for autonomy is what the City of New York
failed to respect—or, perhaps, to understand—in 1992 when it
sued the Hibernians and in 1993 when it tried to deny the group
a parade permit because of disagreement with Catholic theology.
In particular, it is crucial to the autonomy of the religions that
they be allowed to define their own creeds, their own members,
and their own senses of right and wrong. The matter of the gay
and lesbian marchers presented what seemed to many to be an
agonizing clash of plausible moral claims, but actually the
dilemma is quite easily resolved. True, one might perfectly well
argue that the liberal virtue of respect for persons means that it is
wrong to discriminate against people because of their sexual ori-

entation or their private sexual conduct, and I think the argument correct. That is why the state should enact and enforce appropriate legal protection for homosexuals against discrimination in the market—employment, housing, and the like. But religion is different. If the religions are to retain the autonomy that they are guaranteed both by the Constitution and by the liberal virtue of respect for individual conscience, then they must remain free to reject that argument on theological grounds—just as they must be free to reject capitalism or communism, racial equality or racial segregation, or any other state policy.

A religion, in this picture, is not simply a means for understanding one's self, or even of contemplating the nature of the universe, or existence, or of anything else. A religion is, at its heart, a way of denying the authority of the rest of the world; it is a way of saying to fellow human beings and to the state those fellow humans have erected, "No, I will *not* accede to your will." This is a radically destabilizing proposition, central not only to the civil resistance of Martin Luther King, Jr., and Mohandas Gandhi, but also to Operation Rescue, the activist anti-abortion group whose confrontational tactics are rejected by such moderate pro-life groups as the National Right to Life Committee.[34] The legal scholar Mark Tushnet has suggested that it is precisely this ultimate radical possibility of refusing to accept the will of the state that leads to America's political suspicion toward religious belief.[35] Perhaps so; for the nature of religion is finally not just to know, but to act, and to act at times without regard to what others consider the settled facts. "[A]bove all," David Tracy points out, "the religions are exercises in resistance. Whether seen as Utopian visions or believed in as revelations of Ultimate Reality, the religions reveal various possibilities for human freedom that are not intended for that curious distancing act that has become second nature to our aesthetic sensibilities."[36]

Religion, in short, *matters* to people; it is real, and so is its influence on human personality. For some, it is more real than the state, which explains why, for example, the fundamentalist

Christian movement for many decades preached an avoidance of politics, and why, until the 1970s, many fundamentalists could not be troubled to use their vote.[37] Certainly, to many, religion is more real, more alive, more vital than the good opinion of others, which is why Maria went to her Mother Superior for permission to marry and why many followers of the Reverend Sun Myung Moon are willing to grant him the same privilege. The essence of religious martyrdom is the sacrifice that comes from the refusal to yield to what one's society demands. Anyone who believes deeply is a potential martyr, for belief always entails a bedrock principle that will not yield.

The sense that the religously devout hold principles that they will not surrender to societal demand is one reason that so many contemporary theorists of liberal democracy either omit religion from their theories or assign it a subsidiary role. Today's political philosophers see public dialogue as essentially secular, bounded by requirements of rationality and reason. It is not easy to fit religion into that universe, which is why some religiously devout people find themselves at war with the dominant trends in contemporary philosophy (see chapter 11). In the words of Mark Tushnet, religion "poses a threat to the intellectual world of the liberal tradition because it is a form of social life that mobilizes the deepest passions of believers in the course of creating institutions that stand between individuals and the state."[38]

Mobilizes passions, Tushnet says—not *appeals to reason.* The difference is telling. The legal scholar Owen Fiss, musing about the philosopher Martha Nussbaum's work on alternatives to reason as bases for human judgment, issued the following warning: "To devalue passion when it misleads would not only be to neglect its actual place in our lives, but more significantly would transform it into something else, something akin to reason."[39] Similarly, there is real risk that the often sensible liberal concern about the role of religious leaders in public political debate will be at its nadir when the cause on behalf of which the leaders labor is most "progressive"—an approach that would transform religion into "something akin to reason," honored when it reaches right results, despised when it reaches wrong ones. Whereas religion is really an alien way of knowing the world—alien, at least, in a political and legal culture in which reason supposedly rules. The idea that a group of people will refuse to bow, either to law or to what some are bold to call reason, is, of course, a very subversive one in organized society. But religion, properly understood, *is* a very subversive force; subversive, at least, in a state committed to the proposition that religious ways of looking at the world do not count. No wonder, then, that our political culture seems to be afraid of it.

One way of coping with the fear is to try to brush off the religiously devout as fanatics, as is done with depressing regularity. Another way to deal with the fear of the subversive independence of the religions is to try to domesticate them, to demonstrate to the faithful that God is, after all, on the side of a particular political movement, whatever it might be. That, too, happens with depressing regularity, and is the subject of the next two chapters.

3

From Civil Religion to Civil Exclusion

B Y now, many a patient reader will be ready to argue that there is in contemporary America no trivialization of faith, no pressure to treat one's religious belief as a hobby—that, to the contrary, religion is ever-present in American politics and law, and its influence is growing. We read about it, we hear it, and, through the wonder of television, we *see* it—too much of it, some would say. Don't our politicians end every speech with "God bless you"? Don't religious leaders speak up constantly on whatever moral issues grab their attentions? Indeed they do, which is why the patient reader might insist that we lately have run a serious risk of breaching the wall of separation between church and that our courts for the past several decades have read into the First Amendment.

But having lots of public religion is not the same as taking religion seriously, and the presence of religious rhetoric in public life does not mean that citizens to whom that rhetoric is precious are accorded the respect that they deserve. In truth, the seeming ubiquity of religious language in our public debates can itself be a form of trivialization—both because our politicians are expected to repeat largely meaningless religious incantations and because of the modern tendency among committed advocates across the political spectrum to treat Holy Scripture like a dictionary of familiar quotations, combing through the pages to find the ammunition needed to win political arguments.

GOD-TALK

Take as a starting point a line from President George Bush's 1992 State of the Union Message: "By the grace of God," he said, "America won the cold war."[1]

By the grace of God: few phrases are as common in the mouths of political leaders, and why not? With these five short words, a politician conveys the sense of a people specially favored by the Almighty—quite flattering to one's constituents. At the same time, one wraps the mantle of godliness around one's policies. The message is not only that our faith in God helped us, but that God is on our side. We won the cold war not simply by God's grace, but by God's will; we won not only because God was with us, but, in effect, because God is one of us. The message, at bottom, is that God is an American—and maybe even a Republican.

The political year 1992 was a fascinating one for students of the relationship between religion and politics. Never did a political convention seem so relentlessly religious as the August 1992 convention of the Republican party. America's religious traditions were repeatedly invoked in support of the Republicans and in opposition to the Democrats, and several speakers described those traditions as "Judeo-Christian."[2] Once upon a time, broadening traditional references to America's Christianity to include Jews was probably thought progressive. Nowadays, though, that invocation can be more subtly nativist than broadly unifying. As Sanford Levinson has pointed out in a different context, "Hackneyed references to the 'Judeo-Christian' tradition will not prove attractive to growing Islamic communities in Detroit or Brooklyn." Nor does appending another name make necessary repairs: "[O]pportunistic reference to the monotheistic 'Judeo-Christian-Islamic' tradition will prove no more attractive to some of the religious communities of the Far East."[3]

Such problems as defining America's religiosity did not give the Republican speakers pause, however. Indeed, for all the references to the Judeo-Christian tradition, the rhetoric was better characterized as fairly conservative Christian. Former Bush adversary Patrick Buchanan, who called the nation to a holy war, was quite explicit in suggesting that George Bush, not Bill Clinton, was God's candidate. And President Bush himself, speaking to a rally during the convention, charged that the Democratic party platform had omitted the letters "G, O, D"—an echo of the Reverend Pat Robertson's remarks before the convention a few nights before: Clinton, said Robertson, "is running on a platform that calls for saving the spotted owl but never once mentions the name of God."[4]

Since the emergence of Jerry Falwell's Moral Majority as a short-lived political force in the 1980s, and with the burgeoning influence of Pat Robertson's Christian Coalition in the 1990s, the relationship between the Republican party and the religious right has been the subject of much vitriol, and much alarm. After the 1992 Convention, the alarms reached fever pitch. One political columnist warned, "Unless moderate Republicans understand the Houston convention as a wake-up call, . . . they'll find the GOP entirely in the hands not merely of conservatives, but of religious zealots."[5] (Moderate Republicans may be awake at last, for they have formed the Republican Majority Coalition with the avowed intention of saving their party from its right wing—just as the Democrats who formed the Democratic Leadership Council in the early 1980s sought to save their party from its left wing, and wound up electing a president.)[6] The *New York Times* editorialized: "It clanks with sanctimony when the Republicans insist on exclusive alignment with the Almighty."[7] The National Council of Churches (of which Bush's own Episcopal Church is a member) issued a strong denunciation of the attempt to cast the GOP as God's Own Party, warning that the Republicans stood on the threshold of blasphemy.

The conservative commentator William Safire, lamenting the growing number of political speeches that end with "God bless you and God bless America," asked after the 1992 Republican Convention, "[B]y what ecclesiastical authority do politicians, in holy alliance, bestow God's blessing on us and our country?" Seeking an answer, he hit the proverbial nail on its head: "The answer is that the name of the Lord is being used as a symbol for the other side's immorality, much as the American flag was used in previous campaigns as a symbol for the other side's lack of patriotism."[8]

In one sense, these criticisms are obviously deserved, if only because of the frighteningly antidemocratic (small *d*) character of the push by a national political party to replace secular politics with an appeal to religiosity. In a nation founded on the principle of religious liberty, it might even be called un-American to imply, as some at the Republican Convention did, that those with a different set of religious precepts deserve whatever they get. As a committed Christian, moreover, I have always been deeply offended by politicians, whether on the left or on the right, who are ready to seize on the language and symbols of religion in order to grub for votes. When members of the clergy use those symbols as divisively as they did in Houston, presuming to cast their opponents into the outer darkness, I tremble with anger—and, since that decision is not really within the scope of their ecclesiastical authority, I tremble as well for their souls.

Yet I am equally offended by suggestions that our politicians are wrong to discuss their views on the will of God, or that members of the clergy have no business backing what candidates they will, or that voters should never choose among candidates based on their religious beliefs. It is, of course, always fair game to criticize a political party for standing for the wrong causes, and many of the positions of the religious right are both morally and theologically objectionable; it is disturbing, however, to find that much of the criticism seems aimed at the fact that many activists are moved by religious commitments and talk about them freely, rather than the substance of the commitments themselves.

In 1976, a great outpouring of support from Christian evangelicals—theretofore scarcely noticed by the mainstream media—helped elect born-again Christian Jimmy Carter as president, and scarcely a whisper was heard about the impropriety of this vote. From the late 1950s through the mid-1970s, religious activists were at the forefront of many a political struggle (and, sometimes, many a political campaign) without being labeled witch-hunters.

The contemporary concern about the use of religious rhetoric to promote policy was not always a cultural norm, even in recent history. The civil rights movement provides only the most obvious example, for its leading public rhetoriticians were unapologetic about the open invocation of religious imagery. Consider the Reverend Martin Luther King, Jr.'s renowned "God Is Marching On" speech in Montgomery, Alabama, in which he called for "march[ing] on ballot boxes, until we send to our city councils, state legislatures, and the United States Congress men who will not fear to do justice, love mercy, and walk humbly with their God"—a biblical injunction (Micah 6:8) that sounds very much like the rhetoric of the religious right today deemed so alarming.[9] Certainly King and other religious leaders showed no reluctance to claim for their positions an "exclusive alignment with the Almighty." Nor is there any reason that they should have been reluctant, provided that they had come in a prayerful way to a sincere belief that they had discovered the will of God.

During the anti-Vietnam War movement of the sixties and seventies, for example, many liberal activists were driven by and publicly invoked deep religious commitments. From the Berrigans to William Sloane Coffin, some of the best-known antiwar figures were members of the clergy and freely invoked God's name. They were often criticized by conservative evangelicals—but only on the ground that they were taking the wrong position on the war. (*Christianity Today,* for instance, supported the war effort to the end, often in terms more hawkish than those of the government itself.) Rarely, however, were the religious antiwar activists accused of trying to take over the Democratic party for narrow religious ends. Probably the reason was that the causes in which the word of God was enlisted were causes that were more popular, particularly among the opinion makers who have ever since been dumping on Republicans for daring to mix church and state.

The trouble with the attacks on the 1992 Republican Convention is that most of them were misdirected. Understandable opposition to the *causes* that religious conservatives espoused and the Republican party endorsed—prayer in the public schools, severe restrictions on abortion, discrimination against homosexuals—was too often transformed into opposition to what is sometimes called *God-talk.* God-talk is public discussion in explicitly religious terms, rather than, for example, in the generalized spiritual terms with which Americans are often more comfortable. God-talk is what was going on at the Republican Convention. The civil rights movement involved God-talk in a vital cause. I believe that much of the God-talk of the religious right is very much the opposite. But if one dislikes the causes in which the name of God was invoked, it is those causes, not the God-talk itself that should have been the object of criticism. If on the other hand, one does believe that God-talk of all kinds should be forbidden, one had best be prepared to do battle on both political flanks—and to struggle against the weight of American history.

That is why one must be wary of pressing the criticism of the 1992 Republican Convention too far. As noted earlier, the National Council of Churches responded to the 1992 Republican Convention by calling it blasphemy "to invoke the infinite and holy God to assert the moral superiority of one people over another, or one political party over another." The council added: "Any partisan use of God's name tends to breed intolerance and to divide."[10] But these statements cannot be seriously meant. In 1948, the Democratic party was morally superior to the Dixiecrat party, which wanted to preserve the Southern racial caste system, and it is hard to see how a member of the clergy would have been committing blasphemy had he used the word of God to condemn the determination of the Dixiecrats to perpetuate the sin of racial segregation. The moral superiority of the Democrats over the Dixiecrats had nothing to do with the worth of the individuals involved in each and everything to do with the political positions for which the parties stood. In 1992, the political preachers who spoke on behalf of the Republican party—just like those who supported Ronald Reagan through two terms in office—were, in the same sense, claiming that the positions of one party were morally superior to the positions of the other. The National Council of Churches was surely right that God's name should not be used "to breed intolerance and to divide," and it was also right to point out that the Republican Convention's rhetoric did exactly that. But it was wrong to suggest that *any* partisan use of God's name tends to do so. It is quite enough for the council to criticize the *positions* espoused by those who invoked God's name in Houston (plenty of moral error there) without disputing the idea that one party might in fact stand for values that are closer than the other's to the will of God. The Republicans might have been mistaken in their claims—I am confident that on some points they were—but the reason is that I reject their interpretations of Scripture, not that it is morally impermissible for the faithful to use their religious understandings to guide political choice.

CLOTHING THE PUBLIC SQUARE

The arena in which our public moral and political battles are fought has come to be called "the public square," and Richard John Neuhaus, in his well-known book *The Naked Public Square,* tells us that in America, the public square has become openly hostile to religion.[11] I am not sure that Neuhaus has it quite right—nowadays, religion is treated more as a hobby than as an object of hostility—but he and other critics are surely correct to point out that the rules of our public square exist on uneasy terms with religion. We as a nation have come to accept, and even to expect, that our political leaders, when in the public square, will engage in what is known as "civil religion," famously defended by Robert Bellah[12] and nicely defined by Frederick Mark Gedicks as the utterance of "faintly Protestant platitudes which reaffirm the religious base of American culture despite being largely void of theological significance."[13] But the platitudes are important opportunities for cultural definition. "America's civil religion," writes sociologist Robert Wuthnow, "portrays its people, often in comparison with people in other countries, as God-fearing souls, as champions of religious liberty, and in many instances as a nation God has consciously chosen to carry out a special mission in the world."[14] This explains why no less a personage than the president of the United States concluded that America won the cold war by God's grace.

The platitudes of America's civil religion are expected and accepted—but they are only platitudes. They have no theology, except perhaps, as Wuthnow notes, a theology of "America First." It may be that we are comfortable with them precisely

because they demand nothing of us. Not only are they easily
ignored by those who happen to have no religious beliefs, but
they make virtually no demands on the consciences of those
who do. God is thanked for the success of an enterprise
recently completed or asked to sanctify one not yet fully begun.
God is asked to bless the nation, its people, and its leaders. But
nobody, in the civil religion, is asked to do anything for God.

We seem to be far less comfortable with religious people
who publicly invoke the name of God in ways more profound
than the ritualistic incantations of the civil religion. We are troubled when citizens who are moved by their religious understanding demand to be heard on issues of public moment and yet are
not content either to remain silent about their religions or to limit
themselves to acceptable platitudes. Our cultural discomfort does
not, perhaps, rise to the level of the hostility that Neuhaus and
others have observed—but it is not difficult to understand why
religious people seeking entrance to the public square might see it
that way.

Consider two examples. Imagine that you are the parent of
a child in a public school, and you discover that the school,
instead of offering the child a fair and balanced picture of the
world—including your lifestyle choice—is teaching things that
seem to the child to prove your lifestyle an inferior and perhaps
an irrational one. If the school's teachings are offensive to you
because you are gay or black or disabled the chances are that
the school will at least give you a hearing and, if it does not, that
many liberals will flock to your side and you will find a sympathetic ear in the media. But if you do not like the way the school
talks about religion, or if you believe that the school is inciting
your children to abandon their religion, you will probably find
that the media will mock you, the liberal establishment will
announce that you are engaged in censorship, and the courts
will toss you out on your ear. In fact, this happens all the time to
parents who profess religious objections to the curriculum, who
see the schools as encouraging their children to disregard what

they learn at home (see chapter 9). And whatever the grounds for the rejection of the parental protests (as we shall see, some argue that the Constitution requires it), one can understand why parents who feel their life choices threatened will not see the public square as an especially accommodating place.

The second example involves a talk I gave at the law school at the University of Notre Dame a few years ago—a talk in which I discussed some of the themes of this chapter. At a reception afterward, two law students came up to me to tell how their classmates mocked them when, in class, they opposed abortion. The two students were Catholics and were told by classmates that because of their religion, their moral opinions on this matter were out of bounds—and this at a Catholic university. Had they but reached their moral positions with no reference to their religious beliefs, these students believed, they would have been welcomed into the classroom's version of the public square. But since they were accused of invoking, in effect, a forbidden epistemology, they were not.

In this case, again, there are *reasons* that the public square is cautious about religion—reasons linked to history, linked to post-Enlightenment philosophy, linked to the Constitution. In chapters to come, I will have much to say about all of them. For the moment, however, the argument is narrower: from the point of view of religiously devout people whose consciences and visions of reality are influenced by faith, the public square can indeed seem a cold, suspicious, and hostile place. That the hostility might sometimes have a justification does not mean that the hostility is not there.

Many commentators dispute the idea that there is any animus to religion in the public square. Frequently they trot out counterexamples: "It is as if they [proponents of the hostility thesis] had missed the last three decades: the Moral Majority, the Reverends Billy Graham, Martin Luther King, Jesse Jackson, Pat Robertson, Jerry Falwell, Theodore Hesburgh, and others—all have taken their turns in the political limelight."[15] However, as

Kathleen Sullivan of Harvard Law School (who also rejects the hostility thesis) has noted, "The prominence of a few celebrated clergymen does not prove that religious freedom is alive and well, any more than the election of a few black mayors and the judicial internment of Jim Crow signalled an end to race discrimination."[16]

Indeed, the fact that some members of the clergy have attained political prominence may be a symptom of the problem, not evidence against its existence. Perhaps Americans who feel a deep sense of exclusion because they prefer to ponder moral questions in terms of their faith rush to support those few people in public life who seem to speak in language that appeals to just those religious instincts that citizens are often embarrassed to make central to their own public politics. This would explain the lionization of prominent preachers who are often quite ordinary as preachers go; more, it would explain the broad support among many religious people for Ronald Reagan.

Besides, to say that the public square is formally open—that it is not actually hostile and not really "naked"—is hardly the same as saying that religious witness is actually welcomed there. The legal culture that guards the public square still seems most comfortable thinking of religion as a hobby, something done in privacy, something that mature, public-spirited adults do not use as the basis for politics. The legal scholar Sanford Levinson, responding to remarks in which President Bush seemed to link the success of Operation Desert Storm to the New Testament, raised a question about the "propriety" of presidential God-talk: "That one has a legal right to articulate religious convictions in the public square does not mean that one ought to do so." As Levinson further explains, "many liberal theorists argue that one should voluntarily refrain from religious speech in a particular kind of liberal polity."[17]

His reference is to a burgeoning strand in American political theory holding that whatever grounds might lead citizens to their political views, the views must be justified in secular terms—that is, without regard to religion—when they enter the public square and urge other citizens to act. This, in turn, is part of a larger effort by the contemporary liberal* philosophers to create a conversational space in which individuals of very different viewpoints can join dialogic battle, in accord with a set of dialogic conventions that all can accept. The philosophical idea is that even though all of us have differing personal backgrounds and biases, we nevertheless share certain moral premises in common. If we then exclude what we do not have in common, what remains can be the basis for a conversation.

For example, the political scientist Stephen Holmes, in discussing what he calls "gag rules," argues that "[i]n a liberal social order, the basic normative framework must be able to command the loyalty of individuals and groups with widely differing self-understandings and conceptions of personal fulfillment." For Holmes, this is a reason that liberal theory must "steer clear of irresolvable metaphysical disputes."[18] Similarly, the legal theorist Bruce Ackerman has argued that the goal of dialogue is to "locate normative premises both sides find reasonable."[19] Thomas Nagel has called for a dialogue involving "the exercise of a common critical rationality" in which evidence for justification is limited to evidence that all can accept.[20] Unfortunately, all of these efforts to limit the conversation to premises held in common would exclude religion from the mix.[21]

For reasons I explain in detail later on (see chapter 11), I do not find this vision of the public square either welcoming or just. In brief, I would point out that the effort to place limits of this kind on dialogue is less likely to move many citizens to

---

* Here and, with some exceptions, throughout the book, I use the term *liberalism* to denote the philosophical tradition that undergirds the Western ideal of political democracy and individual liberty—a tradition that such conservatives as Robert Bork claim to represent no less than many prominent liberal intellectuals. This usage should not be confused with the polemical use of the term in contemporary politics to signify possession of a particular bundle of policy positions. On the rare occasions that I do mean the term *liberal* to be understood in contemporary political terms, the context will make it clear.

restructure their arguments than to silence them—or, perhaps (if history is any fair teacher) to move them to revolution. (No comments, please, about how people's willingness to kill and die for their religious traditions shows why those traditions must be kept out of the public square—after all, people are also willing to kill and die for freedom and equality.) In an electoral democracy, the revolution may be a peaceful one. The roughly half of Americans for whom religious tradition is very important in reaching moral decisions are, in the long run, likely to turn their backs on a liberal tradition that turns its back on what they cherish most.

I think the legal theorist Michael Perry has it right when he argues that forcing religious arguments to be restated in other terms asks a citizen to "bracket" religious convictions from the rest of her personality, essentially demanding that she split off a part of her self. Says Perry: "To bracket them would be to bracket—indeed, to annihilate—herself. And doing that would preclude *her*—the *particular* person *she* is—from engaging in moral discourse with other members of society."[22]

The point is that the proposed rules to govern discourse in the public square are constructed in a way that requires some members of society to remake themselves before they are allowed to press policy arguments. To suppose that this remaking is desirable, to say nothing of possible, reinforces the vision of religion as an arbitrary and essentially unimportant factor in the makeup of one's personality, as easily shrugged off as a favorite color when, for example, one is called upon to evaluate the views of a politician who never wears it.

HOW *ROE* CHANGED THE RULES

It is, in some ways, a strange and boisterously wonderful time to be an American. As the twentieth century marches toward its close, for the first time in its history America has begun to take halting steps toward an aggressive pride in its diversity, toward respecting and understanding its pluralism rather than dumping everyone into a simmering melting pot intended to boil us all down to a common essence. It is both tragic and paradoxical that now, just as the nation is beginning to invite people into the public square for the different points of view that they have to offer, people whose contribution to the nation's diversity comes from their religious traditions are not valued unless their voices are somehow esoteric. One thinks, for example, of the Colorado school district (mentioned in chapter 1) that ordered, with federal court approval, that the Bible and books on Christianity be removed from a classroom, while books on Native American religious traditions—and, for that matter, on the occult—were allowed to remain.[23] And then there is the prominent feminist who grumbled in the summer of 1991 that there are too many Catholics on the Supreme Court—discussing Roman Catholics the way that Pat Buchanan discusses homosexuals.[24] And consider the fact that for all the calls for diversity in the hiring of university faculty, one rarely hears such arguments in favor of the devoutly religious—a group, according to survey data, that is grossly underrepresented on campus.[25]

What is going on here in America, where religion was once thought to be so important that the Constitution was amended to protect its free exercise? This is an America that once gloried in the smart show of religion in the public square, most notably and most recently in the sixties, when the civil rights and antiwar movements were awash in openly and unapologetically religious rhetoric which politicians fell all over themselves to endorse, to emulate, and to amplify.

What has happened can be captured in one word: abortion. In 1973, the Supreme Court decided in *Roe v. Wade* that the right to privacy (which, despite some sniping, was firmly established in past decisions) was broad enough to encompass a pregnant woman's decision on whether to carry the pregnancy to term.[26]

For many religious conservatives, *Roe* was like a cold shower. All at once, the nascent pro-life movement (which actually began a few years before *Roe*, as a response to efforts to liberalize abortion laws) exploded into the national prominence. The very same Christian fundamentalists who had preached for decades that their followers should ignore the secular world, perhaps not even vote,[27] looked around and decided that the secular world was on the verge of destroying the tight religious cocoons in which they had bound their communities. The Roman Catholic Church saw a nation that had suddenly committed itself to the destruction of lives that the church had, for centuries, called sacred. And so the public rhetoric of religion, which from the time of the abolitionist movement through the era of the "social gospel" and well into the 1960s and early 1970s had largely been the property of liberalism, was all at once—and quite thunderously, too—the special province of people fighting for a cause that the left considered an affront. Since the 1970s, liberals have been shedding religious rhetoric like a useless second skin, while conservatives have been turning it to one issue after another, so that by the time of the 1992 Republican Convention, one had the eerie sense that the right was asserting ownership in God—but that the left had yielded its rights.

Nowadays, public religious appeals are generally associated with conservative causes, which might explain why liberals often seem overenthusiastic in the rush to register their distaste for religion. The sociologist James Davison Hunter, in his fine book *Culture Wars,* quotes a 1981 address in which the President of Yale University told incoming freshmen that politically active Christian evangelicals were "peddlers of coercion."[28] Garry Wills records the objections of some authors to the appointment of a Jesuit as the head of the New York Public Library.[29] And in a widely reported instance that I would like to think apocryphal, a woman who addressed a feminist conference in California and described herself as a Jewish atheist received a ringing ovation, as though by purging herself of religiosity she had somehow accomplished a great good.* Political candidates who make a show of their religiosity—or who show the danger signs of taking their religious commitments seriously—are treated with suspicion by mass media not quite sure how to present this unfortunate malady to the public. (How often one hears on the news a political report beginning, "Her opponent, a born-again Christian . . . ").

Curiously, the mass media seem willing to overlook this difficulty—religiosity—in candidates they like, even as the media emphasize the same factor in those they dislike. Garry Wills has noted the peculiar media attitude toward the two ordained ministers in the 1988 presidential primary campaigns, Pat Robertson and Jesse Jackson:

> While asking what Jackson "really wants," they kept looking for what he was "really" saying under the ornamental flourishes of Scripture language. If reporters had not shown a determination to keep Robertson boxed into his religious past, and an obliviousness to Jackson's religious rhetoric, the similarities of the two preachers would have been more frequently noticed.[30]

Similarly, in the 1992 campaign, the media often treated President Bush's speeches to religious organizations as pandering—but when Bill Clinton spoke, for example, to a black Baptist group, he was given credit for shrewdness. (Notice how both descriptions bespeak an assumption of insincerity.) Nor is this effect limited to political candidates. One can scarcely read about any statement by the Reverend Jerry Falwell without being reminded in so many words of his religious involvement. On the other hand, when pundits discuss the work of the Reverend Martin Luther King, Jr., the only member of the clergy whose life we

---

* This story is usefully compared with a very different and much happier tale about feminist writer Gloria Steinem who was asked how Judaism had led her to feminism and responded, "It was the other way around." See Allen R. Myerson, "Editions of the Passover Tale: This Year in Profusion," *New York Times,* April 4, 1993, Section 4, p. 2.

celebrate with a national holiday, the fact of his religious calling is usually treated as a relatively unimportant aspect of his career, if, indeed, it is mentioned at all.

The liberal reluctance to acknowledge the religious content of the civil rights movement is a close cousin to another societal blind spot: the refusal to admit the centrality of religion to most of the black community itself. As a group, black Americans are significantly more devout than white Americans. By some measures, a recent study concluded, black Americans are "the most religious people in the world." For examples, black Americans are "more likely than any other Americans to have high levels of confidence in the church or organized religion" and "much more likely than other Americans to be church members and to attend church weekly."[31]

One reason for the liberal unease with the black community's religiosity may be that the black Protestant churches—as well as the growing Islamic movement—are characterized by a deep theological and social conservatism. For example, black Americans are much more likely than other Americans to treat the Bible as literal truth,[32] a key element of fundamentalism, are heavily represented in the nation's more conservative Protestant denominations,[33] and are among the most likely to support a return to traditional roles for women, a useful measure of social conservatism.[34] Indeed, black Americans as a group seem to follow the general rule that the degree of measureable religiosity is a good predictor of the degree of social conservatism.

To be sure, there are deeply religious people on the left and there are hypocrites and atheists on the right. But the seeming instinctive mistrust of God-talk by contemporary liberals, and its ready embrace by conservatives, has badly damaged the public image of American religion—and provides strong, sad evidence of the way in which the abortion issue has so distorted our political dialogue that the public square, which once welcomed explicit religious witness, now views with suspicion people who talk about God in public.

The way in which the problem of public religious dialogue is inseparable from the problem of abortion was well illustrated in the spring of 1990, when New York City's controversial Roman Catholic archbishop, John Cardinal O'Connor, wrote an article in a church publication warning that Catholic politicians who supported abortion rights were "at risk of excommunication." (He did not, as was widely reported, actually threaten to excommunicate anyone, although several other Catholic bishops have made explicit threats, and at least one has carried it out.) Perhaps to tweak the nose of New York Governor Mario Cuomo, a pro-choice Catholic who has sparred with the cardinal before, O'Connor cited the martyred saint Thomas More, one of the locquacious Cuomo's favorite philosophers: "While he remained committed to his king, his first obligation was to Almighty God. Catholics in public office must also have this commitment to serve the state; but service to God must always come first."[35]

Excommunication is, formally, a recognition that a Catholic has separated from the church. It does not mean that one is no longer a Christian, for it does not undo the rite of baptism. Nor does it, as some in the media reported, represent a sentence of damnation, which the Catholic Church holds to be the privilege of God alone; but it does separate the excommunicant from the sacraments, including communion and last rites. Over the centuries, the possibility of excommunication has been one of the most dreadful for many Catholics to contemplate; it was the threat of excommunication, so the folklore has it, that led Emperor Henry IV to stand in the snow at Canossa, begging forgiveness from Pope Gregory VII for daring to thwart papal edicts.

But this is pluralistic America in the twentieth century, not theocratic Europe in the eleventh, and the words of a prince of the church no longer cause the nation's leaders to fall on their knees in the snow. Instead, they call press conferences. Pro-choice forces understandably jumped all over O'Connor's statement, calling on the cardinal, almost in so many words, to mind his own business. *Vanity Fair* informed its readers that O'Connor was "a fanatic, in the sense that any religious zealot unquestioningly committed to a rigid set of beliefs is a fanatic."[36] Other critics were more respectful. An editorial in the *New York Times* began by disavowing any intention of judging "the moral discipline that John Cardinal O'Connor imposed on Roman Catholics ... including those holding public office," and ended by accusing him of imposing "a religious test" on Catholic office-seekers and forcing Catholic politicians "to choose between looking like heretics and looking like stooges."[37] Catholic politicians quickly chose up sides. New York's Governor Mario Cuomo, whose position is that he publicly supports abortion rights although personally opposed to abortion, called the cardinal's statement "mean-spirited." Former vice presidential candidate Geraldine Ferraro, also a Roman Catholic, warned that the voters might "get angry at the church's attempt to tell legislators how to vote." Not all prominent Catholics objected. Hugh Carey, Mario Cuomo's predecessor as governor, said he was distressed that his fellow Democrats were "gloating and gleeful that their party will kill more fetuses than the other party."[38]

But not even all Catholics who agreed with the merits of the cardinal's position thought his intervention wise. Joseph Cardinal Bernardin, archbishop of Chicago, the nation's largest Catholic archdiocese, argued that the church would accomplish more through teaching and persuasion than through threats. Father Richard P. O'Brien, the head of the theology department at Notre Dame, worried that if other prelates took O'Connor's approach, "practicing Catholics could not run for office," because non-Catholics would doubt their independence.[39] This, of course, is the very fear that John F. Kennedy tried to put to rest in his 1960 presidential campaign, with his emphatic declaration that "I do not speak for my church on public matters—and the church does not speak for me."[40]

Among non-Catholics, too, the debate raged, and two New Yorkers perhaps captured it best. Asked about O'Connor's remarks, former New York mayor Ed Koch, his long-time friend, shrugged: "That's his job."[41] Burt Neuborne, a law professor at New York University, put the other side of the matter succinctly: "When you accept public office, you're not a Catholic, you're not a Jew. You're an American."[42]

Which is, in a nutshell, the problem. What precisely does it mean to be an American and religious? What is the proper scope of the influence of the religious self on the public self? How hard are politicians, and others in the public square, required to work to make this separation—and is the separation possible or even desirable? Governor Cuomo, in a very thoughtful address at Notre Dame in 1984, argued that the separation can and must be made in order for devoutly religious individuals to function as elected officials in a secular polity.[43] I shall presently return to the question of whether the separation is possible (see chapter 11); for the moment, let us consider only whether it is desirable.

Again, if one but turns the clock back to the 1950s, the battle lines over these tough questions were drawn rather differently. In February of 1956, in the midst of one of the most turbulent periods of the civil rights movement, Joseph Rummel, the Roman Catholic Archbishop of New Orleans, issued a pastoral letter condemning racial segregation as a sin. The letter, which rested on traditional church teachings, came at a delicate but auspicious moment. The Montgomery bus boycott was but two months old. The Southern states were crafting legal strategies to resist Supreme Court edicts to integrate their schools. In the middle of the month, Rummel's letter was read in all 120 Roman Catholic churches in the archdiocese, the South's largest. Next, in an editorial in a church publication, Rummel forbade Roman Catholic legislators to support a pending bill that would have required segregation in all of Louisiana's private schools, warning that to do so would be to risk "automatic excommunication."[44] White supremacist Catholic legislators were quick to blast what they evidently considered a violation of the separation of church and state. Racial segregation, they argued, was not "a

matter of revealed religion" and therefore was "outside the
church province."[45] Sneered one, "The editorial makes no difference."[46] Thus, the rhetoric of the 1950s was just like the rhetoric
of the 1990s, except that in 1956, the liberals cheered and the
conservatives got mad.

Then, in the early 1960s, several prominent segregationists
were excommunicated for refusing to follow the church's teaching that racism was wrong. Again, there was no liberal outcry
that the Catholic bishops who commanded their flocks to take a
public political position against segregation or risk separation
from the sacraments were wrongly interjecting their religious
views into politics; no popular magazines called the bishops
"religious zealot[s] unquestioningly committed to a rigid set of
beliefs." Nobody, except a handful of conservatives, seemed to
think the excommunications mocked Kennedy's promise that
his church did not speak for him, nor he for it. Indeed, given
the strong support of many Southern Protestants for segregation, this controversy places the demands that John Kennedy
disavowed any intention to be bound by the teachings of his
church in a somewhat different light. (After all, Kennedy's
famous disavowal came in a quickly crafted speech delivered in
Houston before a group of conservative white Protestant ministers.)[47]

What is one to make of all this? For one thing, there is
much depressing evidence that the religious voice is required
to stay out of the public square only when it is pressed in a
conservative cause. A few years ago, when Roman Catholic
bishops in the United States overwhelmingly endorsed a
nuclear freeze, only a few nervous conservatives objected. (In
an interesting twist, Defense Secretary Caspar Weinberger, who
opposed the bishops on the merits of their view, defended
their right as religious leaders to get involved in secular political issues.) In many parts of the world (but not all) the Roman
Catholic Church has acted as an independent moral force, calling for change in brutal dictatorships and, at times, leading the

charge. For liberals suddenly to decide that they dislike the image of the Catholic Church as a moral force in human affairs when they dislike the content of the moral message is to emulate those hypocritical conservatives who gleefully (and properly) seize on the reports of Amnesty International as evidence of horror made real in Iraq or Cuba or North Korea, but who (wrongly) consider it politically motivated interference in our domestic affairs when Amnesty turns its critical eye on conditions in American prisons.

Catholicism, like any religion worth its salt, is a mass of complexities. There have been Catholic horrors over the centuries, wars, inquisitions, corruptions, and vast moral silences. There have also been plenty of secular Catholic heroes, the most prominent recent example being Nobel Laureate Mother Teresa, who has achieved folk-hero status for her work among the destitute and dying of India. Indeed, for many liberals, it might be said that Mother Teresa embodies all that is best in public avowals of religious purpose, just as Ronald Reagan, while president, very likely embodied all that is worst. Which is why an interesting coda to this chapter involves a meeting between the two of them. A few months after he was shot by John Hinckley, Reagan had a visit from Mother Teresa, who told him: "You have suffered the passion of the cross and have received grace. There is a purpose to this. Because of your suffering and pain you will now understand the suffering and pain of the world. This has happened to you at this time because your country and the world need you."[48]

Strong words, these, from a Nobel Laureate whom many consider holy and some regard as a saint. Now imagine, for a moment, a Reagan so moved by the words that he suddenly decided to turn his presidency into a political effort to do the will of God, as interpreted by Mother Teresa. Thus he might have declared, for example, a holy war on poverty and disease. Probably he would have been lauded: he would have been no irrational, zealous religionist, improperly mixing church and state, but a man devoted to a good and moral cause. Of course, Mother Teresa opposes poverty and abortion with equal vehemence. Suppose the inspired Reagan had chosen abortion instead of poverty as the object of his religious ire. Would he then have been condemned as a religious zealot by our secular culture? One shudders to think that the answer might turn on which part of Mother Teresa's work he chose to pursue.

4

Political Preaching

THE truth—an awkward one for the guardians of the public square—is that tens of millions of Americans rely on their religious traditions for the moral knowledge that tells them how to
conduct their lives, including their political lives. They do not
like being told to shut up. Consequently, to imagine that politicians aspiring to national office can possibly refrain from openly
(but plain vanilla) religious appeals may be naive. In claiming in
his State of the Union Message the approval of God for the Gulf
War, George Bush simply indulged an old American habit, as
common on the left as on the right, to link one's cause to the
will of God: either we already prevailed because our cause was
godly or we will prevail because our cause is godly. In any case,
the cause is surely godly!

But this old habit is the flip side of the trivialization of religion that comes from the effort to keep it out of the public square—only this time, it is the religiously faithful who are the trivializers, in the relentless effort to demonstrate that the Word of God supports virtually every political cause. The seeming unwillingness of politically active religionists to accept the possibility that their religious traditions might correctly teach a word of God contrary to their secular political predilections is an obstacle, not an aid, to restoring religion to the place of honor that it deserves in the pantheon of American cultural institutions; indeed, if the principal value of religion to a democratic polity is its ability to preach resistance, it is difficult to see any gain to religion from the unswerving effort to take control of the apparatus of the state. If the religiously devout come to treat their faith communities as simple interest groups, involved in a general competition for secular power, it should come as no surprise if everybody else looks at them the same way.

THE POLITICAL PREACHERS

It is not our politicians alone who seek God's blessing for one side or the other in our most bitter public disputes—and it is not only the much-maligned televangelists either. One Sunday in the mid-1980s, my wife and I happened into a Roman Catholic church, just in time to hear the priest deliver a sharp homily against the American Civil Liberties Union. The gravamen of the priest's complaint was that the ACLU interfered with the church's effort to be a moral force in the political world. Now, as it happens, I agree that churches should be moral forces in the political world, and I am not sure that they do much good if they are anything else. But the almost casual lumping together of the ACLU, the forces of liberalism, and the courts—all of which came in for skewering—quickly reduced the priest's homily to little more than a political harangue against the left, with the implication that the left was somehow getting in the way of God's work.

Of course, such excess is hardly limited to the right. For example, shortly after moving to New Haven, Connecticut, my wife and I tried out a church about which we had heard the most marvelous stories. The sermon was delivered with energy by a young woman—a divinity student, I believe—with the light of the zealot in her eyes and the flame of absolute conviction in her voice. She wanted to set us straight on Central America, because, she feared, many among us were misunderstanding God's plan and therefore falling into sin. Her sermon, although fiery, was no masterpiece of coherence. Eventually, however, the message came clear. She was talking about El Salvador and Nicaragua, at a time when the people of both nations were suffering under tyranny or struggling to use their new freedoms, enduring civil war or battered by external subversion, depending on which newspaper one happened to read. And she was, as it turned out, a sort of left-wing Oliver North, whose evident view was that it was our Christian duty to support the good (left-wing) terrorists in their holy struggle to massacre the bad (right-wing) terrorists.

I was struck, eventually, by the realization that the preacher in question had no conception of the possibility of a faith not guided by her prior political commitments. For her, politics should lead faith, rather than the other way around—a proposition that is by no means the special preserve of the left. Her sermon, like many that were preached in support of Ronald Reagan's presidential candidacy, exemplified the problem of the political tail wagging the scriptural dog. Probably, the divinity student who hated the Contras, like the Roman Catholic priest who hated the ACLU, and like Reagan's religious supporters, was sincere: she truly believed that she had identified God's command. Perhaps she had. (I claim little expertise.) Probably, the many political preachers who seem to consider the current Republican party the embodiment of God's will are simply stating what they believe. It may even be that Oliver North, an avowed born-again Christian, and his religious supporters earnestly believe that he was doing God's work when he provided funds to purchase arms for the Contras—even if, to do God's work in that fashion, he had first to sell arms to Iran, the aspect of the deal that led John Gregory Dunne, who has a nice way with irony, to observe, "In nations less fastidious than ours, selling guns to the people responsible for the massacre of 241 of your country's soldiery might be construed as treason."[1]

Indeed, it may be that most of what might be called political preachers—spiritual leaders who try to explain to their flocks what God wants them to do in the political world—are sincere in that sense. All of them believe that the political positions they press are the positions that God would want them to press. It is antireligious error to suppose automatically, as some critics do, that political preachers (if they happened to be on the right) are hypocrites or charlatans.

Still, the political preacher's sincerity is not enough to save political preaching. Ordinarily, a preacher concerned with the world can sensibly turn his or her attention to the relevant holy book and find guidance. Political preachers share this revealed guidance with their flocks. Matters become troublesome, however, when one's theology always ends up squaring precisely with one's politics. At that point, there is reason to suspect that far from trying to discern God's will and follow it in the world, the political preacher is first deciding what path to take in the world and then looking for evidence that God agrees.

The sociologist Peter L. Berger has described the view that "churches should reflect the moral concerns of their social milieu" as a principle that "is false," one that "violates the very core of Christian faith."[2] Yet in America, argues Berger, this is what the Christian churches—at least the Protestant churches—have always done. The mainline Protestant denominations, Berger notes, draw their members from the middle class, and tend to reflect the values of the parishioners they seek to attract. Thus, there is no essential difference between the almost repres-

sive patriotism of many of the churches in the 1940s and 1950s
and the often relentless egalitarianism of many of the mainline
denominations today. In both cases, the churches take the values
of their members and put them in the mouth of God, thus con-
firming for the members their own essential righteousness; the
members themselves remain as middle class as ever, but with different political outlooks than middle-class folk of the past.

One result of this alignment of theology and politics is that
all too often, dissenters in the church are not valued, for their
"incorrect" political views are taken as evidence that they are not
sufficiently committed to doing God's good work on earth. The
ideal that the churches should make their members uncomfortable, proclaiming the word of God without regard to the desires
of the congregation, while much-repeated among the clergy,
does not, evidently, fill the pews, least of all if the preaching is
about politics.

It is not at all unusual for the politically minded among the
faithful to seem to make up their minds in advance of any argument, and then turn around and accuse those who disagree with
them of doing the same. In the early eighties, for example, secular liberals, and not a few conservatives, saw Jerry Falwell's
Moral Majority, Inc., then in its heyday, as the epitome of politics
masquerading as religion, accepting no dissent and no argument.
Falwell himself once identified the enemy as "those people in
government who are against what we consider the Bible, moral-
ist position."[3] Even though many secular liberals have grown
concerned about the Reverend Pat Robertson's well-organized
and well-financed Christian Coalition (see chapter 13), the negative public response to the 1992 Republican Convention was
likely to make the GOP more wary about too warm an embrace
for Robertson the next time around. Still, one conservative
activist argued in 1988, "We should run a massive campaign to
register Christians. We don't have to tell them how to vote. Just
get them into the booth, and 81 percent will support the more
conservative candidates."[4] The idea, one supposes, is that even if

they have to hide the public hoopla, conservative Christians will still wield considerable political influence—because, so some leaders seem to believe, devout Christian voters can be counted on to make up their minds on political questions the same way their leaders do.

The flip side of the same problem occurs when, in its rush to affirm the sinfulness of a given course of conduct, a church neglects to mention many other sins of equal or greater weight in its theology, thus giving rise to secular concern that its doctrines are narrower than they are, or that secular political motivations are driving what is framed as doctrinal analysis. The Southern Baptist Convention recently provided a useful example. The SBC was born in the middle of the nineteenth century as a protest against the northern-dominated Baptist faith, which decided not to allow members who owned slaves to serve as missionaries. Nobody, said the Southern Baptists in one of those fascinating American melds of principle and prejudice, has the right to tell another church how to run its business. The Southern Baptist Convention was thus created in an effort to protect slavery—but its rhetoric suggested that its actual goal was to protect the autonomy of local churches.

Today, the Southern Baptist Convention no longer believes in local autonomy, for it voted in 1992 to withdraw "fellowship" from churches that affirm homosexuality. That, of course, is the SBC's right, and neither government command nor secular protest should alter SBC's view on the will of God. As critics have pointed out, however, it is at least peculiar that the SBC can find no other sin—literally, for there are none listed—for which a member church will lose its fellowship.[5] Consequently, it is difficult to resist the conclusion that rather than consulting their religious consciences and deciding which sins should lead to withdrawal of fellowship, members of the SBC consulted their political convictions and decided which one to enshrine as a new fundamental law of the convention.

But, again, the model of selecting one's political convictions, shaping them into the word of God, and then accusing one's religious opponents of pig-headedness, is certainly not limited to the right. Consider, for example, the Task Force on Human Sexuality of the Evangelical Lutheran Church of America, some members of which worried in 1989 that adding a "conservative" member might "derail" the "purpose of the task force"— implying that *this* task force, at least, knew its conclusions before it started. Other members, in an agony of open-mindedness, consented to addition of a conservative member, but only a "reasonable" one.[6]

Few things are more trivializing to the idea of faith than for believers themselves to adopt an attitude holding that the will of God is not *discerned* by the faithful but *created* by them. To be sure, an important trend in contemporary hermeneutics argues that it is impossible for interpreters to do anything else, that all the reader will ever get out of a text is what the reader begins with.[7] For those who profess belief in a God whose will can be at least partly discerned, however, that is far too nihilistic a theology. If, as most Americans believe, there is a God external to the human mind, and if that God has tried to communicate with us, whether through revelation or some other path, then the human task is surely to discover the contents of that communication, not to surrender that possibility in return for the freedom to call one's own politics God's will. Political preachers from right and left alike sense this. They know that their audiences believe in the possibility of learning God's will, which is why it is rare that the political preacher says anything as self-effacing as "I can't say for sure that this is what God wants, but it's certainly what I want."[8]

Nowadays, one sees religious coalitions on almost every issue: spending more tax dollars on education or keeping sex education out of the schools; preserving a woman's right to abortion or preserving the fetal right to life; putting convicted murderers to death or putting an end to capital punishment; adding to the defense budget or reducing it; giving more money to the poor or protecting the earnings of the entrepreneur.[9] In one sense the existence of these organizations is all to the good, for they represent precisely the sort of private associations, vital to civil life in a democracy, that so entranced Tocqueville. When citizens join hands to push a common cause—any cause—the true liberal democrat should, in principle, stand up and applaud. (Even if, later on, the cause itself must be condemned.)

But America, as so often, carries a good thing too far. For example, lots of public interest groups publish pamphlets for the religiously minded among their supporters, supplying copious biblical quotations to demonstrate that God does, in fact, support the cause. The idea, evidently, is that the religiously devout supporter of the organization can now use the fruits of this biblical exegesis to convince friends of the justice—indeed, the godliness—of the cause. But bear in mind what is occurring. The group does not consult Scripture to determine whether or not the cause is just. Rather, the quotes are selected to prove the justice of the cause. The argument the pamphlets make is political rather than theological. But they keep on being printed. The cynicism, the disrespect for the religious mind, that inheres in this practice seems to pass most everyone by.

Political preaching, some observers argue, has deep roots in the American religious character. The nation was born in an era of often vicious Protestant sectarianism, as religious communities battled each other for power, sometimes, especially in New England, carving out entirely new states when dissatisfied with (or oppressed in) the old one. In the early years of the Republic, preachers with political causes made the most of the freedom they gained from the Protestant invocation of the authority of Holy Scripture itself instead of tradition. Uncabined by the rigorous testing of institutional religions, theological inventions flew fast and furious—and the flocks followed.[10] In America, at least, the idea of adjusting the interpretation of the Word to meet the demands of the faithful is a very old one.

CRASHING THE "MEN'S CLUB"

Within many of America's faith communities, the charge that political preachers are adjusting the Word to gain ideological ends is leveled with regularity against supporters of the ordination of women. My own church, the Episcopal Church, has twice nearly split asunder over this issue—when the first women were ordained to the priesthood and, later, when the first woman was ordained a bishop.

As I stated in chapter 2, I certainly support the ordination of women; more properly, I do not believe that the revealed Word of God, Holy Scripture, creates any explicit bar. I have no doubt—indeed, I am quite certain—that supporters of the ordination of women include many people for whom politics drives spiritual commitment rather than the other way around. But that is no more an argument against ordination of women than the fact that many opponents are sexists is an argument in favor. The question, for the believing Christian, is not what motivates some self-righteous advocates on either side of the question but what God would want us to do. My answer is that the readings of Scripture that are said to prohibit the ordination of women, with some exceptions, are cramped and unconvincing, resting principally not on God's word but on Christ's example: He did not choose any women to serve as Apostles. But He also did not choose any college graduates, or, to our knowledge, anyone with children or anyone with a disability. Yet we do not set these up as bars. Although traditions matter—they are part of how faith communities pass their shared understandings from one generation to the next—one must not confuse their importance with their immutability.[11] Changing a church tradition is not the same as changing church doctrine.

So the opponents, I believe, were wrong. But none of this makes them monsters of sexism. Most of them are sincere people, convinced that they have found the genuine will of God, and their exclusion through a parliamentary device has been a source of pain that can hardly be assuaged through telling them that they are immoral people to read Holy Scripture as they do. Still, the history is instructive.

The first unauthorized ordinations of women in the Episcopal Church occurred in 1974 and were plainly in violation of church law. The ordinations were interrupted by a protest, which one report described this way: "A half-dozen black-suited clergymen suddenly surged to the front of the church. 'Right Reverend Sirs!' they called out. And one by one, they voiced a single objection to the ordination under way: in clear violation of Anglican tradition and the canons of the Episcopal Church."[12] One opponent called the ordinations "unlawful and schismatical" and another warned, "God sees you trying to turn stones into bread!" The supporters of ordination were equally firm: "To carry out the unjust laws of this church which do not affirm the right of females to be priests and bishops is to visit oppression upon women."[13]

The supporters' image of oppression, like the opponents' image of tradition, in effect, claimed to know the mind of God. Of course, God alone knows the mind of God, which is why humans, when speaking on matters of God's teaching, should always proceed with caution. But to proceed with a healthy doubt about one's own moral rightness only means treating one's opponents with respect and granting the possibility of error. It does not mean refraining from action. The legal scholar Michael Perry, himself a Roman Catholic, has put the point nicely: "Although we must resist infallibilism . . . at any given moment our convictions are what they are."[14]

Skepticism, especially about one's own ideas, is a useful facet of human personality, but that does not mean that acting on one's ideas is wrong. In the case of figuring out whether God does or does not will the service of women as priests, one similarly must act from conviction, and one must simultaneously be prepared for the possibility of error. But the error either way, if there is one, is not a secular moral error and should not be described in secular moral terms—it is an error in theological understanding and should be described in theological terms. So if, as many deeply pained opponents charge, the church was wrong, the error was necessarily a misunderstanding of God's will; it would not be proper for those of us who support the ordination of women to say that the Bible cannot possibly wall off the priesthood from women simply because we do not want it to, for then we fall victim to the lure of political preaching.

Unless one wants to trivialize the centrality of the word of God in the lives of believing Christians, this distinction matters—less to women who feel called to the priesthood, oddly enough, than to other believers. If it is God's will that women serve as clergy but they are not allowed to do so, then those who prevent them put their own souls at risk—but not the souls of the women who are denied the opportunity. If, on the other hand, it is not God's will that women be ordained, then the church that ordains them engages in an act of sacrilege. Worse, those to whom the falsely ordained administer the sacraments are also in danger of the judgment. Indeed, if women are barred from the priesthood by God's will, then my wife and I, whose Episcopal wedding was officiated by a woman, have been living in sin since 1981, and our children were born out of wedlock. For a thinking, believing Christian, these are issues of considerable consequence, which is why the correct answer to the question of ordination of women must be found in prayerful consideration. The answer has everything to do with discerning and then enacting the will of God, and nothing to do with the rights of women.

On such issues as the ordination of women—issues that are describable, even though not truly comprehensible, in the simple terms in which we debate the same matters in the public square—the media typically make a mess of matters. We as a nation have made a commitment to sexual equality, a commitment, I believe, that moves us closer to God's will, but traditionalists in many faiths believe that the will of God is otherwise.

Often, the internecine religious battles on this point are fought in public, and the media exultantly choose up sides, referring to "liberals" against "conservatives"—implying that only external political forces can explain the way the battle lines have formed.

For example, during the bitter conflict in the Episcopal Church over whether to ordain women as priests and bishops (a battle, I remind, that I think reached the theologically correct outcome) *Time* magazine referred to proponents of ordination as "supporters of women's rights," as though the theological arguments were mere cloaks for politics.[15] Opponents, as it happens, were sure that this was true. For instance, the *National Review* blasted supporters of ordaining women, claiming (erroneously) that they drew their arguments from every field but theology: "They offer only reasons from sociology, anthropology, female liberation, sexuality, psychology, evolution, behavioral sciences, and, yes, politics."[16]

A similar brouhaha arose several years later, when the issue before the church was the ordination of women not as priests but as bishops, and, therefore, as direct successors to the Apostles. On September 24, 1988, Barbara Harris was elected a bishop of the Diocese of Massachusetts on the seventh ballot of a contentious diocesan convention. When, in accordance with tradition, the assembly was asked to make the vote by affirmation, "most joined enthusiastically in the assent, but a few shouts of 'No!' rang through the cathedral."[17]

Those shouts of *No!* subsequently escalated into a roar of criticism. Much of the debate, as before, was theological, but by the time of Harris's election, that battle, though painful, was essentially over. The principal holding action was the argument that since the rest of the Anglican Communion, of which the Episcopal Church is part, had not yet made a judgment on whether women could serve as bishops, the American church should wait. Supporters responded that they had waited too long already—which, if their theology was correct, they certainly had.

Albert O. Hirschman years ago penned the deservedly

acclaimed monograph *Exit, Voice, and Loyalty,* in which he argued that those who are dissatisfied with the performance of any entity, be it a corporation, a political organization, or government itself, face the choices of ceasing to patronize or obey (that is, exit) or complain (that is, voice). The dissatisfied are more likely to remain loyal and choose voice, Hirschman notes, if they believe that their complaints will make a difference in the entity's behavior at a relatively low cost to themselves. Otherwise, they are likely to exit.[18]

That is what many dissenters from the ordination of women as priests and bishops finally did. They chose to exit. In 1989, disgruntled Episcopalians formed the Episcopal Synod of America. The newly elected president of ESA charged the organized Episcopal Church with a "loss of respect for the authority of Holy Scripture and the embracing of a worldview which ignores history."[19] One ESA member suggested that the split reflected a division "between those who believe the gospel as it is revealed and those who believe the gospel should be modified to suit each successive generation."[20]

Like the believing Christians who deny that one can fully experience God in a world in which women are not allowed to answer the call to the priesthood, the believing Christians who formed the ESA must be deeply pained by a sense of betrayal by and exclusion from their church. And although I think that the ordination of women is closer to God's word, I do not think the pain of ESA members insignificant. I do not think them evil, oppressive, sexist. I simply think them mistaken. Those are my feelings as a believing Christian and a member of the Episcopal Church. On this issue, my feelings as a citizen of the secular political world are irrelevant.

And that, of course, is the key point. Even though the Episcopal Church has tumbled toward schism as a result of the move to ordain women as priests and bishops—a tumble that has not yet stopped—at least it must be said, for all the divisiveness that the ordination of women caused, it was the work of members of

the faith rather than the rule of outsiders, especially that powerful group of outsiders that acts in the name of that great metaphysical abstraction we call the state. Had the ordination of
women as priests or bishops come in response to state command, I would have been unhappily but firmly against it.[21]

THE SERVANT OF POLITICS

Still, the central point bears stressing: there is nothing wrong and
much right with letting religious faith be the wellspring of a citizen's public action. At the same time, one whose moral judgments are driven by religious devotion must be ever careful to
discern whether God's word or human politics is doing the
work. For there is a vital difference between a political inspiration that is fired by one's deepest religious beliefs and a claim of
religious belief that is fired by a preexisting political commitment. It is the job of the religiously devout citizen to understand
and preserve this distinction, one that unfortunately is blurred,
and perhaps disbelieved, by our political rhetoric, as well as by
our mass media.

In this sense—as the *servant* of politics—religion is very
much in the public square. It might be supposed that this appeal
to the will of God in support of nearly every cause is evidence of
the exalted position of religion in our culture.[22] But it is evidence
of the opposite. By calling upon the word of God in service of
every known cause, our society diminishes the weight and the
force of religious belief. Indeed, by readily supposing that the
word of God is so malleable that it can (by coincidence) support
every cause that one's politics also happen to support, we under-
mine the idea of faith as a source of moral guidance.

This is the essence of the problem of political preaching, as
I have named the effort to use God's name to bend one's flock
to the correct political view. It is the problem with George Bush's

effort to link God to America's victory in the Cold War, and it is
the problem with much that passes for liberation theology. To
insist that God is, in effect, one of us—that He is our person,
instead of we being His people—is not much different than the
trivialization inherent in the rather offensive slogan that occasionally adorns the bumpers of cars from North Carolina, where
a minor form of godhead is conferred upon the University of
North Carolina's blue-suited basketball team, the Tar Heels. Says
the bumper sticker: "IF GOD ISN'T A TAR HEEL, THEN WHY IS THE SKY
CAROLINA BLUE?" God, it seems, not only roots for the right countries and the right ideologies, but for the right basketball team as
well. But if religion is to be a prop to support secular social and
political movements, one cannot sensibly speak of it as an independent force in the world. If the role of the religionist is first to
make up his or her mind about which political position to take
and next to search for religious arguments to support the already
selected view, the idea of faith as the *source* of moral inspiration
is trivialized.

Religions are moral forces in the lives of their adherents,
which means, inevitably, that they are moral forces in the political world. And, as with all institutions, a degree of cross-pollination between religion and politics is inevitable. But when secular
political considerations become prior to, rather than subsequent
to, religious considerations, the result is not cross-pollination but
pollution.

Sören Kierkegaard, looking at the established churches of
Europe, said that when Christianity becomes a part of the state, it
ceases to be Christianity, a proposition readily generalized
beyond the Christian churches. Kierkegaard believed that religious triumph was found in suffering rather than in hegemony.
The historian Viscount Bryce made the same point another way:
"The more the Church identified with the world, the further did it
depart from its own best self. The Church expected or professed
to Christianize the world, but in effect the world secularized the
Church."[23] What both had in mind, I think, was much the same

as the theologian David Tracy's idea that religions are at their best when they are forms of resistance. One way of losing the power of resistance is to have the state take it away; another is to surrender it willingly in the rush to become part of the very state against which the religions should ideally serve as a bulwark.

The Inquisition only became possible when church and state merged their authorities, and neither was available to stand against the other. The church, by becoming the state, surrendered the possibility of acting as an intermediary. It yielded its essential role as the protector of the people of God; it ceased to be able to preach resistance. One might even say that in its grasping for power, the institutional church gave up the right to die for its beliefs in exchange for the right to kill for its beliefs.

5

The "Christian Nation"
and Other Horrors

THE religions enjoy no special immunity from the tendency of power to corrupt—and of absolute power to corrupt absolutely. As I write these words, people are being slaughtered for their religious beliefs in India, in Bosnia, and in various parts of the Middle East. Closer to home, as Forrest G. Wood is the latest to document, the African slave trade and the post–Civil War oppression of the freed slaves and their progeny were often justified by reference to a variety of Scriptural passages and Christian doctrines.[1] Indeed, there is virtually no evil that one can name that has not been done, at some time and at some place and to some real person, in the name of religion.

Not long ago, I picked up a sobering little book by James A. Haught titled *Holy Horrors: An Illustrated History of Religious Murders and Madness* (1990). The book is just exactly what it claims to be: a list, with copious illustrations, of horrors performed in the service of religion. Although there is a bibliography, there are no footnotes, so it is difficult to judge whether every story Haught recounts actually occurred. His account is further weakened by his insistence on shoehorning as much history as possible into his model (why in the world, for example, does he consider the nineteenth-century Sepoy Mutiny, which most historians describe as a violent revolt against British imperialism in India, to be an example of *religious* horror?) as well as by what at times seems a willingness to credit every scrap of negative hearsay, as long as it is about a religion.[2]

Still, even if Haught has taken a little license, or repeated hearsay, or blown an incident or two out of proportion, one can hardly sift through the book's 233 pages without repeated sharp intakes of breath as he lays out a litany of Satan's work on earth, done by human beings acting in God's name. It is all there, from the castration of little boys to improve their voices for church choirs in the Middle Ages to the seemingly endless rounds of religious warfare on the Indian subcontinent and in the Middle East to the torturing, drowning, burning, and beheading of the Anabaptists, for the sin of baptizing adults who had already been baptized as infants (a history that helps explain why their descendants, the Mennonites, Amish, and Hutterians, are so suspicious of the secular world) to the burning of children to satisfy the gods of the ancient Phoenecians, as well as those of the thirteenth-century Incans. It is difficult to come away without endorsing Haught's unhappy conclusion: "Religion has a great potential for evil—and that potential has been realized thousands of times through the years."[3]

The historical realization of religion's potential for evil goes a long way toward explaining our cultural distrust of it; but it is an error in analysis to leap from the parade of horrors done in the name of religion to the conclusion that religion is itself an evil thing. The evil that has been done in the name of religion no more justifies the relegation of religion to the status of mere hobby than the evil that has been done in the name of equality means that equality is not an end worth pursuing. In fact, it is rarely accurate to attribute the parade of horrors to religion as such. Generally, it is the alliance of religion and government that makes these evils possible, for with the collapse of the organized religious armies that were common in the Middle Ages, it is government itself that holds the power to oppress. Government, of course, has done great evils even without the assistance of religion, and sometimes, notably in the twentieth century, in an effort to stamp it out, as in the old Soviet Union, in China, and in Cambodia.

As often as it is a force for evil, religion is a force for good. In recent history, we have seen religious witness against oppression around the world, which tyrannical governments have often met with antireligious slaughter. In America, we have seen religious witness against slavery and segregation, against the war in Vietnam, and against poverty. Witness of this kind will be most effective in a nation that truly celebrates its diverse religious traditions, valuing them instead of trying to hide them.

Yet one who argues, as I do, for a strong public role for the religions as bulwarks against state authority must always be on guard against the possibility—no, let us say the likelihood—that some religions will try to use the privileged societal position that the First Amendment grants them as an instrument of oppression. Thus, just as it is important in the abstract to bear witness to the value to the society of opening the public square to the religious voice, it is also important, in concrete cases, to bear witness to the dangers that some religious voices present.

THE "CHRISTIAN NATION"

Most American adults—about 85 percent in recent surveys, but dropping—identify themselves as Christians. So perhaps we should be charitable and assume that this self-description is what led Republican Governor Kirk Fordice of Mississippi to assert, at a conference shortly after the 1992 presidential election, that America is a "Christian nation"—a remark that set off a firestorm of controversy just as the Republicans were dousing the flames sparked by their convention. Perhaps the governor was simply counting heads, and meant his remarks as a shorthand for "most Americans are Christians."[4]

However, this meaning seems unlikely, for the governor's troubling remarks are embedded in a long tradition of treating America as essentially Christian in far more than a demographic sense. For millions of Americans, both historically and in the present day, the vision of a self-conscious Christian nationhood is not only attractive, but imperative—and an easy way to decide who is truly American and who is not. The image of America as a Christian nation is more firmly ingrained in both our politics and our practices than the adjustment of a few words will ever cure. Some of the Founders of the nation worried over the consequences should "pagans, deists, or Mahometans" ever be elected to the presidency.[5] The legal scholars of the nineteenth century proudly and loudly proclaimed that "Christianity is part of the common law." Christmas is a national holiday. Christian rhetoric, and perhaps Christian doctrine as well, fueled the ideology of Manifest Destiny that dominated the nineteenth century and the ideology of anti-Communism that dominated the second half of the twentieth. Thousands, perhaps tens of thousands, of laws currently on the books were enacted in direct response to the efforts of Christian churches.[6] Indeed, as recently as the 1950s, there was a major effort to amend the Constitution to provide that the laws of the United States were subject to the word of God, and to the rule of God's Son Jesus Christ.[7] And in 1892, a unanimous Supreme Court made reference to "a volume of unofficial declarations" that added weight to "the mass of organic utterances that this is a Christian nation."[8]

To those who are not Christians—and to many of us who are—this is potentially scary stuff, which helps explain why the hierarchy of the Republican party distanced itself from Fordice's remarks as swiftly as it was able. The immediate aftermath of Fordice's comment is already the stuff of which political legends are made: South Carolina's Governor Carroll Campbell, a fellow Republican, rushed to the microphone with a gentle correction, emphasizing the importance of the nation's "*Judeo*-Christian heritage." Fordice responded (tartly? jocularly? gruffly?—I wasn't there, and the media have used all three adverbs) that had he meant Judeo-Christian, he would have said it. The Republican party, including Governor Fordice, later issued a firmer correction, and certainly the convention's speakers never failed to include the prefix "Judeo-" when referring to the nation's moral and religious traditions. The trouble is, even if one selects more inclusionary language, it is not clear what the words mean. After the Fordice brouhaha, one Talmudic scholar quoted in a news magazine had this to say: "Governor Fordice erred politically by failing to send out the proper signal. . . . But theologically and historically, there is no such thing as the Judeo-Christian tradition. It's a secular myth favored by people who are not really believers themselves."[9]

Although the rhetoric of the Judeo-Christian tradition may have originated in efforts to overcome entrenched anti-Semitism in the nineteenth century, there is some evidence that the linking of the two traditions was a secular political move around the middle of the twentieth century, aimed at curbing the feared influence of the Roman Catholic Church by emphasizing the commonalities of its theological opponents.[10]

There are important similarities between Christianity and Judaism, most notably that they share a sacred text, which is why they are often referred to as the Biblical religions. There are important similarities of moral principle, especially the adherence to the Ten Commandments and the encouragement of attitudes of forgiveness and generosity. Christians, moreover, believe that the Savior, Jesus Christ, was born a Jew, which is no mere coincidence. As the theologian Karl Barth has written, Christians must not believe that Christ "was an Israelite by chance" who could "just as well" have been born something else. Still, declaring the religions to share *theological* principles might demand too much, for the Christology at the center of the Christian mystery proposes what Judaism necessarily rejects; and despite a common Bible and a common commitment to the Ten Commandments, Judaism and Christianity embrace different visions of the nature of God. These distinctions help explain why one sociologist dismissed the idea of a shared tradition with these words: "The more orthodox a Jew is and the more orthodox a Christian is, the more likely they are to say, 'To hell with the Judeo-Christian tradition.'"[11]

And yet it would be a mistake to dismiss the tradition on such grounds as these, as though the theological differences render impossible any recognition of what Pope John Paul II calls "[t]he depth and richness of our common heritage." As a Christian, I have no doubt of either the continuing validity of God's covenant with Israel (see Rom. 11:29) or of my own spiritual inheritance from the Old Testament tradition. I am perplexed by the insistence of so many believing Christians that Jews can find salvation only by rejecting the special covenant that has nurtured them through centuries of hostility and horror.

Of course, the speakers at the 1992 Republican Convention who talked about the Judeo-Christian tradition were concerned with morality, not theology. But on many of the nation's most searing contemporary moral disputes, the gap between Jewish Americans and white Protestant evangelicals (the convention's core audience) is quite striking. For example, to take one of the convention's key themes, the assault on feminism, 40 percent of white Protestant evangelicals but only 24 percent of Jews believe that women should return to traditional roles in the family.[12] There is a similar division on abortion: 50 percent of Jews as against just 14 percent of white Protestant evangelicals consider the anti-abortion movement "totally wrong."[13] In retrospect, the convention's references to a Judeo-Christian tradition look very much like simple throwaway lines, and it was Governor Fordice, in his description of America as a Christian nation, who came closer to what the speakers really seem to have had in mind. But even his wording was too broad. To speak truth to their twin audiences, the one for whom the message was intended and the one for whom the message was intended to be obscure, the speakers should have made reference to the "white conservative Protestant evangelical tradition"—then, at least, the description would have been accurate.

And this leads to the most significant weakness in the claim of a coherent Judeo-Christian tradition: the fact that the Christian tradition includes a millennium or more of efforts to eradicate Judaism from the face of the earth. Richard John Neuhaus quotes a rabbi who says, "When I hear the term 'Christian America,' I see barbed wire."[14] The Holocaust, while not, perhaps, directly a work of the Christian churches,* was undeniably the outgrowth of two millennia of Christian preaching against Jews, and the stony silence of the Roman Catholic hierarchy during the years of Nazi dominance of Europe could hardly have been taken by the regime as anything but a religious license to continue their slaughter.

Many religionists try to talk their way out of this history by explaining, for example, that the church is not responsible for all of the evil that is done in its name. It is difficult to know what to make of this argument. If one believes, as I do, that religions can and should be independent moral entities, separate from the state and thus able to rally their followers to resistance against it, then one must assume that there will be times when the followers will act. Christians cannot pick and choose—saying, in effect, "The civil rights movement is of our making but anti-Semitism is not our fault." Rather, one must be prepared to acknowledge the evil done in the name of faith, to beg forgiveness for it, and to examine the message with care, in order to understand why and how the fol-

---

* This is not to deny that Nazi ideologues appropriated for their own purposes the Lutheran theological idea of "orders of creation." For an effort to recapture what was taken, see Carl E. Braaten, "God in Public Life: Rehabilitating the 'Orders of Creation,'" *First Things*, Dec. 1990, p. 32.

lowers of the message went so far astray—as Pope John XXIII did in 1960, when he acknowledged and begged forgiveness for the role of the Catholic Church in preaching anti-Semitism.

A couple of years ago, I attended a conference at which a Jewish scholar argued that the trouble with America is not that it is a Christian nation but that it too often is not. He was, in a gentle way, calling Christians to remember what is best, not what is worst, in our traditions. Christ's message, after all, is one of love and inclusion, not of hatred and division. It is painful for me as a Christian to watch the perversion of this message, by the far right wing of my own faith, into a call for holy war—a call which, even if metaphorical, can only raise the terrifying imagery of the wholesale slaughter of the Crusades.

CHRISTIAN EXCLUSIVITY

It is essential to distinguish a disbelief in someone else's religion from a hatred of it or its adherents. Consider the much-quoted and much-criticized statement by Bailey Smith, pastor of the First Southern Baptist Church of Del City, Oklahoma, and, at the time, soon-to-be-elected president of the Southern Baptist Convention. Shortly before a dinner in 1980 (at which presidential candidate Ronald Reagan, who did not overhear the remark, would be the after-dinner speaker), Smith said: "[M]y friend God Almighty does not hear the prayer of a Jew."[15] Now on one level, Smith can be seen as making a simple theological claim, to wit, that the Christian faith possesses a connection to God that other religions lack. Thus, the argument runs, only Christians—people who profess a faith in Jesus Christ as Son of God and Savior—can achieve eternal life. Many Christians do in fact believe this, citing, for example, John 14:6 as authority. (My own view is that exclusivity of this kind betrays a lack of faith in God's charity, but everyone is entitled to choose a religious belief.)

However, given the way it has historically been used against Jews, the notion of Christian exclusivity necessarily partakes of a political as well as a religious dimension. In religiously pluralistic America, lots of faiths make exclusivity claims and, for the most part, although any one of them may be right, the matter does not excite great public interest. But when leaders of large and influential Christian denominations make such claims, danger lurks on the horizon. The lurking danger has nothing to do with truth or falsity of the claim of exclusivity and everything to do with the propensity of religious groups as they grow powerful to take secular action consistent with their claims.

A principal theme of this book, of course, has been that there is nothing wrong when a religious group presses its moral claims in the public square. But one must distinguish between the religious motivation for a moral position that is otherwise within the power of the state to pursue and the religious motivation for a moral position that simply involves the oppression of members of other, less politically powerful faiths. Fighting for an end to the production of nuclear weapons is not the same as fighting for official recognition of the exclusivity of one's faith.

Although some Christians defend the exclusivity idea by arguing that one religion's claims inevitably conflict with every other religion's claims, that argument is both ahistorical and illogical. Nothing about the nature of religion requires either exclusivity or universality. Historians tell us that the religions began as essentially local phenomena, explaining essentially local events. To put the matter baldly, if the group over in the next valley worshipped different gods than mine, it was nothing to me: I sacrificed to the gods who governed my crops, they sacrificed to the gods who governed theirs.

There is some controversy over when religions first began to make claims to universality. Some point to the early Hebrews of the Mosaic era, suggesting that the First Commandment was in effect a claim of religious primacy and a rejection of religious pluralism. Others see universality as a Christian invention, and late Christian at that, probably not taking firm theological hold until after the Donation of Constantine and the subsequent merger of the Roman Catholic Church and the Roman Empire. Whatever the correct answer, it is plain that we live today in a world in which many faiths do claim both exclusivity and universality—but it must be emphasized that many others do not.

A claim of exclusivity is not a moral evil. If one genuinely believes that he or she has found the only route to salvation through the one true faith, one obviously has no choice but to proclaim that other religions are wrong. However, the one doing the proclaiming should make clear what is going on: it is the nature of *that individual's faith,* not the nature of *religion itself,* that dictates the exclusivity. So Christians who insist that Jews (or Muslims or Buddhists or anyone else) cannot find salvation without accepting Jesus Christ as savior should not insist that they are making only the argument that every religion demands; they should confess freely that they are making the argument that their reading of Christianity demands. That is not, by itself, a reason not to make the argument, and if they are convinced that they are right, they should not hesitate. Still, it is useful to strip away the veil. Christian exclusivity turns out to be at best a tenet of faith rather than an argument that follows from the nature of religion. Conceding the sincerity of those who insist on Christian exclusivity, one can still wonder if some, at least, have been wrong-footed by the assumption that religions by nature make exclusive and universal claims. Those who profess exclusivity should be careful to assure themselves that they are correctly reading *their* beliefs, not incorrectly reading the nature of religion itself.

RELIGIOUS "TOLERATION"

Some Christians respond that although Christianity is indeed the one true faith, it is important to tolerate those who hold divergent religious views. But Jewish citizens of the United States and others who are not Christians, rightly object to language suggesting that Christians (or anyone else) should "tolerate" them. The fundamental message of the Establishment Clause of the First Amendment is one of religious *equality*—a message to which the idea of majority and minority religions should be bitter anathema. As Robert Goldwin has observed of the time at which the First Amendment was written, "Religious toleration was amazingly prevalent in America, given the intensity of religious conviction observable everywhere, but political equality for members of different religious groups was rare."[16] Toleration, in short, means only allowing someone to exist—but one may exist and still be oppressed.

The suggestion that those who are not Christians (or not Christians of the right kind) are merely tolerated—that they survive on these shores by forbearance, not by right—implies in turn that the folks in charge, the right-thinking Christians, can withdraw that tolerance at any time, thus destroying the political bases for the survival of all wrong-thinkers.*

Tolerance without respect means little; if I tolerate you but do not respect you, the message of my tolerance, day after day, is that it is *my* forbearance, not *your* right, and certainly not *the nation's* commitment to equality, that frees you to practice your religion. You do it by my sufferance, but not with my approval. And since I merely tolerate, but neither respect nor approve, I might at any time kick away the props, and bring the puny structure of your freedom down around your ears.

Besides, the idea of toleration is, for many Christians, bound up with the notion that Jews will in time come to confess error—that is, that they will come to Christ. For a religiously devout American Jew (or, for that matter, for one who is not

---

* Precisely the same analysis applies to any suggestion that the United States is a "secular" nation in which religiosity is simply tolerated. Once more, the implication is that religious traditions survive by forbearance, not by right, and that the folks in charge—the right-thinking secularists—can withdraw that tolerance at any time, thus destroying the religions wholesale.

devout), such a model of toleration could scarcely be more terrifying. Thus a Jewish reader recently wrote in *Biblical Archaeology Review,* "I am deeply offended by Christians who profess
'love' for the Jewish people while trying to wipe them off the
face of the earth by conversion or other methods."[17]

"Other methods," indeed. Even before the Holocaust, history gave Jews little reason to place their trust in Christian
proclamations of love and promises of tolerance. I have even
heard it suggested that the idea that Christians should tolerate
Jews developed hand-in-glove with the notion that Christians
should try to persuade them to come to Christ. It is hard to be
happy if one's religious choice is tolerated only in order to has-
ten its destruction. America should put no one to that choice. A
vital security of life in a free society should be that, far from
being tolerated, every religious person and every religious group
can claim equal rights with every other.

This is the point that is missed in our national stumbling
about over what should be a nonissue: the placing of crèches
commemorating the nativity of Jesus Christ on public property.
The rule should be simple. If the crèches are maintained at public expense, they should not be there (see chapter 6). The
Supreme Court's ridiculous hemming and hawing over whether
and in what circumstances the crèches have religious significance is an unhappy distortion of the principal value for which
the Establishment Clause ought to stand.[18] The question should
not be whether members of "minority" religions (the Court's
word!) are offended or not. The Establishment Clause does not
regulate psychology. The question should be whether the government is placing its imprimatur on a symbol of a particular religion. That is what a crèche is; and, despite the insistence of
some of the Justices of the Supreme Court that the crèche also
carries a secular or even commercial significance, people who
want the government to pay to establish crèches on public property are not doing so in order to commemorate a secular holiday.
Unlike moral legislation, moreover, the placing of a crèche

serves no conceivable function other than to celebrate a purely religious aspect of a festive occasion at government expense. In a world of religious toleration, this emphasis might be irrelevant, as the Supreme Court suggested; but in a world of religious equality, this plain religious preference by the government is insupportable.*

None of this should be taken to suggest that intolerance for Jews—anti-Semitism—is worse than intolerance of other religious traditions. Although Christians carry a special responsibility to bear witness to the suffering that two millennia of Christian anti-Semitic rhetoric have helped to bring about, we enact a terrible threat to the unity of humanity when we construct a hierarchy of suffering, by arguing that one oppression is worse than another. This argument is what has led to the tragic and absurd spectacle of blacks and Jews occasionally sniping at one another over which was a greater evil, slavery or the Holocaust.[19] Such a debate is probably irresolvable and, to those who suffer under particular oppressions, the answer surely does not matter. Pol Pot's victims in Cambodia did not sit around wishing that they had been born chattel slaves in the United States; those who died under Stalin did not dream, in their last moments, of living as Jews in Hitler's Germany.

However, even though the great horrors of history need no ranking for relative horribleness, they are not the same. Every one of the world's great oppressions is unique, which is why each might demand a different solution. The unique circumstance of the oppression of black Americans, for example, demands a variety of dramatic remedial measures if equal opportunity is to be realized, including strict enforcement of a variety of antidiscrimination laws that limit the freedom property holders would otherwise enjoy, and, in many circumstances, forms of

---

* I would agree, however, that the secular Christmas holiday that the society as a whole celebrates bears about as much relation to the religious Christmas Holy Day that believing Christians celebrate as the secular Sunday day off bears to the Christian sabbath day.

racial preference that might otherwise be constitutional anathema. So it is quite plausible that the unique circumstance of the
oppression of Jews might demand the careful nurturing of a
place—an actual physical location, what William F. Buckley, in
his recent book on anti-Semitism, calls a "geographical promon-
tory"—that can, for Jews, serve as both a symbol of independence and sanctuary from a relentlessly hostile world.[20] And if it
is the existence and security of that place, Israel, that is itself the
remedy, then those who challenge its right to exist or to be
secure might fairly be asked, as the opponents of antidiscrimination law might fairly be asked, whether their true belief is that no
remedy is needed—or deserved.

This does not mean that Israel is beyond criticism, only that
its survival should be beyond question. The ghastly experience
of the Holocaust no more immunizes Israel from moral correction than the ghastly oppressions of slavery and Jim Crow immu-
nize those of us who are black. Thus, it is no more anti-Semitic
to criticize Israel for, say, its policies toward West Bank Arabs
than it is racist to criticize such black Americans as Louis Far-
rakhan for making anti-Semitic remarks.

Of course, in a nation where 85 percent of adults identify
themselves as Christians, it may seem easier to speak of tolerance of Jews and other non-Christians than to speak of equality
of any practical sort. But the language of tolerance is the language of power; and although it is vital that the religions remain
public witnesses to moral evil, influencing policy when they can,
calling their members to civil disobedience when they must, it is
also vital, in order to preserve that precious autonomy of perspective that makes religion unique, that the religions avoid the
grasp for secular power. Unfortunately, we live in an era when
the effort to grasp and hold secular power often proves a greater
temptation than some of the religions are able to resist.

THE SERVANT OF POLITICS

All of this brings us full circle, back to the 1992 Republican Convention, where the Christian right seemed to advertise a desire to become a part of the state. The true difficulty in the 1992 Republican Convention's relentless focus on frankly religious appeals is the transformation of politics into a variety of corporate worship, which is, in turn, another instance of the trivialization of religious faith. Our secular politics is unlikely to become the servant of any single religious tradition; the nation has become too secure in its diversity to allow that travesty to occur. But it is quite possible for religion to become the servant of secular politics, and in the 1980s, some would say, it nearly did.

Ronald Reagan seemed to invoke God more often than any president in memory.[21] He addressed the National Association of Religious Broadcasters during each year of his presidency. He supported virtually the entire social agenda of the religious right—not only prayer in public schools and restriction on abortion, positions common to great numbers of American voters, but tax exemptions for racially segregated schools and the teaching of "scientific creationism" in the public school biology classroom.[22] Many a religious leader preached that a vote for Reagan was a vote for God's truth. Certainly, God seemed ever-present in Reagan's rhetoric, so much so that one columnist was moved to comment that Reagan "has reduced Him to the level of a Cabinet officer," and "made Him a cheerleader for the GOP and considers Him a contributor to his reelection effort."[23]

The appeal to religion worked in the 1980 election. Certain that they had been betrayed (which, in a sense, they had), the Christian right voted heavily for Ronald Reagan instead of for born-again Christian Jimmy Carter. And not just the Christian right. Exit polls showed that white Protestants generally, including those from the less conservative mainline churches—Episcopalians, Lutherans, Methodists, Presbyterians—voted for Reagan by a margin of about 2 to 1.[24]

Once in the White House, Reagan exhibited an interest in corporate worship approximating zero: unlike his predecessor, who had attended church services regularly, prayed in public, and practiced his religion (in the face of considerable secular criticism) by declining to serve alcohol at many White House functions, President Reagan could rarely be bothered even to attend church. This does not mean that Reagan was not a religious man; it does mean that he placed a low value on the process of discerning, in company with others of the same faith, the will of God. He was a member of a faith, but he was not, in any practical sense, a member of a faith community.

Pressed on the issue of why he almost never attended worship services, Reagan's advisers said that the security of the president and congregations could not be guaranteed. They suggested that he was bravely staying away to keep the churches safe from his enemies—but somehow this was never a problem for other presidents; indeed, it did not keep Reagan from attending secular rather than religious gatherings. As has been noted by Reagan's defenders, the greatest of all presidents, Abraham Lincoln, was not a member of any church. But Lincoln's reason was that the churches insisted on membership qualifications beyond loving God and loving one's neighbors.[25] Lincoln, moreover, made no effort to sell himself as the candidate embodying God's purpose for America.

Still, Ronald Reagan's piety, or lack thereof, is not the issue. The point is that many opinion shapers on the religious right argued in the course of the 1980 campaign, and again in 1984, that Ronald Reagan was one of them and that a vote for Reagan was, in effect, a vote for God's candidate. By 1984, it was inconceivable that these churchmen could have mistaken Reagan's patent lack of personal interest in things religious for a deep commitment of faith. Rather, they must have been referring to his politics—that is, Reagan became God's candidate because he was, in their view, politically correct.

In his public rhetoric, and sometimes in his public acts, Reagan took this obligation quite seriously, and so did other members of his administration. Some observers have maintained that Reagan did little for his supporters in the Christian right,[26] but that is demonstrably false. The Reagan administration had not been in office for a year when it began its politically disastrous effort to obtain tax exemptions for church-run segregation academies, many of which had their genesis in the effort by white parents to avoid having their children go to school with black kids. Moreover, according to Charles Fried, solicitor general in the last years of the Reagan administration, the Justice Department gave serious thought to supporting a federal trial judge's claim of the right to overrule Supreme Court precedent on school prayer—a preposterous notion that, fortunately, died aborning.[27]

Some social critics have argued that it is a reaction against Reaganism—the open and enthusiastic melding of the political agenda of a party with the moral agenda of a religious sect—that has driven the left to shed religion like a second skin. But this observation, if true, is ominous. Discrediting all religious witness because of the excesses of some Christian fundamentalists is much like what Jaroslav Pelikan once referred to as "the Enlightenment habit of undercutting all of historic Christianity by attacking Roman Catholicism."[28] Besides, Ronald Reagan was hardly the first American president to make a religious commitment the centerpiece of the public life of his administration. Indeed, in an important sense William Safire was wrong to suppose that the tendency of politicians to drop God's name into virtually every speech is something new. There has been no era in American history when our politicians—and, in particular, our presidents—failed to include routine references to God, and even to particular denominations, in their public rhetoric. George Washington made religious arguments in support of the Revolutionary War and, prior to becoming President, called for a state-supported established church in his native Virginia. He also originated the traditional addition "so help me God" at the end of the presidential oath of office—an addition that is not a part of the constitutionally prescribed language.[29] Woodrow Wilson, in his 1917 Thanksgiving Day proclamation, invited all citizens "in their several homes and places of worship to render thanks to God, the great ruler of nations."[30] Shortly before he died, Franklin D. Roosevelt described the American people this way: "[W]e all hold to the inspiration of the Old Testament and accept the Ten Commandments as the fundamental law of God."[31] And certainly Ronald Reagan made no statement on politics more firmly grounded in religiosity than the following words from Dwight D. Eisenhower: "Without God there could be no American form of government, nor an American way of life. Recognition of the Supreme Being is the first—and most basic—expression of Americanism."[32]

Of course, there are notable exceptions. There is Jefferson, who famously refused to proclaim Thanksgiving, because of concerns about its religious nature. (For a discussion of what Jefferson's fears might have been, see chapter 6.) There is Lincoln, who openly and publicly refused to associate with any organized church, while continuing to insist that he was a Christian. There is Theodore Roosevelt, who, following William James, said that his religion was "good works" and that he went to church only to "set an example."[33]

But such sentiments as these seem to be the exceptions, not the rule. Religion has always been in the public square. The rhetoric of religion has always issued from the mouths of the nation's political leaders. And it has always been a part of the public dialogue of others, too. True, the words "under God" were not added to the Pledge of Allegiance until after World War II, but they were invented as an affirmation of loyalty long before. And during the Civil War, for example, the *Atlantic Monthly* in 1863 described the Confederacy as "rebels trying to build an empire on the ruins of the Ten Commandments," adding that the rebellion was bound to fail, because, it seemed, failure was God's will: "This Western Continent, under God, may it please the despots, is not going to barbarism and desolation."[34]

The Confederate states thought God was on their side too, which is the reason they kept slipping references to the Almighty into the loyalty oaths they began to impose as the states spun toward secession.[35] Indeed, as such historians as Jon Butler and Cushing Strout have argued, there has been no era in the history of the United States when religion did not feature prominently both in the moral lives of citizens and in the public life of the nation.[36]

So when the guardians of the public square inveigh against religious dialogue, or when pundits worry about the influence of religion on politics, they are worrying, as it were, against history. The battle for the public square is already over. The rhetoric of religion is simply *there;* it is far too late in America's political day to argue over "shoulds." The important question is not whether religions can act as autonomous, politically involved intermediary institutions, or whether religious people should have access to the public square. Those questions history has already decided.

The question crying out most vitally for resolution, given the presence of religions in the public square, is whether and how to regulate that presence. More and more, the American answer, as with all tough questions, is to let the courts do it. Harkening to the plea for help, the courts have promulgated and nurtured the sensible doctrine of separation of church and state. The problem is whether the courts have got the doctrine right, or whether, as critics charge, it has become a tool for treating religions worse than other American institutions. That problem is the subject of part II.

II

THE
FIRST SUBJECT
OF THE FIRST
AMENDMENT

6

The Separation of Church and State

B Y now, many a patient reader will be ready with another objection: it is all very well to talk about allowing the religious to enter the public square to participate in political debate alongside everybody else. But what about the Constitution? What about the separation of church and state? Don't we have long-standing constitutional and philosophical traditions that limit the influence of religious sectarianism on government policy?

The answer to the last question—as so often in the law—is "not exactly." The courts do indeed enforce a separation of church and state, and it is backed by some very impressive legal philosophy, but one must be careful not to misunderstand what the doctrine and the First Amendment that is said to embody it were designed to do. Simply put, the metaphorical separation of church and state originated in an effort to protect religion from the state, not the state from religion. The religion clauses of the

First Amendment were crafted to permit maximum freedom to the religious. In modern, religiously pluralistic America, where, as we have seen, the religions play vital roles as independent sources of meaning for their adherents, this means that the government should neither force people into sectarian religious observances, such as classroom prayer in public schools, nor favor some religions over others, as by erecting a crèche paid for with public funds, nor punish people for their religiosity without a very strong reason other than prejudice. It does not mean, however, that people whose motivations are religious are banned from trying to influence government, nor that the government is banned from listening to them. Understanding this distinction is the key to preserving the necessary separation of church and state without resorting to a philosophical rhetoric that treats religion as an inferior way for citizens to come to public judgment.

THE SEPARATION METAPHOR

Religion is the first subject of the First Amendment. The amendment begins with the Establishment Clause ("Congress shall make no law respecting an establishment of religion . . . ") which is immediately followed by the Free Exercise Clause ("or prohibiting the free exercise thereof"). Although one might scarcely know it from the zeal with which the primacy of the other First Amendment freedoms (free press, free speech) is often asserted, those protections come *after* the clauses that were designed to secure religious liberty, which Thomas Jefferson called "the most inalienable and sacred of all human rights."[1] What this means in practice, however, is often quite complicated.

Consider an example: at a dinner party in New York City a few years ago, I met a Christian minister who told me about a drug-rehabilitation program that he runs in the inner city. His claim—I cannot document it—was that his program had a success rate much higher than other programs. The secret, he insisted, was prayer. It was not just that he and his staff prayed for the drug abusers they were trying to help, he told me, although they naturally did that. But the reason for the program's success, he proclaimed, was that he and his staff taught those who came to them for assistance to pray as well; in other words, they converted their charges, if not to Christianity, then at least to religiosity. But this program, he went on with something close to bitterness, could receive no state funding, because of its religious nature.

Well, all right. To decide that the program should not receive any funds, despite the success of its approach, might seem to be a straightforward application of the doctrine holding that the Constitution sets up a wall of separation between church and state. After all, the program is frankly religious: it uses prayer, and even teaches prayer to its clients. What could be more threatening to the separation of church and state than to provide a government subsidy for it? The Supreme Court has said many times that the government may neither "advance" religion nor engage in an "excessive entanglement" with it.[2] On its face, a program of drug-rehabilitation therapy that relies on teaching people to pray would seem to do both.

It is doubtless frustrating to believe deeply that one has a call from God to do what one does, and then to discover that the secular society often will not support that work, no matter how important it is to the individual. Yet that frustration is itself a sign of the robustness of religious pluralism in America. For the most significant aspect of the separation of church and state is not, as some seem to think, the shielding of the secular world from too strong a religious influence; the principal task of the separation of church and state is to secure religious liberty.

The separation of church and state is one of the great gifts that American political philosophy has presented to the world, and if it has few emulators, that is the world's loss. Culled from the writings of Roger Williams and Thomas Jefferson, the concept of a "wall of separation" finds its constitutional moorings in the First Amendment's firm statement that the "Congress shall make no law respecting any establishment of religion." Although it begins with the word "Congress," the Establishment Clause for decades has been quite sensibly interpreted by the Supreme Court as applying to states as well as to the federal government.[3]

For most of American history, the principal purpose of the Establishment Clause has been understood as the protection of the religious world against the secular government. A century ago, Philip Schaff of Union Seminary in New York celebrated the clause as "the Magna Carta of religious freedom," representing as it did "the first example in history of a government deliberately depriving itself of all legislative control over religion."[4] Note the wording: not religious control over government—government control over religion. Certainly this voluntary surrender of control is an indispensable separation if the religions are to serve as the independent intermediary institutions that Tocqueville envisioned.

Over the years, the Supreme Court has handed down any number of controversial decisions under the Establishment Clause, many of them landmarks of our democratic culture. The best known are the cases in which the Justices struck down the recital of organized prayer in the public school classrooms, decisions that for three decades have ranked (in surveys) as among the most unpopular in our history.[5] But the decisions were plainly right, for if the state is either able to prescribe a prayer to begin the school day or to select a holy book from which a prayer must be taken, it is casting exercising control over the religious aspects of the life of its people—precisely what the Establishment Clause was written to forbid. But although the separation of church and state is essential to the success of a vibrant, pluralistic democracy, the doctrine does not entail all that is done in its name. I have already mentioned the school district in Colorado that thought it the better part of valor to forbid a teacher to add books on Christianity to a classroom library that already included works on other religions. The town of Hamden, Connecticut, where I live, briefly ruled that a church group could not rent an empty schoolhouse for Sunday services. (Cooler heads in the end prevailed.) These rulings were both defended as required by the separation of church and state; so is the intermittent litigation to strike the legend IN GOD WE TRUST from America's coins or the phrase "under God" from the Pledge of Allegiance, an effort, if successful, that would wipe away even the civil religion. In short, it is not hard to understand the frequent complaints that the secular world acts as though the constitutional command is that the nation and its people must keep religion under wraps.

Proponents of the hostility thesis believe that the Supreme Court bears a heavy burden of responsibility for what they see as the disfavored position of religion in America. Justice Hugo Black, in *Everson v. Board of Education* (1947), often is said to have started the ball rolling when he wrote these words: "The First Amendment has erected a wall between church and state. That wall must be kept high and impregnable. We could not approve the slightest breach."[6] A year later, Justice Stanley Reed warned that "a rule of law should not be drawn from a figure of speech."[7] One critic wrote years later that Black had simply penned a few "lines of fiction."[8] The critics are not quite right, but they are not quite wrong, either. There is nothing wrong with the metaphor of a wall of separation. The trouble is that in order to make the Founders' vision compatible with the structure and needs of modern society, the wall has to have a few doors in it.

SOURING ON *LEMON*

The embarrassing truth is that the Establishment Clause has no theory; that is, the Supreme Court has not really offered guidance on how to tell when the clause is violated. Since 1971, the Justices have relied on the "*Lemon* test," so named because it was framed (quite awkwardly, one is compelled to add) in the

Court's 1971 decision in *Lemon v. Kurtzman*.[9] The case is so often cited that legal scholars tend to forget what it involved: a state program to reimburse all private schools, including religious schools, for expenses of textbooks, materials, and, in part, salaries used to teach nonreligious subjects. (The general problem of aid to religious schools is discussed in chapter 10.) The Court held the program unconstitutional and, in so doing, enunciated the *Lemon* test—a lemon indeed, for it has proved well nigh impossible to apply. In order to pass Establishment Clause muster, the Justices wrote, the statute in question must meet three criteria: "First, the statute must have a secular legislative purpose; second, its principal or primary effect must be one that neither advances nor inhibits religion; finally, the statute must not foster 'an excessive entanglement with religion.'"

Thus conceived, the clause exists less for the benefit of religious autonomy than for the benefit of secular politics; that is, to borrow from the test itself, the Establishment Clause was written to further "a secular legislative purpose," trying to erect around the political process a wall almost impossible to take seriously. It is perhaps needless to add that *Lemon* left the critics in their glory. Did the legislation enacted at the behest of the religiously motivated civil rights movement have a secular purpose? If granting tax relief to parents whose children attend parochial schools advances religion by making the schools cheaper, does refusing to grant them inhibit religion by making the schools more expensive? If competing factions within the same church both seek control of the same church building, does judicial resolution represent an excessive entanglement?

When it promulgates complex multipart tests for constitutional violations, the Supreme Court is almost always luckless, but the *Lemon* test has been extraordinarily unhelpful to the lower courts. Indeed, the courts have reached results that are all over the map—sometimes quite literally, for one of the more interesting cases involved a rather bland "Motorists' Prayer" to God for safety that North Carolina printed on its official state maps. A federal court, missing the significance of America's civil religion, held the practice to be a violation of the Establishment Clause.[10] Another federal court ruled that the clause prohibits religious groups from petitioning the Congress for private laws (available to all other groups) in order to secure copyrights when they are unable to meet the statutory criteria.[11] The list goes on and on—but *Lemon* remains.

The Supreme Court itself has not fared much better than the lower courts in applying its test. The *Lemon* framework might not work too badly, could the courts but take the requirement of a "secular legislative purpose" to mean, as one scholar has proposed, any "political purpose"—that is, any goal the state legitimately is able to pursue. Recently, however, the courts have seemed to fumble this point, confusing the political purpose for which the statute is enacted with the religious sensibilities of legislators or their constituents.

A majority of the Supreme Court missed this point in *Edwards v. Aguillard* (1987), with the suggestion that a law requiring schools to teach scientific creationism is unconstitutional because most of its supporters were religiously motivated—a suggestion that would also render unconstitutional the religiously motivated teaching of evolution, or, for that matter, a religiously motivated nuclear arms freeze.[12] A similar suggestion has been made by some pro-choice scholars who have argued that pro-life legislation violates the Establishment Clause because of the religious motivation of many supporters. For the religiously devout citizen, faith may be so intertwined with personality that it is impossible to tell when one is acting, or not acting, from religious motive—and this is certainly true for legislators, unless we dismiss as hypocritical cynics the entire Congress of the United States, where over 90 percent of the members say that they consult their religious beliefs before voting on important matters. Indeed, by some estimates, an absolute majority of the laws now on the books were motivated, at least in part, by religiously based moral judgments. That is why inquiring into *why* legislators have voted as they have, rather than *what* their legislation does, is almost always a mistake. "That values happen to be religious," New York's Governor Mario Cuomo has warned, "does not deny them acceptability" as part of "the consensus view" needed to support public policy.[13] The result in *Edwards* is probably correct (see chapter 9), but not because of the Court's discussion of what was in the minds of the supporters of the statute.

The idea that religious motivation renders a statute suspect was never anything but a tortured and unsatisfactory reading of the clause. As one scholar has put the matter, there is good reason to think that "what the religion clauses of the first amendment were designed to do was not to remove religious values from the arena of public debate, but to keep them there."[14] The Establishment Clause by its terms forbids the imposition of religious belief by the state, not statements of religious belief in the course of public dialogue.[15] The distinction is one of more than semantic significance.

Consider the call by Reinhold Niebuhr and others back in the 1920s for the "Christianization" of American industry.[16] Their use of the word "Christianization" did not mean the imposition of ritual and doctrine; it meant, rather, the transformation of industry into a new form that would accord with a principle of respect for the human spirit that Niebuhr and the rest found lacking in industrial organizations of the day. Critics called it socialism, or perhaps communism. But whatever it was, religious faith was plainly at its heart.

Niebuhr struck a chord, not only with any number of left-leaning Protestants, but also with a good number of socialists, many of them Jews, and with other reformers of no religious persuasion. (A well-known support group was Atheists for Niebuhr.) Suppose the response had been greater, that public support had burgeoned; suppose that legislatures had begun enacting programs that matched the socialist spirit of Christianization. This reform legislation would be purely secular in operation and could certainly be justified in secular terms. But under an establishment clause that is read to equate *acting* out of religious motivation with *imposing* religious belief, the programs might be unconstitutional, because both those who proposed them and many of those who voted for them would have done so out of religious conviction.

That should be a deeply troubling result. A rule holding that the religious convictions of the proponents are enough to render a statute constitutionally suspect represents a sweeping rejection of the deepest beliefs of millions of Americans, who are being told, in effect, that their views do not matter. In a nation that prides itself on cherishing religious freedom, it would be something of a puzzle to conclude that the Establishment Clause means that a Communist or a Republican may try to have his or her world view reflected in the nation's law, but a religionist can not. Although some critics fear we are already at that point, the truth is that we have a good long way to go; but we are heading in the wrong direction in our jurisprudence, and if the courts continue to read *Lemon* as they have, the Establishment Clause might well end up not antiestablishment but antireligion.

Recognizing this danger, the Justices, and the scholars who support their Establishment Clause jurisprudence, have simply ignored the rules of *Lemon v. Kurtzman* when applying them might prove too disruptive.[17] In particular, they have tried to tiptoe around many widely accepted practices that seem to run afoul of *Lemon*. But squaring *Lemon*'s rules with the accepted usages of the society's civil religion often requires some fancy footwork. How, for example, does one justify the expenditure of government funds to provide armed forces chaplains, which looks like government sponsorship of religion? Answers one observer; "This is not so much 'setting up a church' as providing access to churches already existing for those removed by government action from their normal communities."[18] Okay, but how to explain the use of public funds during the Christmas season to build and maintain a crèche, which celebrates the nativity of Jesus Christ? The Court itself tackled that one: "The display engenders a friendly community spirit of good will in keeping with the season" and any advancement of particular religions "is indirect, remote and incidental."[19] Oh, really? Well, what about the offering of prayers at the opening of legislative sessions? The Justices had an answer for that one too: "In light of the unambiguous and unbroken history of more than 200 years, there can be no doubt that the practice of opening legislative sessions with prayer has become part of the fabric of our society."[20]

Part of the fabric of our society—it is easy to see why the Court is reluctant to hold that the fabric of society includes some threads of unconstitutionality, but it is difficult to imagine how that can be the right test. Racial segregation was once part of the fabric of our society; so was prohibiting the women's vote, and corrupt patronage politics in the big cities. The idea, for example, that a crèche does not advance religion is ridiculous; the point of the crèche is to celebrate the birth of the Lord. So if the Court is willing to ignore *Lemon* and hold that government funds can pay for one, it is simply not doing its job.[21] If the Justices dare not even follow their own rules, it may be time to find a new way to look at these problems. Yet the Supreme Court, although hinting around the edges, has not yet decided to make a full retreat.

Part of the problem is figuring out where the Justices can possibly retreat to. For even if the Court's *Lemon* test is insupportable, it is far from clear what should be put in its place. On this point, not surprisingly, there is a considerable scholarly battle, in which it is healthiest to be a spectator. Michael McConnell has proposed a standard based on coercion of belief, which he has labeled the "lost element" of Establishment Clause jurisprudence.[22] Douglas Laycock has shot back that this test would leave the Establishment Clause void of content.[23] Justice Sandra Day O'Connor has proposed a test asking whether the government is endorsing religious belief or not.[24] Mark Tushnet has answered that Christian judges in a Christian-dominated society are not in the best position to tell whether a message of endorsement is being sent.[25] Steven D. Smith, distinguishing between religious individuals and their organizations, has suggested prohibiting only concerted action by state and religious institutions.[26] Kathleen Sullivan has taken the opposite position, proposing to use the clause to guarantee a secular public order.[27] And one could go on this way at some considerable length.

Constitutional provisions all too rarely, alas, have easily discernible meanings, and there are elements of truth in all these readings of the Establishment Clause. Yet what is most vital, in coming to a sensible understanding of the clause, is to avoid the ahistorical conclusion that its principal purpose is to protect the secular from the religious, an approach that, perhaps inevitably, carries us down the road toward a new establishment, the establishment of religion as a hobby, trivial and unimportant for serious people, not to be mentioned in serious discourse. And nothing could be further from the constitutional, historical, or philosophical truth.

A BIT OF HISTORY

This is not the place to write a detailed history of the views of the Founders on separation of church and state; that is a subject that has usefully occupied many a learned tome.[28] Yet it is useful to summarize what history teaches. Unlike the case of many a constitutional provision, we actually know a great deal about the history of the Establishment Clause and about the development of the ideal of a separated church and state. We know so much, in fact, that it is something of an embarrassment that we so enthusiastically ignore our knowledge in our church-and-state jurisprudence.

In particular, we know that for most members of the Founding Generation the idea of separating church from state meant protecting the church from the state—not the state from the church. No one doubted that the churches should and must be

harsh moral critics of politics; but the Founders did not believe
that the state should be engaged in trying to regulate religions.
Thus, for example, when Roger Williams wrote of the "wall of
separation between the garden of the Church and the wilderness
of the world," he was expressing a popular New England Free
Church ideal of toleration and religious plurality, the ability of
the believer to worship without the interference of the state.[29]

James Madison's *Memorial and Remonstrance,* written in
1785 in a successful effort to defeat Patrick Henry's bill to support all churches in Virginia by assessments from the population
at large, is often, and correctly, cited as a fundamental document
on the separation of church and state. Yet the *Memorial and
Remonstrance* is decidedly of a religious, not a secular, cast. For
example, the *Memorial* is regularly quoted for the proposition
that "the opinions of men, depending only on the evidence contemplated by their own minds, cannot follow the dictates of
other men." For Madison, however, this was a defense of the
right to hold one's own religion, and his reference was to religious opinion. Indeed Madison proclaimed with some pride that
the obligation of man to God was prior to the obligation of man
to the state, which meant, he said, that the state was subordinate
to God. Similarly, Madison is frequently quoted for the following
passage: "Whilst we assert for ourselves a freedom to embrace,
to profess and to observe the Religion which we believe to be of
divine origin, we cannot deny an equal freedom to those whose
minds have not yet yielded to the evidence that has convinced
us." But the very next line is striking: "If this freedom be abused,
it is an offence against God, not against man."[30]

The point is that the *Memorial and Remonstrance,* although
it plainly defends the separation of church and state, frames the
argument principally as a protection of the church, not as a protection of the state. Indeed, the entire disestablishment movement
in Virginia was a movement to rescue religious freedom from state
oppression, not to rescue the state from religious oppression.

Thomas Jefferson is often cited as an exemplar of secular

politics, but Jefferson's vision of the relationship between government and religion was strongly shaped by his vision of religion itself, which he considered a matter of individual conscience rather than of corporate worship. Jefferson, a deist, did not think churches important; he thought the individual important. But although Jefferson might therefore be thought to value religion no more than any other aspect of conscience, he did not consider religion an ordinary matter of conscience—rather, religious liberty was for Jefferson "the most inalienable and sacred of all human rights."[31]

Some scholars argue that Jefferson believed that religion had no role in government, pointing as evidence to his refusal to issue a Thanksgiving proclamation. One scholarly objection has been registered by the legal scholar Akhil Reed Amar, who notes that "while *President* Jefferson in 1802 refused to proclaim a day of religious Thanksgiving, he had done just that as *Governor* Jefferson some 20 years before."[32] Whatever his views while serving as president, Jefferson's gubernatorial proclamation was quite religious indeed, calling for "a day of public and solemn thanksgiving and prayer to Almighty God."[33] Of course this may be evidence that Jefferson distinguished between support for religion by the national government and support for religion by the governments of the states. It is also possible that his views on this matter evolved over the decades. In either case, it is likely that at the time of the Founding, Jefferson shared the general view that government support for religion was not in itself an evil, but that the state had to be prevented from exercising coercive authority over the religions, especially those dissenting from the established churches—once more, a very Tocquevillean approach to the purpose of protecting religion.

The same spirit animated the drafting of the First Amendment and its twin clauses prohibiting religious establishments and guaranteeing free exercise. It is plain that the Founders conceived of these clauses less as distinct entities than as parts of a coherent whole—and, to the extent that they were distinct, the distinction had nothing to do with the way that we read the clauses today.

The language of the Establishment Clause, of course, prohibits the Congress from making any law "*respecting* an establishment of religion." The evident purpose of this first word was to prevent the Congress from interfering with state establishments of religion. Indeed, there is good reason to think that the principal purpose of the Establishment Clause, and maybe the sole one, was to protect the state religious establishments from disestablishment by the federal government.[34] If the clause is antidisestablishmentarian in design, however, it makes little sense to speak of applying the Establishment Clause as a limitation on the power of the states, a point noted by Akhil Amar: "To apply the clause against a state government is precisely to eliminate its right to choose whether to establish a religion—a right explicitly confirmed by the establishment clause itself!" Amar would, however, apply the Free Exercise Clause against the states, with the interesting result that each state "would be free to establish one or several churches, but would be obliged to respect the free exercise rights of dissenters to opt out."[35] In fine, there would seem to be nothing odder, from a historical perspective, than the idea that the Establishment Clause prohibits state support for religious institutions.

But need we be bound by this history? Many scholars think not. In the first place, the Constitution has changed since the adoption of the First Amendment in 1789. Following the Civil War, the nation adopted the Fourteenth Amendment, which granted to all citizens rights against their state governments that previously they had only held against the federal government. The courts have read the antiestablishment right to be among them. Besides, the nation itself has changed. The legal scholar Harold Berman argues that "The religious context of the First Amendment as originally understood—and as understood at least until World War I—no longer exists, and the public philosophy generated in that context no longer exists."[36] In other words, says

Berman, the original understanding may no longer bind us because contemporary reality is so sharply discontinuous with the world of the Founders.[37]

Berman is right: the religious self-image of the American people *has* changed. In particular, since World War II, Americans have come to accept religious pluralism with a sincerity that the Founders could not have envisioned.[38] The data certainly bear this out, but it is not a recent phenomenon. One study suggests that as long ago as the early years of this century, the state courts—notoriously responsive to political trend—were already moving away from the vision of the United States as a "Christian nation" that so influenced much of the church-and-state rhetoric of the eighteenth and early nineteenth centuries.[39]

However, relatively few Americans draw the sharp distinction between religion as a public force and a private one that the guardians of the public square suppose. The data suggest that although Americans are less likely than in the past to respond rigidly to hierarchical commands of religious authority, their religious beliefs tend to be deep and, on many moral issues, seem to be controlling.[40] There is little evidence to support the idea that most Americans prefer to think of the religions as remaining outside the public square. So although it is true that the image of religion possessed by most Americans today is different from the image of two hundred years ago, one wants to be cautious about reading so much into the differences that one ends up with a radically new account of the Establishment Clause.

Berman offers a useful synthesis of the unambiguous history of the religion clauses and the contemporary understanding of religion and politics. He argues against the formally established churches that the Founders wanted to preserve, but suggests that in order to meld their vision of religious America with the religious America that now exists, the Establishment Clause should be read to permit "government support of theistic and deistic belief systems more nearly comparable to the government support which is permitted to be given to agnostic and atheist belief systems."[41] In other words, the clause should not place religions in a second-class status but should, at minimum, allow them to compete side by side with secular groups for the largess of the welfare state.

The history, in sum, suggests that Founders intended to allow states to establish religions, and, certainly, did not intend to proscribe state support for religion. Amar's historical approach would allow state establishments, provided that the religious liberty of the dissenter is protected. Berman's sensible modern gloss would proscribe establishments but would allow support on the same basis as other groups. Although I do think that Amar has the history right, I cast my constitutional lot with Berman.

When one combines the recognition of a greater religious pluralism than the Founders envisioned with the realization that faith communities themselves are more open to internal debate than they once were, two fantasies should collapse. First, the Founders' evident desire to protect the power of states to establish religions is today an irrelevancy, and, second, the fear of religiously motivated automatons doing in politics what their leaders command is today a delusion. One would therefore want to say that the government must not advance the interests of one religious tradition over another, which is why the state should not pay for crèches and why organized prayer must stay out of the public school classroom. But one should not try to oversimplify the human mind by making religious conviction a ground for invalidating law, which is why (although I revisit the issue in more detail in chapter 10), ordained moments of silence to begin the school day probably do not violate the Establishment Clause.

SEPARATION OF CHURCH AND . . . WHAT?

All of which brings us back to the religious drug-treatment program that opened our discussion of the separation of church and state. We are still left with the original question: should the program receive state funding or not?

We have already seen that the Establishment Clause should not be read to prohibit all state support for religion, and, should it be read that way, churches would lose their charitable exemptions. Consequently, one can immediately deduce the rule that religious organizations should be able to compete on the same grounds as other groups for the largess of the welfare state—they should not, on Establishment Clause grounds, be relegated to a second-class status. Consequently, if the program involved no prayer, it would certainly have been eligible for state support: plenty of religious institutions run secular programs that compete for the largess of the welfare state. So the question is whether the fact that the beneficiaries were prayed over—and taught to pray—means that the program should not be eligible.

Many readers might challenge the minister's claim of efficacy, which would make it unnecessary to consider the Establishment Clause claim. However, the claim that the program works well is not wholly implausible. I had no more than a single conversation with the man who runs it, so I honestly do not know whether the program's success rate was unusually good or unusually bad. Drug rehabilitation, unfortunately, is an area in which data are notoriously unreliable. In particular, although claims of this kind are legion, no convincing studies confirm that religiously oriented approaches do a better job than other programs at ending drug habits.* I once saw some data suggesting that strongly religious people are less susceptible than others to drug and alcohol dependencies and are more likely to kick the habit once begun—but this is where the scholar must apply a degree of statistical caution. The data do not and cannot reveal

---

* Although the highly successful twelve-step program pioneered by Alcoholics Anonymous and emulated by many other dependency-treatment programs is frequently characterized as religious—significantly, this characterization usually comes from the program's detractors—AA supporters insist that its reference to a "higher power" is susceptible to many interpretations that do not partake of the supernatural.

whether possession of a strongly religious character is the *reason* that the habit is kicked, or whether the strongly religious character, and the ability to kick the habit, in fact flow independently from some other valuable character trait.

Still, for the sake of argument, suppose that clear and unambiguous data showed, for reasons unknown, that rehabilitation programs involving religious teaching or even conversion were more successful than other drug-treatment programs in helping addicts to return to normal lives. In other words, suppose that this religiously oriented program turns out to be better than the various secular approaches that now receive government aid—with the important distinction that the most successful of its graduates enter with an addiction to drugs and leave with a commitment to God. The program, then, could fairly be described as proselytizing—but, unlike some forms of proselytization, its work is in a secular cause. Should the state then be prepared to fund the program?

Under the *Lemon v. Kurtzman* test, one would probably be forced to conclude that the statistics do not matter, and that assistance to the religiously oriented program, no matter how worthy it might appear, is barred by the "primary effect" test—for, plainly, if the program proselytizes, the effect of the subsidy is to advance the religion in question. But the program might pass muster on some of the alternative tests that have been proposed. For example, support for a drug-treatment program that includes prayer would not involve any coercion, provided that nobody was required to participate.[42] Many observers would surely argue that support for the program involved an endorsement, and therefore it fails Justice O'Connor's test. It is not clear that this is correct, however, for a voluntary drug-treatment program is hardly like the public display of a crèche; besides, if subsidizing a drug-treatment program constitutes an endorsement of religion because the patients learn to pray, the charitable tax deduction for contributions to religious groups would seem to be in terrible jeopardy.

The potential transformation of the Establishment Clause

from a guardian of religious liberty into a guarantor of public secularism raises prospects at once dismal and dreadful. The more that the clause is used to disable religious groups from active involvement in the programs of the welfare state, or, for that matter, from active involvement in the public square that is the crucible of public policy, the less the religions will be able to play their proper democratic role of mediating between the individual and the state and the less they will be able to play their proper theological role of protecting the people of God.

The problem does not stop with a silly fight over the rental of a public school building by a religious group or the unhappy order to wipe the Motorist's Prayer from state road maps. We have also seen enthusiastic litigation—so far unsuccessful—that challenges the tax-exempt status of the Roman Catholic Church because of its antiabortion advocacy.[43] And why not? After all, it is a well-understood rule that tax-exempt contributions cannot be used for lobbying or to support or oppose political candidates. Doubtless the same high principles will soon lead the same protesters to demand withdrawal of the tax-exempt status of the church where my wife and I heard the preacher command support for the Sandinistas (see chapter 4), or, for that matter, to question the tax-exempt status of the many churches where the civil rights movement was nurtured. Or maybe not: maybe there are not any principles involved. Maybe it is just another effort to ensure that intermediate institutions, such as the religions, do not get in the way of the government's will. Perhaps, in short, it is a way of ensuring that only one vision of the meaning of reality— that of the powerful group of individuals called the state—is allowed a political role. Back in Tocqueville's day, this was called tyranny. Nowadays, all too often, but quite mistakenly, it is called the separation of church and state.

7

The Accommodation
of Religion

To be consistent with the Founders' vision and coherent in modern religiously pluralistic America, the religion clauses should be read to help avoid tyranny—that is, to sustain and nurture the religions as independent centers of power, the democratic intermediaries we have been discussing. To do that, the clauses must be interpreted to do more than protect the religions against explicit discrimination. Nowadays, the government hardly ever adopts laws aimed at burdening particular religions.* Consequently, the question of religious freedom arises most frequently when the religious ask for exemptions under the Free Exercise Clause from laws that apply to everybody else. And it must not

---

* Sometimes, of course, uncommon things happen. In June of 1993, the Supreme Court struck down on free exercise grounds a municipal ordinance aimed at making it difficult for adherents to the religious tradition of Santeria to practice animal sacrifice. Whatever the degree of one's affection for animals, it was plain that this statute was enacted out of antireligious animus.

be missed that those "laws that apply to everybody else" often reflect, albeit implicitly, the values and teachings of the nation's dominant religious traditions.

Consider an example: virtually unnoticed in the brouhaha surrounding George Bush's 1992 Christmas Eve pardons of Caspar Weinberger and other officials implicated in the Iran-Contra scandal were pardons for two Jehovah's Witnesses whose crime was refusing to register for military service in the 1940s and 1950s. The law has long allowed the Witnesses, and others with religious objections to combat, to register and then seek "conscientious objector" status; but it does not exempt from the registration requirement itself those with moral objections to war.

By seeking an exemption from a law that applies to everybody else, the war resisters are asking for what is called an "accommodation" of their religious belief.[1] A few constitutional scholars—not many—believe that granting accommodations violates the Establishment Clause, because it provides to the religious something that others cannot have.[2] President Bush's pardons of the Witnesses, then, might be seen as a version of religious preferment in which the government must not engage.

The Supreme Court, fortunately, has never accepted the idea that all accommodations are unconstitutional. So the government can generally allow religious exemptions, as the Congress did in the statute allowing the religious to wear unobtrusive religious apparel while on active military duty (see chapter 1). However, after a brief flowering of judicially created exemptions, the Court has looked increasingly askance at claims of a free exercise right to violate laws that everyone else must obey. The most notable recent example is the Court's 1990 decision in *Employment Division v. Smith,* which upheld the application of a state antidrug policy to state employees who, as members of the Native American Church, were required to use peyote during religious rituals.

In this chapter and the one following, I argue for a broader understanding of religious freedom and, in consequence, a wider set of religious exemptions from laws of general application. In no other way can we enable the religions to stand as intermediaries between sovereign and citizen, thus limiting the prospect of majoritarian tyranny; and in no other way can we translate the Founders' ideal of religious freedom in a relatively simple society into a new ideal for a new era, one characterized by a regulatory regime far more intrusive than the Founders could possibly have contemplated.

WHAT ARE ACCOMMODATIONS?

The accommodation of a religious group's faith traditions in an otherwise applicable legal framework can best be envisioned as a form of affirmative action. Recognizing both the unique historical circumstances of the religions and the importance of nurturing their continued existence, the state chooses to grant them a form of differential treatment. When President Bush pardoned the Jehovah's Witnesses, he was not endorsing their religious claims, but he was seeking ways to accommodate them within a political structure that generally favors the adherents of the mainstream religions.

Indeed, the domination of our politics by citizens raised in the mainstream religions helps explain why accommodations are so often necessary. Consider for a moment the Supreme Court's 1990 decision in *Employment Division v. Smith*.[3] The case involved the dismissal of two state employees who had violated policy by using a controlled substance, peyote. The employees protested that the Free Exercise Clause was a shield, because they had used peyote as part of a religious ritual. The majority scoffed at this claim, not so much disbelieving it as disregarding it: the fact that the peyote use had religious significance, the Court said, was irrelevant, as long as the state law was not "an attempt to regulate religious beliefs, the communication of reli-

gious beliefs, or the raising of one's children in those beliefs"—
which, plainly, it was not.[4]

Employment Division v. Smith is a much criticized—and
justly criticized—decision, and it shows clearly just where the
current Court's Free Exercise jurisprudence is heading: toward a
clear separation of church and self, a world in which citizens
who adopt religious practices at variance with official state policy
are properly made subject to the coercive authority of the state,
which can, without fear of judicial intervention, pressure them to
change those practices.

Formally, the *Smith* decision turned on the question of
whether the Free Exercise Clause imposed the weightiest constitutional burden—the requirement that the state demonstrate a
"compelling" interest—before the courts would uphold a seemingly neutral statute that interfered with the practice of a religion.
The *Smith* majority lamented that insisting on a heightened standard "would open the prospect of constitutionally required religious exemptions from civic obligations of almost every conceivable kind." One can understand the Court's worry about how to
stay off of the slippery slope—*if peyote, why not cocaine? if the
Native American Church, why not the Matchbook Cover Church
of the Holy Peyote Plant?*—but the implications of the decision
are unsettling. If the state bears no special burden to justify its
infringement on religious practice, as long as the challenged
statute is a neutral one, then the only protection a religious
group receives is against legislation directed at that group. But
legislation directed at a particular religious group, even in the
absence of the Free Exercise Clause, presumably would be prohibited by the Equal Protection Clause.

After *Smith* was decided, critics tumbled all over one
another in the rush to be the first to offer the obvious hypothetical situation. Prohibition, implemented by the Volstead Act of
1919, included an exemption for religious use of wine—but suppose it had not. If a Christian or Jew were prosecuted for defi-
ance of the act, would a conviction really be sustained against a

free exercise challenge? (At least one dry state, Oklahoma, apparently made no exception during Prohibition for religious use of wine, for the state was dominated by Baptists who did not use wine and who saw it as an indulgence of Catholics and Jews.)

Perhaps the dissenting Christian or Jew would have to go to jail, because a nation prepared to pass a Volstead Act without a religious exemption would be a nation no longer as heavily dominated by its religious mainline. And that, of course, is the point of the story. In America as it is today, the hypothetical case about the prohibition on the religious use of wine is a hypothetical case that would never occur precisely because the nation's dominant religious traditions—Catholic, Protestant, and Jewish—all use wine for religious purposes. The great majority of Americans profess one of these faiths, and they will not countenance a state effort to shut down their religious observances; indeed, the state would never try. As the legal scholar Kathleen Sullivan has pointed out, "not a single religious exemption claim has ever reached the Supreme Court from a mainstream Christian religious practitioner."[5]

The judgment against the Native American Church, however, demonstrates that the political process will protect only the mainstream religions, not the many smaller groups that exist at the margins.[6] It is as though the relevant legal principles have been designed in order to uphold state regulations infringing on faith traditions that lie far from the mainstream; perhaps the courts are unable to appreciate the concern about "incidental" infringements precisely because judges are not drawn from religious traditions likely to suffer them.

Justice Antonin Scalia, perhaps unknowingly, made this precise point at the conclusion of his opinion for the *Smith* majority:

> It may fairly be said that leaving accommodation to the political process will place at a relative disadvantage those religious practices that are not widely engaged in; but that unavoidable consequence of democratic government must be preferred to a system in which each conscience is a law

unto itself or in which judges weigh the social importance of
all laws against the centrality of all religious beliefs.[7]

What Justice Scalia misses is that it was in order to avoid
this "unavoidable consequence of democratic government" that
the Free Exercise Clause was crafted in the first place. The fact
that the defense of religious liberty burdens the courts is hardly a
reason, as he implies it is, to forbear.

A more practical danger also lurks, one that the legal
scholar Frederick Mark Gedicks has noted: "Without exemptions,
some religious groups will likely be crushed by the weight of
majoritarian law and culture. Such groups pose no threat to
order. However, majoritarian dominance could radicalize some
believers into destabilizing, antisocial activity, including violence."[8] Of course, the dominant culture can do what it has
always done in the face of threats to order, especially threats
from people the nation itself has oppressed, such as Native
Americans and slaves: it can declare the marginalized and violent
dissenters to be criminals, and thus rid itself of them, their movements, and their religions all at once.

THE REDUCTION OF RELIGION

Smith is part of a recent and unfortunate line of cases that
reduce the scope of the Free Exercise Clause until it lacks independent content, forbidding by its own force no more than do
the document's other clauses that protect individual rights (here,
equal protection, in other cases, free speech or assembly). So, for
example, the Court has held that religious people (*not* religions
as such) have the rights to proselytize or seek contributions without government permission;[9] to give sermons without an official
license;[10] and to meet and worship without first seeking state
approval.[11] All of these rights resemble, and perhaps are identical

to, rights that would be upheld on free speech grounds even if there were no religious freedom clause. In a sense, this might be seen as a triumph. Justice William Brennan, in a slightly different context, has put the matter this way: "religionists, no less than members of any other group," should "enjoy the full measure of protection afforded speech, association and political activity generally."[12] However, this glowing account of the similarity between speech rights and religion rights masks a danger. The question is whether those are the only rights that religionists hold. For the cases upholding religiously motivated actions that look like other protected speech exemplify what the legal scholar Mark Tushnet has labeled the "reduction principle" of religious freedom, a doctrine holding "that religious belief is indistinguishable from other types of belief, so that neither the free exercise nor the establishment clause constrains governmental action any differently than the free speech clause does."[13]

Indeed, Justice Scalia's focus in his majority opinion on the ability to *communicate* religious beliefs, whether to others or to one's progeny, fits the traditional free speech model so snugly that one can assume that those protections would be available even if there were no Free Exercise Clause. The vision of the clause as protecting communicative acts rather than acts of worship or public acts carries with it precisely the message that the separation of church and self entails: you are free to believe as you like, but, for goodness sake, don't act on it!

Now, one will not find many serious scholars of the Free Exercise Clause who find *Smith* convincingly reasoned, and it does seem inconsistent with earlier cases in which the Court did command accommodations of religious belief. For example, the Old Order Amish won a rather spectacular victory when, in *Wisconsin v. Yoder*,[14] the Justices allowed them to cease sending their children to school after the eighth grade. (For more on *Yoder*, see chapter 10.) And then there is the challenging line of cases that began with *Sherbert v. Verner*, wherein the Justices ruled that if an employer refuses to accommodate the religious needs of an employee and the employee is subsequently dismissed, the state cannot deny unemployment compensation.[15]

But those decisions seem increasingly shaky. The Justices have refused to extend *Yoder*-type protections to any other group, or, for the Old Order Amish, to any other activity. As for *Sherbert,* the Justices warned, in *Frazee v. Illinois Department of Employment Security* (1989), that the protection of religiously based refusals to work (at least on Sunday) might vanish if "Sunday shopping, or Sunday sporting, for that matter, [would] grind to a halt."[16] In other words, if accommodating a religious tradition is inconvenient, no accommodation is necessary.

In light of reasoning of this kind, it is small wonder the Justices showed such little sympathy for the Yurok, Karok, and Talowa Indians who challenged the Forest Service's decision to allow a road to be built through an area used by the tribes for sacred rituals. As noted in chapter 1, the Court, in *Lyng v. Northwest Indian Cemetery Protective Association,* ruled that even though road building might have "devastating effects" on the Indians' religious practices, "government simply could not operate" if forced to "satisfy every citizen's religious needs and desires."[17] Again, as in the case of the Native American Church, the Court seems to fear the slippery slope. After all, were the Court to require the Forest Service to take account of the Native Americans' religious practices, thus enabling them to block the road, goodness knows who might be next. Hunters, maybe, or the Sunday shoppers who so concerned the justices in *Frazee;* maybe even (gasp!) environmentalists.[18]

The legal distinction, of course, is that the other potential objectors would not be able to call upon the special protection of the Free Exercise Clause. The practical distinction is that none of the other potential objectors represent religious traditions that are on the margin of America's religious culture. It is no coincidence that the losers in these cases are Native Americans, just as, in an earlier era, they were Mormons; after all, only the religions that are political outsiders are likely to object to what the state requires or forbids them to do. And if, as I have been arguing, the religions are at their most useful when they serve as democratic intermediaries and preach resistance, then it is at precisely that moment, the moment when the religious tradition most diverges from the mainstream, that protection is both most needed and most deserved.

"COMPELLING STATE INTEREST"

To say that the courts should pay greater heed to the claims of outsider religions—or perhaps even to the claims of insider religions, on the rare occasions that the state interferes with their traditions—is not to say that the religions should always win and thus always be exempt from the laws that apply to everybody else. Rather, the rule would be that the state, in trying to enforce a law impinging on the religion's ability to sustain itself, would be required to demonstrate a compelling interest in enforcement of the questioned statute. A compelling interest is one of greater weight than is ordinarily demanded to sustain regulation, and the state would be required to demonstrate that its goal is sufficiently weighty and that the goal could not be accomplished through a less intrusive means.

It is possible that the state antidrug law at issue in *Smith* would have been sustained under a higher standard, but it is not likely, because a majority of states *do* in fact exempt Native Americans from certain drug regulations. Similarly, even under a compelling interest test, the Forest Service might have been able to build its road and destroy the sacred lands, and the Air Force officer mentioned in chapter 1 might properly have been disciplined for wearing a yarmulke. But we can only guess what would have happened under a higher standard of scrutiny, because the Supreme Court has never demanded one in cases calling for accommodations of religion. To apply such a standard, wrote Justice Scalia for the *Smith* majority, "would be courting anarchy." His language recalls the language that the Court chose a century ago (see chapter 2) in rejecting the claim of Mormons for an exemption from antipolygamy laws. To grant the exemption, the Court wrote then, would be "subversive of good order." In other words, the big religions win and the little religions lose.

THE CASE FOR
SUBVERSIVE ANARCHY

As a general proposition, order is a good thing. Nobody much likes anarchy. Justice Scalia lists in his opinion many of the modern statutes from which the religious might demand exemptions—everything from traffic laws to environmental laws to child labor laws—but he misses a crucial historical point. When the First Amendment was written, none of those laws existed. None of them existed because the modern concept of a welfare state, a state in which the government's duty was caring for its citizens, did not exist.

Justice Scalia's conception of a free exercise clause that only protects the religious against discrimination is an example of what is called "neutrality" in the legal literature, the idea that the state should not favor religion but also should not oppress it. The ideal of neutrality might provide useful protection for religious freedom in a society of relatively few laws, one in which most of the social order is privately determined. That was the society the Founders knew. In such a society, it is enough to say that the law leaves religion alone. It is difficult, however, to see how the law can protect religious freedom in the welfare state if it does not offer exemptions and special protection for religious devotion. To offer the religions the chance to win exemptions from laws that others must obey obviously carves out a special niche for religion, but that is hardly objectionable: carving out a special place for religion is the minimum it might be said that the Free Exercise Clause does.

Nowadays, the government rarely if ever enacts legislation intended to oppress a particular religion, which is why Michael McConnell has written that the difference between neutrality and accommodation "is the difference between a Free Exercise Clause that is a major restraining device on government action that affects religious practice and a Free Exercise Clause that will rarely have practical application."[19]

That practical distinction is not, however, the important theoretical distinction. What matters more is the different attitudes that neutrality and accommodation evince toward the role of religious belief in a democratic polity. Neutrality treats religious belief as a matter of individual choice, an aspect of conscience, with which the government must not interfere but which it has no obligation to respect. This was the significance of Justice Scalia's almost snide closing reference in *Smith* to a land in which "every conscience is a law unto itself."[20] In this sense, neutrality treats religious belief like any other belief, controlled by the same rules: the choice is free, but it is entitled to no special subsidy, and, indeed, it can be trampled by the state as long as it is trampled by accident.

Accommodation, however, can be crafted into a tool that accepts religion as a group rather than an individual activity. When accommodation is so understood, corporate worship, not individual conscience, becomes the obstacle around which state policy must make the widest possible berth. Accommodation is therefore closer to Tocqueville's (and the Founders') conception of religious groups as autonomous moral and political forces, intermediate institutions, separate heads of sovereignty vital to preventing majoritarian tyranny. Thus, the reason for accommodation becomes not the protection of individual conscience, but the preservation of the religions as independent power bases that exist in large part in order to resist the state. To allow the

state, without very strong reason, to enforce policies that interfere with this corporate freedom would be antithetical to the
understanding of religious purpose as resistance.

There remains the question of what it means to speak of an
accommodation of religion that takes account of the intermediary
function of religious autonomy, especially in a nation, as Justice
Scalia's opinion reminds us, where the laws are diverse and all-
embracing. The problem of making accommodation work in the
welfare state is the subject of the next chapter.

8

Religious Autonomy in the Welfare State

WHAT would it look like, an accommodation of religion that is driven by the demands of autonomy—autonomy not simply of believers, but also of the religions themselves? Once more, let us proceed by way of example.

THE APARTMENT PROBLEM

Suppose that you, a religious person, decide to rent out an apartment over your garage. Along comes a possible renter who seems to meet all of your requirements, except that he lets slip, in casual conversation, that he is a Satanist. He tells you that he intends, while living in your apartment, to conduct certain rituals demanded by his faith. Now, it happens that your state's fair housing law prohibits religious discrimination,* and you share the moral premises of that law. On the other hand, you cannot, consistent with your own religion, allow Satanic rituals on your property. What do you do?

If you follow the law—a law you generally support—then you must allow on your property activities that your religion forbids. You might even fear the hellfire. (As many as 82 percent of Americans believe Hell to be a real place.)[1] But if you reject the tenant because he happens to be a Satanist, you will be in violation of the law and could face a heavy fine. You might want to plead in defense your constitutional right to exercise your religion freely, asking for an accommodation of your beliefs, which means, in this case, an exception to a valid statute that applies to everybody else. But that would seem something of a long shot. As we have seen, the Supreme Court has made such a mess of the right to exercise one's religion freely that there is little chance the claim for an exemption would succeed. So you would, in the name of nondiscrimination, be stuck with the Satanist.

Of course you have an alternative. You could take the apartment off the market entirely. Or you could try. It might not work, because overcoming such devices as the withdrawal of a listing is the sort of thing any good lawyer can do in her sleep. Then, assuming you were to get away with it, you would have saved your religious beliefs, but at the cost of getting out of the market, which means losing income. If no exemption is forthcoming, your unattractive choice is between going to Hell by renting to someone who will engage in activities you are religiously forbidden to allow on your property and not renting at all.

The dilemma is not entirely hypothetical. Consider a case that arose in California not long ago, when an unmarried couple

---

* The Federal Fair Housing Act does not apply to rentals of single-family homes by their owners or rentals of rooms in such homes or to buildings with fewer than five units if the owner actually occupies one of them. (See 42 U.S.C. Section 3603.)

found their application for an apartment refused because their potential landlords, John and Agnes Donahue, believed they would be "putting themselves in the position of eternal, divine retribution" if they allowed the sin of fornication, as they described it, on their property. Because housing discrimination on the basis of marital status is forbidden in California, the rejected applicants filed a complaint. The Donahues responded that their religious freedom was at stake.[2] At the time of this writing, the case was pending before the California Supreme Court.[3]

The case poses precisely and painfully the liberal dilemma when religious liberty runs up against the regulatory ubiquity of the welfare state. In late twentieth-century America, nearly everyone seems to operate with the general presumption that the government can and should regulate in whatever areas suit its constituents' fancy—unless opponents can interpose a claim of constitutional right. And as federal constitutional rights go, the right to exercise religion freely is quite near the bottom of the totem pole. But the states are free under their own constitutions to protect more than the federal Constitution does, and a friend-of-the-court brief in the Donahue case, signed by religious organizations across the political spectrum, has urged the California Supreme Court to demand that the state meet a heavy burden of justification before it can apply the antidiscrimination law to the Donahues—perhaps even the "compelling interest" test that the Supreme Court rejected when, in *Smith*, it allowed punishment for Native Americans required to use peyote in their religious rituals (see chapter 7).

The Donahue case, although many may find it especially poignant, is not unique. Antidiscrimination law is one of the cutting edges of the accommodation problem, not least because many religious traditions encourage or even require discrimination on grounds that we as a nation have rejected or are on the way to rejecting. Although few American religious traditions will admit any longer to relegating people of color to an inferior status—even the Mormons at last experienced a new revelation, that black members can be priests of the Inner Temple after all—there are many that understand the word of God as barring women from the priesthood, notwithstanding that the equality of women is firmly established in secular law. And many more religions do not allow as ministers individuals who engage in homosexual activities, even as the gay and lesbian rights movement makes important secular inroads.

No one—yet—proposes state regulation of the ministry, but the organized churches are large and complicated operations, and most have many lay employees. Given the broad protections that exist in law against employment discrimination, the potential problems are obvious. Should a church be able to require that the gardener be a coreligionist? That the plumber take a religious oath? That the painter tithe?

In general, the Supreme Court has seemed indecisive in the face of religious objections to statutes regarding employment practices. So, for example, the Justices ruled in 1979 that the National Labor Relations Board cannot exercise jurisdiction over lay teachers in Catholic schools.[4] Then, six years later, the Court ruled that the Labor Department can enforce minimum wage laws on behalf of at least some employees of religious foundations.[5] Now, that is another view, not quite consistent with the first. But at least the justices are in there punching.

When forbidden discrimination is the issue, even Supreme Court justices who might otherwise be considered accommodationists tread warily. In the best-known case, *Corporation of Presiding Bishop of the Church of Jesus Christ of Latter-Day Saints v. Amos* (1987), the Court upheld a provision of federal law exempting secular nonprofit activities of religious organizations from the general prohibition of discrimination on the basis of religion. The decision, though, was narrow, resting on the conclusion that the exemption was intended to avoid "significant governmental interference with the ability of religious organizations to define and carry out their religious missions."[6]

One might argue, as the legal scholar Kathleen Sullivan has

done, that what is at issue in these cases is a "religious opt-out from the redistributive programs of the welfare state."[7] We are talking, after all, about employment rights that exist because of the statutes of the New Deal and the Second Reconstruction: the rights of employees to organize unions, to be paid a fair wage, and to be free of market discrimination. The same might be said of the California housing discrimination case that opened the chapter, even though the rights of unmarried couples there asserted are of more recent vintage. Thus, one might conclude, with Sullivan, that "[j]ust as religionists must pay for the secular army that engineers the truce among them, they must pay for the other common goods of the civil public order."[8]

Now, even if one concedes the bemusing notion that a major task of the armed forces of the United States is to avoid religious strife, there is still trouble in this welfare state paradise. If the religions are properly called upon to make the sacrifices that the law requires because the statutes in question all involve the provision of common goods, one might then conclude that the *Smith* case (discussed in chapter 4), sustaining the punishment of Native Americans for using peyote in worship as required by their religion, was rightly decided after all—a sacrifice that they must make in order to enable a common war on drugs. Sullivan, however, is certain that *Smith* is wrong, and that it represents discrimination against—indeed, a certain judicial "blindness" about—a minority religion, which it certainly does. Sullivan's distinction seems to be that *Smith* involves a judgment made by an adult about drug use, whereas the cases she comfortably considers examples of the welfare state in action involve the employment relationship, which is different.

One is tempted to respond, welfare state or none, that the employees are also adults, and may work for low pay for their religious organizations as willingly as the state employees in *Smith* used peyote in their rituals.[9] But a different answer is also possible. Imagine that we are in the United States not of the late twentieth century but of the late nineteenth, when state laws required racial discrimination in many areas of life, and when, for example, religious groups that ran integrated schools in the South were threatened with prosecution. These statutes were defended—implausibly, but never mind—as improving the society. Would Sullivan really suggest that a religion should not be allowed to opt out of generally applicable secular regulations on education? One might answer that greater religious autonomy was needed in an oppressive American South of the nineteenth century than is needed in the liberal democracy we are said to enjoy today. But while I, like Sullivan, tend to be a supporter of regulatory government, many religions see the welfare state, for all its virtues, as oppressive of their liberties.

What is needed, in order to bring coherence to the problem of accommodation, is a richer understanding not of the nature of the welfare state, or, indeed, of government, but of the nature of the religions themselves, particularly the nature of religious autonomy. To gain that richer understanding, one must think not of the way the society looks at religions but of the way religions look at themselves. In the 1987 *Presiding Bishop* case, a separate opinion by Justice Brennan, joined by Justice Thurgood Marshall, got the point right:

> For many individuals, religious activity derives meaning in large measure from participation in a larger religious community. Such a community represents an ongoing tradition of shared beliefs, an organic entity not reducible to a mere aggregation of individuals. Determining that certain activities are in furtherance of an organization's religious mission, and that only those committed to that mission should conduct them, is thus a means by which a religious community defines itself. Solicitude for a church's ability to do so reflects the idea that furtherance of the autonomy of religious organizations often furthers individual religious freedom as well.[10]

What Brennan understood—and what the Court, and the literature, too often do not—was that religion is more than a matter of what an individual chooses to believe. Religions are communities of corporate worship, or, as one might say in this postmodern world, communities of sense and value, groups of believers struggling to come to a common understanding of the world. So when one speaks of autonomy, one is speaking not just of the individual, but also of the group.

The group, moreover, will often be engaged in what David Tracy calls acts of resistance (see chapter 2)—interposing the group judgment against the judgment of a larger society. Worshipping together, endeavoring jointly to discern the will of God, if honestly done, will lead frequently to that result. When the state tries to block that process of discernment in a faith community, it is acting tyrannically by removing potential sources of authority and meaning different from itself. This, too, Brennan plainly understood in a way that the Court as a whole rarely has:

> The authority to engage in this process of self-definition inevitably involves what we normally regard as infringement on free exercise rights, since a religious organization is able to condition employment in certain activities on subscription to particular religious tenets. We are willing to countenance the imposition of such a condition because we deem it vital that, if certain activities constitute part of a religious community's practice, then a religious organization should be able to require that only members of its community perform those activities.[11]

Brennan was concerned about what abuses this rule might invite, and he added a sensible caveat: "religious organizations should be able to discriminate on the basis of religion only with respect to religious activities, so that a determination should be made in each case whether an activity is religious or secular."[12] One can see Brennan's point: hiring a plumber to fix the sink in the parish hall is not the same as hiring a counselor to work in a religious program to fix dysfunctional families. Still, what Brennan does not say—but what his line of argument implies—is that the key "determination [of] whether an activity is religious or secular" must give considerable, if not decisive, weight to the religion's own vision of the distinction. If one does happen to encounter a religion that considers the repair of the sink God's work, one must not respond blithely—as the courts too often do—with, "Really? Well, we don't."

Translating this principle into law, one would say that the central acts of faith of a religious community—the aspects that do the most to produce shared meaning within the corporate body of worship—are entitled to the highest solicitude by the courts, and, therefore, when infringing on those central acts, the state must offer a very convincing reason. As the acts of faith that the state seeks to regulate or forbid become less central, the state's burden of justification grows less.

In terms of the cases, this would mean that before punishing an obviously central act such as the use of peyote by the Native American Church (the *Smith* case) or before destroying the land that makes a religious tradition possible (the *Lyng* case, cited in chapter 7), the state would have to meet a very high burden of justification, perhaps even show a compelling interest, before it is allowed, through a seemingly neutral policy, to trespass upon the central faith-world of a religion. In those cases, it is not likely the burden could have been met, so the decisions are probably wrong.

The welfare state cases—those involving employment or housing discrimination—might at first seem more difficult to resolve. After all (one might object), in *Smith* and *Lyng* the government is acting against people who simply want to worship, but the Donahues are trying to make money. If their religion will not let them make it by the rules the state has set out, can't they just put their money somewhere else? But the objection is a non sequitur. It in particular does not distinguish *Smith:* the reason the state of Oregon punished the Native Americans for using peyote was that they were state employees. Presumably, if they do not like the rule, they can work for somebody else.

More fundamentally, however, the objection misses the critical difference between living in a society that does much regulating and a society that does little. The First Amendment was written for a world in which regulation was expected to be rare and would almost never impinge on religious liberty. We live instead in a world in which regulation is everywhere, and the idea that the religious citizen can escape it, through a careful search, is a fantasy. Besides, even were escape easier, the problem remains that religious people might wind up finding it more costly to participate in the market than others who do not share their views. Of course these additional costs—such as the cost of not being able to discriminate—might be justifiable. The accommodation test here proposed would only demand that the state offer more than an ordinary justification for them.

It is not possible to resolve here all the many cases that might arise from pursuing this approach, so I will limit myself to making two points. First, it would be both a secular and religious disaster were religions by the dozen suddenly to come forward claiming a free exercise right to engage in all the many forms of discrimination that secular politics has decided to forbid. However, it would also be a secular and religious disaster were we to rule out entirely the possibility that a few religions could come forward and meet the test I have proposed. Deciding when to allow exemptions would place a tremendous burden on the courts—but there is no reason that the hard work of protecting freedom should be easy, and, certainly, the fact that the task is difficult is no reason not to undertake it.

Thus, resolution of the cases involving the minimum wage or labor-organizing rights for employees not directly connected with the central religious function of the church would require more searching inquiries than the Supreme Court generally likes to see the federal courts undertake. The case of the refusal of the Donahues to rent to an unmarried couple, however, may be a simple one. If, as the Donahues claim, their religious tradition teaches that they will be damned if they allow fornication on their property, it is hard to see why anything other than a compelling interest should allow the state to put them to that risk.

Still, in crafting a sensible understanding of religious autonomy, the courts ideally should play only a minor role. The more important role is the one that the society itself must play, in its politics and its rhetoric. As with every fundamental human right, the ultimate security of religious liberty lies not in judges' opinions but in citizens' commitments; it is vital that we ourselves, the people of the United States, before allowing our government to trespass on religious freedom, balance the depth of our moral commitment to the policy in question against the value of religious autonomy. If our commitment to the policy wins every time, then we really have become the majoritarian tyrants against whom Tocqueville warned us a century and a half ago.

One of the reasons that the asserted political influence of religious groups is so feared is that some people believe that the religions, if politically empowered, might try to impose on the secular society their own visions of the good life. This is, of course, a real danger, although there is reason to doubt that more harm to individual freedom *necessarily* occurs when a religion seeks to impose its vision of the good life than when an entirely secular political movement does it. Indeed, it is not easy, in a nation committed to religious liberty, to understand why the risk that the religions might try to impose on secular society their religious visions of the good life is more to be avoided than the risk that the state and its powerful constituents might try to impose on the religions a secular vision of the good life.

THE PROBLEM OF STATE COERCION, REVISITED

Sometimes, the government does try to force a church to change its practices. To be sure, the matter is almost never put that way, and it is rarely intended that way either. For example, in the *Smith* case, discussed in chapter 7, the antidrug policy under which the two state employees were dismissed was not aimed particularly at the Native American Church, of which they were members; it contained no exception for the religious observances of other churches either. And the question of whether the statute is neutral or not, or whether it is aimed at the religion or not, does not change the fact that the existence of the statute pressures the religion to alter its practices.

The late legal scholar Robert Cover suggested that the centrality of a proposition to a particular faith is not truly tested until the state places its weight on the other side. When government says to members of a religion that they will be penalized if they do not change their practices, the members are forced to decide how much the practices really matter. If they are willing to change in order to avoid punishment, Cover argued, that is evidence that the belief was not as central as the members might have thought. He offers as an example the fact that some Christian denominations, threatened with loss of tax-exempt status for some of their activities because of racial discrimination, suddenly "discovered" that God did not, after all, mandate racial segregation.[13] True, they caved in to government pressure—but they might not have yielded so readily had the state threatened to penalize them for proclaiming, say, the divinity of Jesus Christ.

In contemporary politics, the metaphor of the wall of separation between church and state is used most frequently to explain why religion is not supposed to influence governance, and, particularly, why the government is not supposed to endorse or further the aims of religious organizations. But the wall of separation is also intended to protect religion from the state. Some critics of religious power suggest that the wall of separation is being breached, that religions are gaining too much influence in governance. But the breach, if it exists, also runs the other way, for government may be gaining too much influence over religion. Some of this is the fault of a chaotic political system that has ceased to accept the need for intermediate institutions that serve as bulwarks against both majority tyranny and an overweaning centralization of power. But much of it is the fault of the religions themselves, which have entered into a Faustian bargain under which they accept favorable tax treatment from the state. Now the bill for that special tax status is coming due—and the price is turning out to be much higher than anticipated.

The fact that state pressure often tests the depth of a religion's world view is not the same as saying that pressure is always, or even often, a good thing. It may be that the religions, by accepting the state's offer of tax exemptions for their property and activities and charitable deductions for the donations that they receive, have taken the wrong side of a Faustian bargain. (I take no position here on whether special tax status represents a state subsidy.)[14] The trouble is that if the state is able to manipulate the content of religious doctrine through its power to extend or deny the favored tax treatment, the religions are already well down the road to compromising their autonomy. Yet the autonomy of the religions is, at bottom, what makes them worth protecting, most of all when their autonomy leads them into controversy; one scarcely needs a free exercise clause to enable the devout to do what the state would allow them to do of its own free will.

Which brings us back to chapter 2's tale of the effort by the City of New York to force the Hibernians to allow gay and lesbian marchers of Irish descent to join the St. Patrick's Day Parade. The city's principal argument was that the Hibernians had a special responsibility to observe the city's human rights laws because the St. Patrick's Day Parade marches along a chunk of city property, a questionable argument that one judge accepted, at least in part, by declaring the parade to be a "public" activity within the meaning of the city's human rights law. As we have seen, a federal court formally ruled against the city. But the fact that the argument became plausible at all (the city would never have made it had the celebration been held in a church) helps illustrate the Faustian bargain that many of the religions have made in order to gain access to the many benefits that the welfare state supplies. The claim that city property is involved was plainly a bootstrap, one that was available only because the Order of Hibernians, although styling itself a religious organization, nevertheless wanted to use public property—Fifth Avenue—for its march. I have no constitutional quarrel with the desire of the Hibernians to march on public property. But it is useful to consider that a parade license is much like a subsidy, for it allows the use of a street maintained at public expense. Had the Hibernians not sought this use of public property, the city would have had no argument, which is an example of one way in which the growing breach in the wall of separation between church and state is the fault of religions themselves.

This is not to say that the Hibernians should have lost the case. As Judge Duffy noted, the argument pressed by the City of New York was legally shaky.[15] Just consider another case that might fall under the same rubric of "public" activity that the state can regulate. During his visit to the United States, Pope John Paul II celebrated mass on one of the most famous properties in America—the Mall, in Washington, D.C. The Mall was needed because the Pope was expected to draw a huge crowd, which he did. And yet it would be a supreme irony to suppose that precisely because he is sufficiently famous that the faithful would fill that space by the tens of thousands, the Pope was therefore required under appropriate antidiscrimination laws to accept the assistance of female clergy, a concept that the Roman Catholic Church treats as an oxymoron. Nor does it matter that the Pope planned to celebrate Mass while the Order of Hibernians proposed to parade. The Pope might have marched along the Mall after mass, and the analogy would be nearly perfect.

Some of the defenders of the Hibernians—the *New York Times,* for example—were cautious, offering what lawyers call "slippery slope" arguments rather than tackling directly the issue of the opposition of religious freedom to antidiscrimination laws.

If the wall of separation is low enough to allow this regulation, we learned, there are many others who will cry for "equal time" waiting in the wings. The slippery slope argument is effective, too. It takes little imagination to visualize the case of a pro-choice religious group planning a public march and pro-life demonstrators demanding a place in the procession on the ground of freedom of speech; or a public interfaith service for racial harmony, with the Ku Klux Klan insisting on a role.

This is a sensible, clean argument, but it does not come to grips with the central issue of religious autonomy. The truth is that the City of New York's theory carries within it the seeds of tragedy. The effort to force the Hibernians to allow marchers to whom they objected on religious grounds is an example of secular leveling, the sense that government should use its authority to ensure that every organization, in its internal organization, reflects government policy. At one level, the state in bringing such an action simply offers a moral critique of a religion's theology. At another level, however, the state is using its political authority to enforce the moral critique; it is, in effect, demanding a change in theology.

Ordinarily, the government would not dare try. The Free Exercise Clause, and the principle of religious pluralism that remains deeply embedded in American ideology, would make such an effort unthinkable. The only difference, however, between the attempt to regulate the Hibernians in their march and an attempt to limit what a religion is allowed to preach in its place of worship is that the Hibernians were on public property. But it is absurd to say that because a public license is obtained, traditional religious freedom is surrendered. The religious significance of an event does not disappear because permission is granted to perform it on public ground. Religious significance does not even diminish. And if the religious significance entails discrimination—or other policies that the state could never accept for its own activities—that is simply a cost of a freedom that the society should scrupulously protect.

THE FAUSTIAN BARGAIN,
REVISITED

I have already explained (chapter 2) the importance of viewing religions as intermediate institutions. In the ideal democratic vision, these intermediaries would much influence government, but government would little influence them. However, we live in a welfare state. For better or worse, the government is deeply involved in offering special treatment to and, therefore, the regulating of intermediary institutions (consider, for example, the brouhaha over all-white and all-male "private" clubs). In such a world, it is foolish to imagine that religious organizations can remain free of any connection to governance. Through their tax exemptions and charitable deductions for contributions to them, the religions receive favored treatment through the tax code. Moreover, many religions provide social service functions in their communities and, in that capacity, they receive direct governmental assistance. Thus the welfare state has already trapped the religions, and the day will doubtless come when they, too, face pressures to behave correctly with respect to race, sex, and many other issues, or lose valuable government patronage. (Indeed, the day may be here already, as the Roman Catholic Church, a major operator of a variety of welfare services and thus a major consumer of government largess, is learning.)[16]

An interesting harbinger of such a situation was the case of *Bob Jones University v. United States,* decided in 1983, in which the Supreme Court sustained Internal Revenue Service rules denying tax-exempt status to educational organizations that discriminate on the basis of race, as Bob Jones University did.[17] The *Bob Jones* case arose in part because of the alliance of President Reagan with the least attractive forces in the Christian conservative movement. The IRS, at least since the Nixon administration, had cracked down on religious schools that used their tax-exempt status to perpetuate racial segregation at public cost. The

1980 Republican party platform, on which Reagan was elected by a landslide over Jimmy Carter, promised to "halt the unconstitutional regulatory vendetta launched by Mr. Carter's IRS Commissioner against independent schools."[18] The Reagan administration, to the astonishment of nearly everybody, actually followed up on this promise and decided not to dispute in the Supreme Court the right of Bob Jones University to segregate with tax dollars because of its religious nature. The Justices showed more fortitude than the administration, however, and made short work of the argument.

By the time the case was decided, the religious freedom claim had essentially dropped out of the case. Formally, the argument in the case was about government structure: since the Congress had not explicitly authorized the withholding of tax-exempt status because of racial discrimination, the Treasury Department should not withhold the status on its own initiative. This is a technical but important legal point—government authority always needs a source—which the Supreme Court, perhaps wisely, circumvented, holding that the statute in question did indeed authorize the actions of the Treasury Department.

Still, there is more to the religious freedom claim in *Bob Jones* than might first appear. Stripped of frills, the question was whether the government, through the tax code, should be able to pressure the religions to alter their practices, or whether the Free Exercise Clause requires that the government supply a compelling justification for doing so. Bob Jones University would have lost even under a very stringent test; given the nation's history, the elimination of racial discrimination in education is as compelling a justification as one might demand. Discrimination against groups that the nation has long oppressed is illegal, immoral, and sinful, which would seem to cover all the bases.

One must be careful, however, not to be so blinded by the immorality of racism that one misses the glaring problem for the religions that the *Bob Jones* case illustrates. By accepting the offer or special tax treatment, the religions themselves may have paved the way for a future in which they are told that they will lose their treasured tax status unless they reflect, in theology and practices, whatever the current government policy might be: pro-life or pro-choice, pro-nuclear weaponry or pro-nuclear freeze. This bears thinking about, not because Bob Jones University is an admirable party—it isn't—but because special tax status for the religions may not after all be an admirable development.

"The power to tax," Chief Justice John Marshall wrote in 1819, "involves the power to destroy."[19] He might have added, had he but known what was in store, that the power to grant tax relief also involves the power to destroy. Churches are not the only intermediate institutions that have become addicted to government aid, even through the indirect form of tax exemptions and charitable deductions. But addictions carry costs, not the least of which is the sad fact that, in the end, the supplier always controls the addict—something to ponder, surely, as one contemplates how to avoid the trivialization of religious faith in America. One way might be to put the religions beyond the power of government not only to regulate, but to purchase; and the only way to stay beyond the reach of the government's power to purchase obedience is to remain beyond the long arm of government assistance. That would mean, of course, giving up the cherished deductibility of contributions to, and other tax exemptions for, religious organizations, a terrifying thought to religious groups in this era of financial stress.[20] But when one makes a deal with the devil, one must be prepared to hold up one's end when the debt comes due. Or, to switch to a metaphor perhaps more appropriate, the religions should ponder the possibility that it might be time for the religiously devout once more to render unto Caesar that which is Caesar's, instead of rendering Caesar's due to the church and then writing it off.

PRIVATE REGULATION

Not all the benefits that religions receive in the Faustian bargain flow directly from the state. Some of them flow rather indirectly, as, for example, through the accrediting authority of educational organizations that control the credentials schools must obtain to survive. For example, the Association of American Law Schools forbids its member schools from discriminating against students because of race, sex, or religion. The rules are not mere hortatory recommendations: the AALS regularly inspects its member schools and those that discriminate may find themselves dropped from the roster of approved schools—not, surely, as great a punishment as loss of accreditation, but a loss of status that few deans would like to try to explain to the alumni at the next fund-raising event.[21]

Now the AALS may be poised to trespass, with full knowledge, on what the Catholic Church considers a fundamental moral teaching. Since 1990, the association has listed "sexual orientation" as another forbidden ground of discrimination. Schools operated by religious institutions, however, have been exempt. Recently, the AALS has considered dropping that religious exemption, on the perfectly sensible, but also deceptively simple, ground that no other exemptions from antidiscrimination provisions are allowed to religious schools. For example, a law school run by a religious institution would lose its approval were it to discriminate on the basis of race or sex. Some members of the AALS—much like the California Fair Employment and Housing Commission in the case that opened the chapter—have argued that discrimination is discrimination, period.

The substance of this response seems, at first, exactly right. If schools run by religious organizations are to be allowed to discriminate on the basis of sexual orientation, logic indeed dictates that they must be allowed to discriminate on the basis of race and sex as well. However, the position of the schools raising the original objection is exactly right as well. A respect for religious freedom does indeed entail the proposition that religious schools must be free to follow their doctrines. Thus the clash is not of wrongs but of rights, and the clash cannot be avoided. One must come down on the side of equality or on the side of religious freedom, for in this conflict it is impossible to do both.

Here again, the late Robert Cover made a thoughtful contribution. Writing about the *Bob Jones* case, Cover suggested that it was a mistake to describe the choice as one between equality and religious liberty in the abstract. Rather, he argued, one could say that our national commitment to the eradication of racial discrimination has of necessity grown so great that every arm of the government must participate, and every regulated entity must yield, even if it would otherwise be able to claim a right to insulate itself against the coercive authority of the state. Cover lamented that the Supreme Court, which treated the case as raising a mundane question of administrative law, was unwilling to justify its decision in these terms.[22] Still, the Court plainly was caught up in the sweep of precisely the commitment that Cover describes. The Justices could hardly have been unaware that, had they sustained the right of Bob Jones University to practice racial discrimination while receiving federal tax relief, they would have looked as cruel, and as ridiculous, as the Reagan administration did for pressing just that proposition.[23]

Another way of putting the matter is this: once societal consensus has been reached that a form of discrimination is wrong, religious organizations, when they consume the largess of the welfare state, will not be allowed to engage in it. If on the other hand the society remains deeply divided over whether a given form of discrimination should be allowed or not, the religions, protected as they are by a constitutional right of free exercise, should remain free to engage in it until consensus arises. (I pass for the moment the question of how one can tell when a consensus has come to exist.) This argument would mean that the AALS would be right to crack down on schools—even religious schools—that discriminate on the basis of race or sex, but would be wrong to crack down on religious schools that discriminate on the basis of sexual orientation.*

Yet this answer in the end is unsatisfying. It suggests that those religious institutions that regulatory entities can reach, especially educational institutions that need federal funds and the approval of accreditors and associations, can practice some forms of otherwise forbidden discrimination but not others. The test to determine which discriminations can be practiced, moreover, is a secular one—and the secular questions it raises are fundamental matters of the spirit. The society might end up saying to the religious school, "You may discriminate against homosexual students but not black students because we are less sure in the first case than in the second that discrimination is wrong. When we decide, we will let you know." So frustrating an answer is necessarily anathema to the forces of both egalitarianism and religious liberty. Indeed, there is about it a Solomonic aspect of cutting the baby in half, which is not the way to be sure that the baby grows up strong. True, our society resolves most of its difficult questions through enacting compromises that leave nobody fully satisfied. This solution certainly fits that description, for nobody is likely to be happy with it. Indeed, if one takes seriously both equality and religious autonomy, there may be no good answer.

This chapter began with the proposition that obedience to laws prohibiting discrimination is one of the cutting edges of the accommodation problem. There is, however, another cutting edge, one that most Americans probably see as slicing much closer to the center of their lives, a cutting edge that affects not religiously devout adults but their children. It is to the complicated dilemmas of educational accommodation that I next turn.

---

* I would strongly support the decision of an individual school to prohibit discrimination on the basis of sexual orientation, including the banning of recruiters for firms (and government agencies) that engage in it. Yale Law School, where I teach, takes exactly that position.

9

In the Beginning

"LET us put away childish things," wrote Sigmund Freud of religion, dismissing the subject, and, ever since, the American legal and political cultures have struggled to follow his advice. In a sense, America has gone Freud one better. Having battled to a draw in the effort to purge government of religious rhetoric (although not, of course, religious influence), all sides in the fight over the proper role of religion in public life have more and more turned their attentions to where much of the battle began nearly a century ago—the public schools, where "childish things" are, by definition, a part of the curriculum. And the ensuing struggle over prayer, curriculum, and other matters is often nasty and usually depressing.

ANOTHER MONKEY TRIAL

In 1991, an Orange County, California, high school biology teacher named John Peloza created a minor cause célèbre when he insisted on his right to teach the theory of creationism along with the theory of evolution. Many parents complained, and the school district reprimanded him. This being the era of litigation, Peloza responded with a $5 million lawsuit—and, once more, the battle was joined.

Creationism, popularly, but not quite accurately, associated with Christian fundamentalism, is actually the catchword for a variety of approaches to the origin of life and the universe adopted by people whose approach to Biblical interpretation involves a belief in its literal inerrancy. The most important commonality among these approaches is a confidence that the development of life, particularly human life, was directed by God, rather than the result of natural selection. The accounts of creationism that most concern the media are those that rest on the creation story (or stories, for there are two) of Genesis and deny the Darwinian theory of evolution, reserving particular scorn for the idea that human beings descended from lower forms.

Creationism as science is not new. On the contrary, until Charles Darwin's *Origin of Species,* first published in 1859, became popular in the years after the Civil War, most natural scientists were creationists in the sense that they accepted as truth the essence of the Genesis creation story. Many noted scientists—the most famous was Louis Agassiz of Harvard—rejected Darwin's work precisely because it seemed inconsistent with divine creation. As time passed, however, natural selection proved to be a powerful tool for analyzing and explaining the natural world. By the early twentieth century, despite some efforts to find a middle ground, a sharp split had developed between scientists and theologians who continued to treat the Genesis account as literally true and the increasing number of natural scientists who rejected it.[1] By the time John Peloza entered the fray, the battle was officially over.

Peloza was careful to note that he was not telling his students about creationism in the sense that the term is usually meant. "I never quote Genesis in my classroom," he told an interviewer. "I have taken God out of this." Still, Peloza must have had in mind something like the classic creationist position: "When I give my presentation," he said, "I give two sides, one that we are here by chance and the other that we are here by design."[2] *Here by design:* in other words, created by a designer— or, more properly, a Designer—which is probably why an attorney for the school district shot back, "Creationism is not a scientific theory, it is a religious belief. It is inappropriate to teach religion in a science class."[3]

The Peloza case raised specters that many had thought were put to rest, either in 1968, when the Supreme Court overturned an Arkansas statute prohibiting the teaching of evolution,[4] or in 1987, when the Court struck down a Louisiana statute requiring that "scientific creationism" be granted equal time with evolution in high school biology courses.[5] It is into this uneasy arena that John Peloza stepped in 1991, when he risked official disciplinary action for insisting on his "right" to teach creationism. Some saw an ironic parallel between the Peloza case and the fabled 1925 "Monkey Trial," in which high school teacher John Scopes was prosecuted for violating a Tennessee statute forbidding the teaching of evolution. Scopes was defended by Clarence Darrow who, although he lost the case, famously devastated evangelical hero William Jennings Bryan on the witness stand.[6] Noted Benjamin Hubbard, a professor of religion at California State University at Fullerton, "Scopes was forbidden to teach evolution and he threw down the gauntlet and taught it. Now we have somebody who is forbidden to teach what Scopes was supposed to teach, and he is throwing his own gauntlet."[7]

If Peloza, in demanding the right to teach creationism to public school biology students, was throwing down the gauntlet, plenty of opponents were prepared to pick it up. One well-known biologist warned, "[T]he issue is not evolution. It's the survival of rationality. What do we teach children in our schools? Do we teach science? Are we allowed to teach superstition, or astrology rather than astronomy?"[8] This language typfies the way that much of our culture addresses the creationism phenomenon—and, indeed, the creationists themselves. Creationism is frequently compared with Lysenkoism, the disastrous Soviet rejection of modern genetic theory, a decision, some say, that led to millions of deaths and lingering problems in agriculture in Russia and the other former Soviet republics. But the critics do not stop with that comparison. During the litigation over the Louisiana equal-time statute, an article in *Omni,* a magazine devoted to popularizing science, complained that "intolerance has raised its pea-brained head." The author went on, in what was doubtless designed as a great show of tolerance, to ridicule creationism as "the latest surreal joke in a deranged world."[9] The distinguished literary critic Harold Bloom derides creationists by quoting H. L. Mencken: "They are everywhere where learning is too heavy a burden for mortal minds to carry."[10] World-renowned anthropologist Richard Leakey perhaps summed up the scientific community's views with his dismissal of the notion of balanced treatment as "utterly stupid."[11]

All of this adds up to a perception of creationists as backward, irrational, illiberal fanatics—not too smart and not too deserving of respect. Thus, at the height of the Peloza contratemps, another faculty member at the same high school publicly invited the embattled science teacher to share with professionals in the field the evidence for his rejection of evolution, but doubted that he would be able to produce any: "Although [Peloza] is qualified to teach high school biology, his background does not qualify him to make changes in the prescribed curriculum pursuant to his 'discoveries.' I'm sure most Americans would agree, especially knowing that his students will enter a system of higher education that rejects his view."[12]

Such concern for the teaching of children sounds sensible, but it is not at all clear that most Americans would agree. Survey data indicate that 82 percent of American adults believe that God created human beings. This figure includes the 44 percent of adults who accept the Genesis account of creation and the 38 percent who believe that God guided evolution.[13] Those numbers are not, by themselves, enough reason to teach scientific creationism. But they do suggest that an attack on creationists as a minority trying to foist its views of science on an oppressed majority are a little bit overdrawn. They also suggest that for most Americans, the relationship between religious belief and scientific understanding is not capable of the neat separation that our legal rhetoric sometimes seems to suppose.

The notion of the supernatural—the idea that some sentience beyond the human plays a role in mortal affairs—took firm hold on the national imagination in the early days of the Republic and has never loosened its grip. As Yale historian Jon Butler demonstrates in his fascinating study *Awash in a Sea of Faith* (1990), most Americans have never drawn a neat line between the religious and the secular, either on questions of politics and morality or on questions about the natural world.[14] Plainly, a legal culture trying to separate church and state must specify the line between the two anyway; but there is no reason to think that most Americans will be happy with the location of the line merely because it happens to exist.

The short of the matter is that most Americans might actually approve of Peloza's decision to teach creationism in the biology classroom—discomfiting though that may be to nearly all scientists and to just about anybody who does not agree with Peloza's particular understanding of the origin of life.* And whether or not most would approve, these putative know-nothings actually number in the tens of millions—hardly the tiny

---

* Peloza was also accused of pressuring students to agree with his religious views, for example, by inviting them to his home to discuss creationism and by arguing with them about their own religious convictions, a charge that he denied and against which none of his many supporters, as far as I am aware, made any attempt to defend him.

fringe of American society that is usually described in media accounts of the creationism phenomenon.

I should make clear that I am no creationist—not, at least, in the popular sense. So-called scientific creationism, the effort to dress creationism in the language of natural science, seems to me shoddy science, not science at all, really. And scientific creationism challenges more than just evolution. As Nobel Laureate Murray Gell-Mann has noted, "the portion of science that is attacked" by creationism "is far more extensive than many people realize, embracing important parts of physics, chemistry, astronomy, and geology as well as many of the central ideas of biology and anthropology." He adds,

> In particular, the notion of reducing the age of the earth by a factor of nearly a million, and that of the expanding universe by an even larger factor, conflicts in the most basic way with numerous robust conclusions of physical science. For example, fundamental and well-established principles of nuclear physics are challenged, for no sound reason, when "creation scientists" attack the validity of the radioactive clocks that provide the most reliable methods used to date the earth.[15]

Not only do I reject the scientific conclusions and the scientific method of scientific creationists, but I, as a committed Christian, also do not share the particular vision of biblical inerrancy that motivates many of its adherents. I would be distressed were creationism to be offered as part of the curriculum at a public school supported by tax dollars, but it is important to note the reason. I would be distressed because I think it bad science—no more and no less. I would be equally distressed were a scientifically illiterate legislature to decide, as the Indiana legislature nearly did in 1897, to teach that the value of pi (the ratio of the circumference of a circle to its diameter) is somewhere in the vicinity of 9.2—a value nearly three times too large, and one that, if seriously applied, would cause bridges to fall.[16] And I would be just as distressed were my children taught (as I was, years ago, in the public schools of Washington, D.C.) that the slaves in the antebellum South were generally content with their lot and that most aspired to nothing more than a kind master. Or if they were taught that the moon is made of green cheese. Or that the earth is flat.

These propositions are all factually in error, and it is those factual errors that I do not want my kids to learn. Perhaps I have no legal recourse against these errors—no way, for example, to obtain a court order forbidding the schools to teach that the slaves were happy—but they are every bit as objectionable to me as the thesis that the earth is only 20,000 years old. And the fact that the motivation for teaching them is racism or scientific illiteracy rather than religious certainty does not render them any less objectionable. The federal judge who struck down an Arkansas "equal-time" statute, in an otherwise thoughtful opinion, let slip this disconcerting line: "The facts that creation science is inspired by the Book of Genesis and that [the words of the statute are] consistent with a literal interpretation of Genesis leave no doubt that a major effect of the Act is the advancement of particular religious beliefs."[17] But this cannot be right. If my children attended a public school that decided, for purely religious reasons, to begin offering a modern calculus course not previously part of the curriculum, I would be the first to cry "Hallelujah!" It would not matter one whit that the calculus course was consistent with some religion's holy book—and I doubt that anybody would sue.

So, no, creationism does not belong in the public school science classroom. But the principal reason it does not belong there has nothing whatever to do with the motivation for putting it there. The principal reason is that it is bad science.

THE ENEMY OF SCIENCE

It is our habit in this technological age to treat religion as necessarily the enemy of scientific progress. All too often, it has been.

But a generalization is not at all fair. Many great scientists—Sir Isaac Newton is a frequently mentioned exemplar—saw their work as adding to the glory of God. "The time is long gone," the sociologist Robert Nisbet has written, "when Newton's *Principia* can be treated as something separate from the religious and biblical studies with which he occupied himself throughout most of his life." Nor did it stop with Newton. Puritanism, Nisbet points out, "endowed knowledge—theoretical, practical, above all scientific—with millenarian importance."[18] Indeed, the Western religious traditions have always been associated with the ideal of human progress, with scientific progress very much to the forefront.[19] To be sure, the relationship between science and religion ultimately grew more complex. Today, scientists are less likely than the general population to describe themselves as religious. (Intriguingly, however, natural scientists are much more likely than social scientists to describe themselves that way.)[20]

Still, despite the publicity that still attends the battles over creationism, it is not true that science and religion are *naturally* enemies, and not all the history relied upon to prove the point is good history. Although America once taught its school children, for instance, that the Roman Catholic Church insisted that the earth was flat until Columbus proved the contrary, this has been shown to be an anticlerical canard invented in the nineteenth century. True, there are spectacular examples of religious resistance to scientific change, the trial of Galileo being perhaps the best known. But there are also spectacular examples of secular resistance to scientific change; one thinks of the aforementioned Soviet agricultural disaster under Lysenko's genetics and the (fortunate) Nazi resistance to relativity and other aspects of what the regime derided as "Jewish physics." And it is by no means clear where the advantage lies. Science is the natural enemy not of religion as such but of power, at least power that rests on the preservation of the status quo. (Racism, for example, has lost much ground to the advance of science.) A religion concerned with the preservation of its secular authority might well fight sci-

ence, just as it likely will fight any autonomous source of knowledge; but any other entity concerned with the preservation of
secular authority will do the same.

The no-doubt sincere effort to foist upon the public an
image of creationists as know-nothing zealots is profoundly disturbing in part because it implicitly endorses this mistaken vision
of the historical relationship between science and religion. That
error alone is likely to alienate millions of citizens who might
otherwise gradually be brought to accept more of the conclusions of modern science. (I do not exclude the possibility that
they might also, in fair dialogue, convince others that modern
science is in error.) Few recall that when the Tennessee Supreme
Court sustained the conviction of John Scopes for teaching evolution in violation of state law, it justified the statute on the
ground that only by banning any talk of evolution was it possible to get the people of the state to allow a modern science curriculum in the schools, which they might otherwise have rejected
altogether.[21] This is a telling reminder that in a democracy,
change is not always rapid.

The virulence of the verbal assaults on creationists is not
just unfair. It is also politically foolish. "The creation story is not
going to go away as a political issue," Garry Wills has written,
"for the obvious cultural reason that the Bible is not going to
stop being the central book in our intellectual heritage."[22] That is
why, as long as those who oppose the teaching of creationism in
the public schools cast its supporters in the role of the narrow-
minded oppressors, it will be a simple matter for those who support it to cast the opponents as attacking the Bible itself—and
thus attacking what tens of millions see as a fundament of American society. That is why Robert L. Simonds, the head of Excel-
lence in Education, a conservative Christian organization that
monitors school curricula, doubtless scored some political points
when he attacked the school district that censured John Peloza,
claiming that school officials displayed "an anti-Christian bias."[23]

The caricaturing of the creationists is doubly tragic because it is so unnecessary. It has the feel of elitist posturing, the knowledge snobs at work. Very well, let it be conceded that the creationists do not have science on their side. In that case, the charge of "bad science" seems an entirely adequate response to the pressure to teach scientific creationism. It is not response enough, unfortunately, for our secular society. Indeed, the usual criticism of the so-called equal-time statutes, which require that creationism be taught alongside evolution, has less to do with science than with religion. The usual, and more strident, criticism is that the statutes are simply masks for the official endorsement of religious belief, proselytizing hidden behind the smoke and mirrors of scientific jargon. Plainly, there is *something* to this critique. Murray Gell-Mann, in the article already quoted, goes on to say: "We are dealing with attempts by lobbyists and legislatures to force entry into science classrooms on behalf of a particular kind of fundamentalist religion dressed up as science."[24] This is precisely the understanding of creationism that underlies the Supreme Court's 1987 decision in *Edwards v. Aguillard,* which held the equal-time statutes to be an unconstitutional violation of the separation of church and state.[25]

What is intriguing about the Supreme Court's decision in *Edwards* is that the majority of the Justices focused so closely on the *reason* that the legislature mandated the teaching of scientific creationism—in other words, the Justices looked into motive. Improper motive, I have already argued (see chapter 6), is not a particularly useful test for determining whether a law violates the Establishment Clause. *Edwards* helps illustrate why. After all, there is little except the conflict with science to distinguish religiously motivated legislation requiring the teaching of creation theory from religiously motivated legislation to implement the Biblical injunction "Thou shalt not kill"—or religiously movitated legislation in response to the Roman Catholic bishops' call for a more equitable sharing of the nation's wealth. A prohibition of murder, like a forced distribution of wealth, might be religiously motivated, but only the teaching of creationism conflicts with natural science.

Scientific creationists, of course, do not believe that a conflict exists. Evolution is just a theory, the creationists insist, and it must, as a theory, be open to challenge. And challenge it they do, pointing to mountains of what they say are errors, exceptions, and inexplicable transitions in the fossil record.[26] To be sure, the scientific community fires back hard and, more often than not, blows the creationist "evidence"—other than the Bible itself—right out of the water. But creationists are undeterred.

One bloody battleground was the elementary school curriculum known as MACOS, an acronym for *Man: A Course of Study,* which hit the public schools in the 1960s. By the early 1970s, many conservative Christians were furious at its seeming depiction of human beings as just another animal, its purported moral relativism, and its insistence on treating evolution as a literal truth. Politicians—Ronald Reagan very much to the fore—joined the fight against MACOS. The scientific community once more thundered its anathemas, but the popular revolt harmed the federally funded MACOS series immeasurably. More important, the successful struggle against MACOS established a precedent; conservative Christians now realized that they, just like other parents, could try to challenge any public school curriculum program that they saw as threatening their core religious values.[27]

What is interesting about the MACOS fight and other similar struggles, as Dorothy Nelkin of Cornell University has pointed out, is that some of the changes demanded by the critics probably made the textbooks more accurate—even if the accuracy might be confusing to school kids. For instance, sentences stating the conclusions of scientists as facts were altered to read, "There is evidence" or "evidence that is often interpreted to mean." Instead of learning that birds developed "after" flying reptiles, children would be taught that birds "appear in the fossil record" after flying reptiles. Qualifiers were added: evidence now *seemed to* show, and students were frequently reminded "we don't know why."[28] Some in the scientific community protested that any compromise with creationists, even a seemingly reasonable one, might lead to the deluge—which is, as it happens, the same way that the fearful creationists talk about secular science.

But the MACOS struggle was, for creationists, at best a kind of holding action. To the biblical literalist, after all, the most important evidence against evolution theory is not the complexity of the fossil record or the debate over falsifiability of the theory of evolution, but the beginning of the Book of Genesis, comprising, as one creationist has written, "eleven chapters of straightforward Bible history which cannot be reinterpreted in any satisfactory way."[29] This approach is an application of the traditional interpretive rules of literalism and inerrancy, and it is best expressed by the combination of the following propositions, drawn from the Articles of Affirmation and Denial adopted in 1982 by the International Council on Biblical Inerrancy: (1) "the normative authority of Holy Scripture is the authority of God Himself"; (2) "the Bible expresses God's truth in propositional statements, and . . . biblical truth is both objective and absolute"; (3) "since God is the author of all truth, all truths, biblical and extrabiblical, are consistent and cohere, and . . . the Bible speaks truth when it touches on matters pertaining to nature, history, or anything else"; and (4) "Genesis 1–11 [the creation story] is factual, as is the rest of the book."[30]

The point bears emphasis because the critics of creationism often overlook that the creationist rejection of evolution theory rests on a nontrivial hermeneutic and a rational application of it to the evidence—although, obviously, creationists dispute what counts as evidence.* As Loren Graham, a prominent historian of science, has noted, there have always been charges by critics of "the epistemological bases of science" that science "is, at best, so specialized that it misses the most significant modes of reality, and, at worst, fundamentally alienating to the human spirit." Graham is no fan of creationism, but he recognizes it for what it is: a

---

* Many fundamentalist Christians, in fact, insist that their faith itself is based on reason, rejecting both the thesis that an unexplainable "leap of faith" is needed to account for religious belief, and the modern understanding of a sharp separation between the task of religion and the task of science.

part of a larger movement toward "alternative modes of cognition."[31] Adds the liberal theologian Harvey Cox of the Harvard Divinity School, "The conviction supporting [the creationist] position is that science, rightly understood, supports and confirms religious belief—or at least *this* religious belief. This is not an antiscientific attitude. It expresses an idea of the relationship between religion and science which, though Isaac Newton held it, is no longer in fashion."[32] Thus, opponents of creationism who stress its religious roots as a means of dismissing it as proselytizing largely miss the epistemological point. The creationist position is no mindless assault on modernism in general or on secular science in particular, although obviously it contains elements of hostility to both. Creationism rests centrally on a claim about what counts as authority, a claim that has been central to the fundamentalist movement in American Christianity for decades. The hermeneutic of literalism, after all, arose as part of an effort to provide an interpretive rule to express what fundamentalists believed that Christians had always done—a tradition that was threatened by a variety of modernist approaches to biblical interpretation around the beginning of the twentieth century. Thus, as one observer has written, "The emphasis on biblical inerrancy, so puzzling to liberals, was at least in part a *rational* search for a form of authority strong enough to resist encroachments on traditional doctrine by liberal and modern ideas."[33] In *Edwards v. Aguillard,* however, the Supreme Court told the fundamentalists that in the battle over the content of public school science courses, their preferred source of authority lost out.

WHO DECIDES?

None of this should be taken to mean that *Edwards* majority reached the wrong result. *Edwards v. Aguillard* is correctly, if perhaps tragically, decided. The decision is correct because of the difficulty of articulating the precise secular purpose for the teaching of creationism: even if dressed up in scientific jargon, it is, at heart, an explanation for the origin of life that is dictated solely by religion. That is not the same as saying that the explanation is not true (which is impossible to show) or that the people who believe it are irrational (which simply is not true)—two points generally missed in the rush to ridicule creationists. Still, even if justified in more moderate terms, *Edward* represents a humiliating constitutional slap in the faces of millions of Americans who are unwilling to make the separation of faith and self that secular political and legal culture often demand.

From the beginning, the constitutional case against the teaching of creationism in the public school classroom has been inextricably bound up with the scientific case against the claims that creationism makes. This strikes me as perhaps an inevitable course, but an awkward one as well. A statute cannot be said to further religion merely on the ground that a majority of scientists do not believe that it furthers science. Even if the "scientific" case for creationism is appallingly shoddy and naive, nothing follows for constitutional purposes.

Murray Gell-Mann, no doubt reflecting prevailing sentiment in the scientific community, concludes his analysis this way: "Fundamentalists have a perfect right to their beliefs but no right to control the teaching of science in the public school."[34] Now, aside from the adoption of this common, vaguely pejorative, and certainly misleading use of the term "fundamentalist" (not all fundamentalists are creationists, not all creationists are fundamentalists) Gell-Mann actually poses a question about power. Very well, suppose he is right that parents who believe that God created the universe and the earth in a relatively short period of time have "no right" to decide what gets taught as science in the public schools. Query, then: Who does have "the right"?

It is no answer to say that the majority of the people should have the right to decide what is taught in school, because in many jurisdictions the creationists *are* the majority. Nor is it much of an answer to say that professionals—educators or scientists—should always get to decide what is taught, not least because millions of parents are not really interested in having their tax dollars spent for education in accordance with the views of experts whose knowledge the parents may find inaccessible and threatening and who in any case often heap abuse on the opinions of the parents themselves. Indeed, one of the strongest arguments in favor of public assistance for private school tuition is that only in that way can parents choose for themselves the education their children should have, rather than having some other entity, one over which they may have little control, make the choice for them. (See chapter 10.)

It is the effort to exercise control of this kind that leads to the depressing spectacle of open disputes between parents and schools—disputes that frequently end in litigation—over whether parents can, on religious grounds, exempt their children from sex education, some parts of biology or history, or condom distribution programs. Often, although not always, the complaining parents are politically conservative Christians who believe that what the school offers their children is a threat to their efforts to raise those children in their religion. One frequent target of parental ire is *Impressions,* a very successful series of books designed for use in elementary school classrooms. Many parents complain, for example, about recommended classroom exercises involving exposure to what they insist is magic and the occult. The publisher has responded by noting that these selections are meant to be used mostly at Halloween—probably not the reassurance that the dissenting parents are seeking, for many consider the celebration of Halloween a pagan ritual. The liberal People for the American Way (PAW) has blasted the attack on *Impressions* as "the biggest mobilization of Far Right censorship groups" since PAW began keeping track in the early 1980s.[35] But calling the effort to control the curriculum censorship simply evades the question of who *should* have the power to decide what is taught.

Perhaps a more explosive battleground is sex education in all its various manifestations. When the New York City Board of Education decided not to require that parents be informed before children are given condoms in the public schools, the decision was an unintentional slap at those parents who prefer that the educational system not interfere with their efforts to raise their children in their religion. An editorial in *Commonweal* lamented that the program should be "[p]rotecting and promoting, rather than undermining, the authority of the family," which "is essential in fostering the kind of moral responsibility that will keep young people alive."[36] The Catholic archbishop of New York, John Cardinal O'Connor, reportedly encouraged parents to sue.[37]

When disputes of this kind wind up in litigation, the dissidents rarely prevail. At this writing, the Peloza case has not been tried, but it is easy to predict that he will lose, because the courts have rejected both the mandated teaching of creationism and the claim that a biology teacher has the constitutional right to discuss it in the classroom.[38] Parents who have tried to keep certain books out of the public school classroom, citing religious objections, have generally lost.[39] When Brevard Hand, a federal trial judge in Alabama, ordered the removal from public school classrooms of forty-four books said to promote the "religion" of "secular humanism," he was quickly slapped down by an appellate court.[40] But although his opinion was something of a legal blunderbuss, Judge Hand might have been on to something important. Even if what some religionists call secular humanism—an educational philosphy characterized by an emphasis on moral relativism and the celebration of self—is not a religion, it might properly be labeled an ideology.[41] As Alan Freeman and Elizabeth Mensch have pointed out:

> Perhaps Judge Hand is straining the legal doctrine in declaring secular humanism a religion for establishment clause purposes, but his basic point—that the schools do convey a pervasive message of extraordinary spiritual shallowness— cannot be ignored, nor can the fact that the message is not

simply "neutral" and 'objective' but, rather, deeply ideological and alienating to those whose perspective is more spiritually based."[42]

That, perhaps, is the tragedy in a nutshell: much about the system of public education *is* deeply alienating to many people "whose perspective is more spiritually based." Yet the First Amendment, which is designed to protect religious freedom, turns out to mean that little can be done about that alienation. Obviously, public educaton would face disaster should federal courts get in the business of banning books.* On the other hand, parents who have raised religious objections to mandatory AIDS education programs in the public schools have achieved small victories, with their children winning at least potential exemption from sections of the curriculum that touch on drug use and sexual activity.[43] And in what remains the most spectacular single exemption, the Supreme Court ruled in *Wisconsin v. Yoder* (1972) that members of the Old Order Amish could follow the dictates of their religion and keep their children out of school entirely after eighth grade.[44]

Yet matters are less clear than they seem. When a court allowed religious parents the possibility of exempting their children from AIDS education, the exemption was conditioned on their "showing that the education they offered their children was the functional equivalent of the AIDS curriculum," which suggests that the case involves less an exemption than a transfer of the costs of education.[45] The parents, it seems, are not allowed to shield their children from the state-imposed educational program, but only to adapt and interpret it through the lens of their religion—not a small right by any means, but a very long way from the right to insist that their religion allows them to opt out. As for the Old Order Amish, the Supreme Court's decision was

---

* Although, to be sure, at least one federal court has taken it upon itself to sustain a school district's refusal to allow a teacher to put a Bible where the students can see it (see chapters 1 and 6).

so heavily qualified (the Justices kept emphasizing that the Amish live apart from society) and so laden with rhetoric about how special (one can almost read "peculiar") is the Amish way of life, that the broad exemption from schooling has never been granted by any other court to any other group.

The short of the matter is that it is not at all clear that the public educational system is prepared to make compromises with parents who raise religious objections to the curriculum— even though educational authorities often seem more than ready to make peace (as, very often, they should) with people who object to parts of the curriculum as racist or sexist. Religion, however, is treated as an inferior ground for objection; and even the courts, to which the Constitution remits the duty of protecting the free exercise of religion, seem unwilling to interfere very much when the question involves the education of children.

One might argue—many smart philosophers do—that this is, in fact, the point, that education in a secular society is and must be aimed at a sort of mainstreaming.[46] The leading twentieth-century thinker on public education, the estimable John Dewey, was of the plainly stated view that one of the reasons for public schools was to remove the irrational religious influence that the children might otherwise retain from their parents. In *Wisconsin v. Yoder,* Justice William O. Douglas disagreed with the majority's decision to allow the Old Order Amish to remove their children from school. Wrote Douglas: "While the parents, absent dissent, normally speak for the entire family, the education of a child is a matter on which the child will often have decided views." Thus, Douglas argued, "It is the student's judgment, not his parents', that is essential."[47] But in the battles over the education of students, the judgment that turns out to be essential is neither the parents' nor the student's, but the school's. It is most certainly this vision that continues to motivate, for example, the conclusion that nothing as trivial as a religious objection can stand in the path of the right kind of AIDS education.

The trouble is that so relentlessly secular a measure of what counts as valuable is probably not in accord with the world views of most Americans; certainly, there are plenty of religious citizens, from a variety of faiths, who reject entirely the notion that the secular world should tell them how and what to teach their children. The truth, for better or worse, is that we live in a world in which epistemology sometimes reflects religious belief, a world in which religious belief may move people to decide, quite sincerely, whether to accept or reject both moral and factual propositions. People so guided may often seem aberrational, in the sense that they refuse to accede to the authority of others; but that is a trait that liberal politics should value, not oppose, for it yields precisely the diversity that America needs.

For this reason, parents should be entitled to broad rights to exempt their children from educational programs to which they raise religious objections. Perhaps it is not appropriate to allow the parents to control the curriculum that others must learn, but there are important societal reasons to allow them a degree of control over what their own children learn. The courts should not cooperate in efforts to make the family, in effect, an extension of state policy, as, for example, by allowing parents to opt out of sex education for their children only if the parents provide some substantially equivalent teaching at home. Only in this way can the society take seriously the epistemological diversity that leads some parents to prefer to learn science from the Bible.

For similar reasons, the challenge of a John Peloza should not be viewed simply in the legalistic terms that are needed to make out a constitutional case. There is an essential difference, one that our secularized culture tends to miss, between the claim that creationism is wrong and the claim that it is irrational. Scientific creationism may well be wrong, in the sense that it represents shoddy analysis of shaky data—but that analysis and that data form only a part of its source. To the extent that creationism is the result of the application of the hermeneutic of inerrancy to the opening chapters of Genesis, it is certainly rational.

Kent Greenawalt, in his thoughtful book *Religious Convictions and Political Choice,* reflects on a hypothetical case quite similar to the creationism problem, and ends by challenging the idea that the tools of natural science and the tools of biblical inerrancy are equally rational. "The scientists," writes Greenawalt, "are relying on premises that have so far been confirmed by common human experience and by techniques of discovery that would be accepted as valid by those capable of understanding them intellectually." The religionists, however, rely on premises that "are less securely rooted in common human experience and in techniques whose validity will not be contested by anyone capable of an intellectual grasp of them."[48]

But no creationist is likely to be persuaded by Greenawalt's argument, because creationism rejects the notion that the methods of natural science—especially as applied to the origin question—have been "confirmed by common human experience." Creationist parents would insist that their own "human experience" confirms a very different set of truths. Perhaps the most central of these truths is that God is real, a truth confirmed by a sense of closeness felt every day—a sense that much of the secular world seems prepared to deny. More directly, there is no way to disprove, for example, the old creationist claim that physical evidence that appears to run against the biblical account is only a trap set by the devil for the unwary. (One is reminded of the scene in Douglas Adams's comic science fiction novel *The Hitchhiker's Guide to the Galaxy,* when an alien being assigned to build the Earth mutters apologetically, "It's only half completed, I'm afraid—we haven't even finished burying the artificial dinosaur skeletons in the crust yet.")[49] Given its starting point and its methodology, creationism is as rational an explanation as any other. The trouble is that both the starting point and the methodology reflect an essential axiom—literal inerrancy—that is not widely shared. In this sense, the wrongness of creationism becomes a matter of power: yes, it is wrong because proved wrong, but it is proved wrong only in a particular epistemological universe. To say that the creationism battle is ultimately over epistemology, not religion, is not to defend the so-called equal-time statutes, but only to say that those who demand them are not irrational or fanatical. They are merely wrong.

For much the same reason, it is imprecise to suggest that the "equal-time" statutes necessarily represent officially authorized proselytizing. It is something of a commonplace in our politics to treat parental attempts to control the school curriculum as efforts to impose religious beliefs on others, but this is not the only possible explanation and it may not be the most plausible one. More likely, the parents are frightened of the conflict between religious authority on the one hand, and the authority of secular society—as represented by the public schools—on the other. It is all very well for the critic to say that the creationists simply want the government to endorse their religious beliefs. But for the creationist parent whose child is being taught the theory of evolution, there is no religious question, only a question of fact. Indeed, for the parent the matter is quite simple. The child is being taught a pack of lies. The parent wants the school to teach the truth.

Obviously, the scientific community will dispute the means by which the creationist parent has arrived at the truth, but that has nothing to do with the sincerity of the parent's conviction. The fact-value distinction so dear to Western philosophy since the Enlightenment in this case runs up against a blank wall, for the creationist parent will never be convinced that the war is between his or her religious belief on the one hand and scientific fact on the other. Rather, the war is between competing systems of discerning truth—and creationist parents, much like the scientist Murray Gell-Mann, want to know why it is that the school has the right to teach their children lies.

TRUTH AND EXPERTISE

Objections to the role of professed expertise in finding truth, when it conflicts with the central tenet of one's system, are common, and they are hardly limited to the scientific creationists. Consider, for example, those who cherish the market theory of value. If one considers value properly measured by the prices of goods and services in a market, it is easy to understand the wrath that is directed at government regulation seen as distorting the market. Take the idea of "comparable worth"—the notion that experts can study the nature of a task, compare it with other tasks, and decide whether the market has valued it properly. Outside of committed advocates, one can find few economists who take the idea of comparable worth seriously. The late Clarence Pendleton, head of the United States Civil Rights Commission, was roundly attacked for his reference to comparable worth as "the looniest idea since looney tunes." But his rhetoric was not appreciably different from the way in which, for example, pro-choice forces refer to efforts by self-proclaimed experts to prove that human life begins at conception. One can run down the list of crucial issues in America and see that mistrust of the experts is everywhere. Critics question expert views on the degree of racial bias in standardized testing, the mechanism for transmission of the AIDS virus, the safety of nuclear power, and the likelihood that prayer can heal diseases.

Nobody, it turns out, much likes to defer to experts whose judgments might interfere with the ability to follow the call of one's most cherished value. Disagreement with the self-proclaimed expertise of others is as old in America as George Washington's complaints about interference by the Continental Congress with his military strategy during the Revolutionary War. But when the claim interposed against expertise is of a religious nature, the specter of irrationality rears its head. So if, for example, parents who believe in the literal inerrancy of the account of creation in the opening chapters of Genesis refuse to let their children learn what the experts say is the better answer, they are derided in terms strongly suggesting that they are fanatics, and quite out of their heads besides.

Because we do not usually consider people crazy or fanatical just because they refuse to accept the counsel of scientific experts, the reason for the verbal assaults on the parents who believe in creationism cannot be their rejection of scientific method. The one thing that distinguishes the creationist parents from other dissenters from expert advice is the *ground* on which they make their rejection. Parents who accept and insist on the biblical account of creation are motivated by their religious faith—and that motivation, evidently, makes all the difference.

Of course one can understand why the religious motivation might make a *constitutional* difference. After all, whatever the controversy among legal scholars on the proper interpretation of the Establishment Clause of the First Amendment, there is broad agreement that the government cannot endorse a particular religious belief, and the teaching of creationism does seem to constitute such an endorsement. But whatever the legal status of efforts to teach scientific creationism in the classroom—whether by government mandate, as in the Louisiana case, or because the teacher wants to, as in the case of John Peloza—it is terribly troubling to see what a vast rhetorical difference religious motivation makes. For the rhetorical case against the creationist parents rests not merely or mostly on arcane questions of constitutional interpretation; the case rests principally on the sense that they themselves are wrong to rely on their sacred text to discover truths about the world.

TRUTH AND POWER

For the creationist parents, of course, this bottom-line judgment—that their epistemology is *wrong*—is precisely the reason for anger. The parents, very devout and very worried, are trying to protect the core of their own beliefs. It is not that they want the public schools to proselytize in their favor; it is rather that they do not want the schools to do what Dewey implied that they must, to press their own children to reject what the parents believe by calling into question a central article of their faith. The parents are fighting to preserve their sense of community, a sense engendered in part through a shared religious faith. The response of the creationist to the teaching of evolutionary theory, like the resistance to AIDS education or condom distribution, might best be viewed as a reaction to a fear of indoctrination: religion demands one intellectual position, and the state seeks to command another. Liberalism, in this case, is curiously intolerant of what certainly may be viewed as a classic case of conscience interposed before the authority of the state. Nor have the consciences of the protesters been formed without any thought. They understand quite well that the hermeneutic they have chosen has interpretive implications, not just for their sacred text, but for the entire natural world, and devout literalists understand and accept them. The creationist parents, in short, are not a superstitious rabble. They are independent thinkers who insist on a right to their own means for seeking knowledge of the world, and they deny the right of the state to tell their children that their parents' world view is wrong.

On this vision, a public school curriculum perceived as secular and modernist is a grave and obvious threat to the efforts of parents to raise their children in their religious belief with its hermeneutical implications. Thus, the question that moves the debate—who shall control the education of children?—is starkly posed. Educators might insist that the public schools should be neutral on questions of religious belief, but the parents protest that this insistence is simply window dressing for something more sinister. What the schools are offering, the parents charge, is not a neutral curriculum, but one that can only call into question—or hold up to ridicule—some of their most cherished religious beliefs. Parents who want scientific creationism taught in schools do not share the view that they are asking the schools to teach their religious beliefs. Their view is that they are asking the school to teach the truth—not the moral truth with which religion is commonly associated in our dialogue, but a truth about the material world. In this sense, their battle is not with the courts or with the First Amendment, but with the distant and disdainful experts who insist on teaching children an account of creation and evolution that the parents believe to be fraught with factual errors.

One of the lawyers who waged the successful battle against the Arkansas "balanced-treatment" statutes correctly understood this point but misapprehended its significance. He wrote: "[N]owhere has creation-science been added to public school curricula because of the sheer force of its ideas. Its inclusion in science classes has always been the result of irregular political intervention in the curriculum development process."[50] To which the creationist parents would reply, with vigor, "Yes, exactly! We were forced to turn to politics because the so-called experts wouldn't listen to us!" Whether the experts *should* have listened or not has little to do with whether "political intervention in the curriculum" is, on its face, always something to be resisted.

The demand for the teaching of scientific creationism, so understood, is much like the demand for what is described as a multicultural curriculum. Concerned that "expert authority" is replete with distortions and evil influences, the critics of the curriculum insist that other points of view be included or, in some cases, allowed to dominate. Many on the left find it easy to embrace the multiculturalist movement but are deeply offended by the creationists; on the right, there are those who would defend the effort to require the teaching of creationism but fight furiously against multiculturalism. In a sense, those who support one and oppose the other are missing the critical connection between the two, for both are exercises in resistance to central authority in the teaching of children. (The "home schooling" movement, which many intellectuals oppose because it grants too much authority to parents (!), is an example of the same effort to resist state authority.) Again, we see Tocqueville's scheme at work, even though it continues to frustrate liberal political theory: those who organize to propogate a different idea are crucial democratic bulwarks against majority tyranny, or, as we near the end of the twentieth century, the tyranny of experts. Neither the creationists nor the multiculturalists see much reason to be impressed with supposedly "expert" conclusions that run counter to what they themselves are certain is correct. At the same time, the political divisions that play out among the supporters of creationism on the one hand and multiculturalism on the other are instructive, for they suggest the possibility of taking both ideas seriously as just that—as ideas—and, therefore, arguing over the consequences.

This point is crucial to an assessment of the movement for scientific creationism. The fact that creationist parents are driven by concerns about epistemology and the survival of their way of life does not distinguish them from lots of other worried people, and it should not insulate their claims from criticism. The criticism, however, should be of the claims themselves, on their merits as good or bad ideas, rather than of the motivation for the claims. There is no need, and less reason, to single out religion for special treatment or special disability. If one dislikes a teaching, one can argue against it, as my parents did when I was taught in junior high school that slaves were essentially happy in the antebellum South. My parents did not want their children taught that only a few of the slaves wanted to be free because it was not true.

Of course, parents who believe that Genesis contains a literally accurate story of creation would make the same statement: they do not want their children to learn the theory of evolution because it is not true. In rejecting their cosmology, I have no answer to give them, none that will satisfy. When I mentioned this point in a lecture at Duke University, a member of the audience responded that the answer was simple: we already had the Enlightenment, and their side lost. That answer, of course, states the simple historical fact of the matter, but it is less an argument than an explanation. We win because you lose. We have the power and you don't. On such distinctions, all too often, is the modern notion of truth premised.

10

God:
A Course of Study

IN the preceding chapter, I quoted the dissent of Justice
William Douglas in *Wisconsin v. Yoder,* the Supreme Court's 1972
decision allowing the Old Order Amish to keep their children
out of the public schools after eighth grade. It is useful now to
consider Douglas's words once more: "While the parents, absent
dissent, normally speak for the entire family, the education of a
child is a matter on which the child will often have decided
views." Having set up the worrisome conflict between the parents and the child, Douglas went on to reinforce the point: "It is
the student's judgment, not his parents', that is essential."[1]

The implication of Douglas's reasoning is that parents who
choose a religious education for their children are involved in
conduct that is somehow suspect, that the state therefore needs
to be a monitor to ensure that the child's wishes are being pro-

tected—in a way that the state need not monitor, for example, the parents' decision on a reasonable bedtime. If it turns out that the child does not want the religious training that the parents prefer—well, what is the state to do then? Even Douglas did not quite suggest that the state should intervene to prevent the parents from forcing the dissenting child to accept their religion, and that is a good thing. The right of parents to choose a religious upbringing for their children is older than America, and ought to stand as an unshakable fundament of national life. Nobody talks seriously about taking that right away (although if one takes seriously the rhetoric of some philosophical critics of religion, one must wonder why). And yet the right is under pressure of another kind, the pressure exerted by an educational system that is too often unresponsive to the needs or desires of parents concerned about their children's religious upbringing, and by a legal and political system reluctant to take any steps that might be seen as "supporting" religion—and, as a result, burdening parents who seek religious educations for their children with costs that other parents, even those sending their children to private schools, need not bear.

That battles over the proper interaction between religion and education are so heated is painful, but should not be surprising. After all, religion and education share a characteristic that so many human activities lack: they matter. This chapter discusses four additional areas of controversy: classroom prayer, school funding, the teaching of values, and teaching about religion in the curriculum.

CLASSROOM PRAYER

My children pray in school, in an organized fashion, each morning before classes begin. They do so because they attend a private religious school, which, fortunately, my wife and I are able

to afford. One of the reasons we prefer private to public
school—the main one, in fact—is our determination to educate
our children in an environment that celebrates, not demeans,
their religious beliefs, one that is responsive to our concerns
about morality and parental responsibility. Group prayer is part
of that celebration, and we are glad that it is a part of their
school day. But we would never impose that preference on anybody else.

As a child in Washington, D.C., I attended a public school at
which, each morning, one of the children would read a psalm
aloud. But only the Christian children participated. There were, as
I recall, perhaps three Jewish children out of a class of twenty-
five or thirty. As the rest of us listened to the psalms, they would
read books. I do not recall ever thinking that what the other kids
and I were doing was better than what they were doing, or that
they were wrong not to participate, and I do not recall any of my
classmates expressing such sentiments either. What I do recall
was feeling with the sharp empathy of a seven-year-old the exclusion of the Jewish kids: how, I often wondered, do they feel at
this moment? I didn't know then, I don't know now. I have talked
to some Jewish adults who have told me that their parents were
glad that the Christian kids prayed in school: a reminder, they
were told as children, of just what you are up against in the
world. But I am not proud to be a part of a world in which Jewish kids have to be reminded what they are up against.

Prayer is a crucial part of our family life. We pray before
important events: meals, trips, sleep. We give thanks for our good
fortune, pray for those less fortunate, beg forgiveness for our sins,
and ask forgiveness for the sins of others. For us, prayer is an
affirmation of our connectedness to God. We have no way of
knowing whether God approves of us, and that is not what our
prayers are for—we are only mortal, after all, and have no right to
presume. Yet the activity of prayer is our tradition as well as our
comfort, and we cannot, as a family, imagine life without it.

I have described one approach to moral life. There are many

others. Different religious people pray in different ways. And there are of course religious people who do not like to pray, or who do not pray publicly, or do not pray in groups. There are also people who are not religious. It is not possible to find a way to join all of these diverse groups in a "nonsectarian" prayer, still less in an openly sectarian one. By choosing among possible prayers, and then forcing its choice on impressionable children who look to their schools for guidance, the state in effect coerces religious adherence. This is the reason, as I have already explained (see chapter 6), that the Supreme Court was correct to forbid organized prayer in the public school classroom.

It is important to stress what the Court banned and what it did not. What the First Amendment does not allow, according to the Justices, is organized classroom prayer, whether led by a teacher or by a student, as a part of the regular school day. This does not mean that students cannot pray quietly and nondisruptively, whether before meals or (as many of us have) before exams. It does not mean that students cannot organize their own prayer groups to meet outside of regular classroom time, a right that the Congress has guaranteed by statute. It does not mean that students are forbidden to follow the teachings of their religions on school property or even to preach them. In short, it does not mean that God is not allowed in the classroom, a metaphorical banishment that would be a metaphysical impossibility. It does mean that the state, in the person of the teacher, the classroom's authority figure, cannot tell the students whether to believe in God, whether to worship, or how. Organized classroom prayer is forbidden because there is no way to organize it without having the state do just those things.

Not everyone is happy with those Court decisions, of course, and, in particular, the decisions are unpopular with parents who want their children to pray in school but are unable to go into the education market and purchase access to a school where they can do so. Even though support has fallen a bit, most Americans since the 1960s have supported the effort to amend the Constitution to overturn the school prayer cases—a movement celebrated quadrennially in the Republican party's presidential platform.

As in the case of the fundamentalist parents (discussed in chapter 9) who seek to force the schools to teach creationism, it is a mistake to look at the movement for school prayer as an effort to enlist the state as an aid to proselytizing. A cleaner and more realistic view is that the parents genuinely believe that study of the Bible is essential to education because the will of God, expressed in the word of God, is the moral fundament on which we Americans should build our nation. To open the school day with a prayer, then, is to acknowledge and reinforce what seems to them a simple but indispensable moral truth. Pat Buchanan was ridiculed for his apparent effort at the 1992 Republican Convention to link the Los Angeles riots of April 1992 with the ban on organized classroom prayer, and the criticism was mostly deserved. And yet there are Americans for whom he expressed in his demagogic style a vital aspirational belief—namely, that America would be a better nation if only it took more seriously the reinforcement of strong moral character in its children. With this sentiment one can hardly disagree, which is why it is a shame that religious conservatives keep ruining it by saying that the real problem is how the liberals have kicked God out of the schools.

It is impossible to test scientifically the intuition that many supporters of school prayer hold, the intuition that Buchanan so badly misused, the intuition that says that daily worship improves the society. One can marshal powerful counterexamples—at the time that half the nation was run as a slaveocracy, there was prayer aplenty in what schools existed—but they do not quite disprove the thesis either. Yet the point of religious freedom and religious equality ultimately must be that it does not matter whether the intuition is true or not. Even were it the case that classroom prayer would make us more moral, that would not justify the state in what amounts, for the dissenter, to a coercion of religious belief at the moment in time when children are most impressionable and their intellects most vulnerable. Coercion might not be the intention; it is, however, the effect.

It is possible, of course, to carry this concern to extremes, and some critics believe the Court did just that in the 1992 case of *Lee v. Weisman*. The case involved a Long Island public high school graduation ceremony at which a rabbi delivered an invocation and benediction. This was not daily prayer of the sort with which earlier decisions were concerned, but it was still, said the Court, unconstitutional. The Justices described the rabbi's spoken prayer, which occurred just once in the students' school careers, as "in effect requir[ing] participation in a religious exercise." In a public school setting, the court majority concluded, "the choice imposed by the State constitute[d] an unacceptable constraint" prohibited by the Establishment Clause of the First Amendment.[2]

The case was controversial in part because school prayer has been for the last three decades a principal battleground for the separation of church and state. Since the Court began in 1962 the long process of disentangling religious worship and public education,[3] it has been routinely accused of shoving God out of the classroom. Over the years, intermittent reports have indicated that the school prayer decisions are ignored in parts of the Bible Belt. Even now, thirty years later, public opinion surveys continue to indicate overwhelming popular support for a constitutional amendment to allow organized classroom prayer.[4]

Yet the Justices were always correct to build the wall that they did, even in the face of public disapproval. The powers of the state should not be used to coerce religious belief, and it is impossible to design a noncoercive approach to school prayer. Probably the court had it right in *Lee v. Weisman* too, although this was about as close a case for school prayer as one is likely to see. Justice Scalia noted in dissent that "from our Nation's origin, prayer has been a prominent part of governmental ceremonies and proclamations." He cited, with some force, the Declaration of Independence.[5] But his opinion reads most powerfully as a justification for prayer at public meetings for mature adults, at which attendance is optional. It has little obvious relevance to public schools, where the attendance of impressionable children, except for those wealthy enough to make different choices, is compulsory.

A harder case is *Stone v. Graham,* decided in 1980, in which the Justices struck down one school's practice of posting the Ten Commandments on classroom walls.[6] Perhaps the practice did reflect a desire to circumvent the school prayer decisions, but circumvention is not itself a fresh constitutional violation; if the effect of the posting was to teach the students religious law, then the Establishment Clause was surely violated. If, on the other hand, the school sought to inculcate some of the admittedly spiritual but not necessarily religious values with which many of the Commandments are concerned, it is difficult to see why any constitutional issue arises.

One federal court that almost certainly was wrong was the United States Court of Appeals for the Tenth Circuit, which held, in the case of *Roberts v. Madigan* (1990), that a school district violated no religious freedom rights when it forbade a teacher to display his personal Bible where the students could see it, or to read it silently when his students were involved in work that did not require his direct supervision (see chapter 1). Indeed, the judges suggested, even had the district not implemented the ban, the Establishment Clause would probably have provided a basis for a court order including the same prohibition.[7]

The separation of church and state should prohibit the use of the apparatus of government to coerce religious belief, but it must not be made a metaphor for government pressure *not* to be religious. *Roberts v. Madigan* is therefore wrong, but the basic school prayer cases are right. They are right as a constitutional matter, but they are also right as a moral matter. No government should take steps that amount to enforcing a religious orthodoxy on its people, and organized prayer in the public schools, however benignly intended, does precisely that.

That is not the same as saying that nobody should be *allowed* to pray in school. Were our children in public schools, we would still expect them to pray before meals, as our son did, alone but proud, at his preschool. Similarly, students who want to organize religious clubs outside of school time but on school property should be placed on the same footing as other student organizations. Such activities as these harm or coerce no one, although when Congress adopted legislation requiring schools to allow "equal access" to religious meetings on the same terms as other student groups,[8] some critics understandably worried what else other than small voluntary prayer groups the tide might sweep in once the flood gates swung wide open.[9] The fears might be well founded, which is why school officials and courts must remain vigilant—as long as they never make the mistake of thinking that the enemies of freedom are the children who choose to pray.

Many observers have reported over the years that the Court's decisions on school prayer are honored in the breach. Especially in the Bible Belt, but elsewhere as well, there are said to be some public school classrooms in which organized prayers are recited, and there are many school events that are opened and closed with spoken prayers led by school officials or clergy. Often, these tiny acts of civil disobedience continue without a murmur of dissent, because they are undertaken in religiously homogeneous communities, in which nearly everyone wants prayer in the schools. Occasionally, of course, a suit is brought, and the plaintiff always wins, as everyone understands the plaintiff will—and, bit by bit, the local schools fall into line.

The cases involving a state-mandated "moment of silence" before the school day begins present a more complicated issue. The Supreme Court, in *Wallace v. Jaffree* (1985), struck down an Alabama statute allowing schools that so desired to set aside one minute for "meditation or voluntary prayer."[10] The Justices argued that the only purpose of the legislation was a religious one—to return prayers to the public schools—and noted that nothing prohibited students who desired to pray or meditate from doing so.

The Court's reasoning majority reflects the contemporary

suspicion of "accommodations" of religion that I discussed in chapter 7. It is not clear, however, that the answer the Justices reached is the only one possible. Taking as given that the state might choose to allow, or even require, schools to set aside a moment of silence, why should it matter that some legislators hope that many students will pray? The dynamics of the classroom should matter to the Court, as they mattered in *Lee v. Weisman,* but the motivation of legislators should be irrelevant (see chapter 6).

And what are the likely classroom dynamics? I have nothing on which to base an empirical judgment, but I can hazard an educated guess. Many students *will* pray—we can take that as given—but if the effect on the dissenter of silent prayer during a moment when all students are silent is as coercive as the majority feared, then the Court is probably wrong to suggest that, in the absence of the moment of silence, nothing prevents those students who want to pray from doing so. After all, if the knowledge that many of one's classmates are praying during the moment of silence produces pressure to pray (and the Court might be right), then surely the knowledge that many of one's classmates are *not* praying as the school day opens will produce pressure *not* to pray. There is, in short, no neutral position. To reach the outcome that the moment of silence is unconstitutional, then, the assumption must be that when faced with the necessity of choosing between a course that will have the effect of encouraging silent prayer and a course that will have the effect of discouraging it, the government must choose the second. This is not a happy outcome, especially for the millions of Americans who see religion as a positive good rather than as a malevolent evil, but it might be the outcome that a concern for classroom coercion commands.

Still, my wife and I are glad that our children pray in their private school and that they begin each day with mandatory chapel. We are glad that the school reinforces our religious training rather than interfering with it. And if anybody happens not to like it, that is not our problem—not so far, anyway. I suppose that if one takes seriously Justice Douglas's opinion, the state should intervene to be sure my wife and I have made the decision that our children want—that is, the state should somehow undertake to learn whether our children really want to attend a religious school. William Douglas was a very smart man, but some of his ideas were, let us say, on the eccentric side. This time, fortunately, nobody took him seriously. If the time comes when the government does, I am quite sure that my family, and many others too, will pack up and leave the United States, for no nation that strips away the right of parents to raise their children in their religion is worthy of allegiance.

SCHOOL FUNDING

Of course, it is in a sense unfair that my children attend a school where there is organized prayer because my wife and I are able to afford it, and other children whose parents want the same for them cannot, because it is too expensive. One might respond that that is simply the way that market economies work—if we have more money, we can purchase things for our children that others cannot.

This sense of unfairness is evidently widely shared, and some leading politicians—most notably and recently George Bush—have responded to this concern by pressing for a voucher program that would offer parents federal dollars (probably through a tax credit) with which to purchase private education, including, if they so choose, education at private religious schools. In 1983, the Supreme Court upheld a state tax deduction for tuition paid to private schools, including parochial schools, notwithstanding its indirect effect of supporting religious schools.[11]

The principle of choice that vouchers represent is in many ways attractive. After all, parents select health care providers for their children, and if the nation continues its steady march toward national health insurance, that choice will receive a hefty government subsidy. Parents who are financially able to do so select neighborhoods for their children to grow up in, and the home mortgage interest deduction subsidizes that choice too. Even when parents select a religious faith in which to raise their children, aspects of that choice may, in a sense, be subsidized too, through the charitable deduction for contributions to religious groups.

Among the vital pillars of civic life, then, only primary and secondary education requires parents to allow the government to choose for them if they want to receive a subsidy. Thus, a program of vouchers to allow the purchase of private education can be seen as a way of extending the principle of government-funded choice—a staple of the modern welfare state—into another important field of civic endeavor.

Sounds good, doesn't it? But of course, matters are hardly that simple, and a voucher program possesses obvious drawbacks. Quite apart from the traditional concern over whether a voucher program would be a subsidy for private segregation academies,* the most significant criticism is that a voucher program would allow the private schools to skim off the cream, taking the best students, leaving those who cause trouble to the

---

* In other work, I have expressed reservations about voucher systems on the ground that a subsidy for private education might lead to an increase in racial segregation. See Stephen L. Carter, *Reflections of an Affirmative Action Baby* (New York: Basic Books, 1991), pp. 147–48. Since that time, however, I have been confronted with statistics showing that even though the aggregate ratio of black students to white students is lower in private schools than in public schools, the actual distributions are such that the median private school is more integrated than the median public school—in other words, that the median private school is less likely than the median public school to be all white or all black. As for the median religious school, it is likely to be even more integrated than the median private school. James Coleman et al., *High School Achievement: Public, Catholic, and Private Schools Compared* (1982), pp. 29–37. One might fairly question whether these data would hold up were a voucher system universally available, but the data certainly must give pause to those of us whose knee-jerk reaction has been that vouchers are *certain* to lead to greater segregation.

public schools, a prospect that would in effect destroy the project of public education in the United States. Supporters of vouchers counter, with some force, that much of the cream is already gone—that the well-heeled can afford to send their children elsewhere and generally do, so that the project of saving the public schools by refusing to aid those who make different choices really means preserving our consciences by burdening the working class. Polling data indicate that strong majorities of the public support voucher programs and other tax support for private schools, including religious schools.[12]

This is not the place to resolve the wisdom of a voucher program generally, which promises to be a contentious political issue for years to come. It is the place to argue that if voucher programs are established, the Supreme Court was right to hold that religious schools *can* be included as a constitutional matter, and, as a policy matter, religious schools should not be left out.

One must note at the outset that the overwhelming majority of private school students (about 85 percent, perhaps more) are in religious schools, and that most parents (especially in lower income brackets) who desire private school educations but cannot afford them would evidently send their children to religious schools. This means that a voucher program that omits religious education would leave out most of the parents who most need it. Thus, the effect of such a plan would be to make it more costly to send children to religious schools than to other private schools. Quite apart from whether the state may constitutionally create such a disincentive—many scholars think not[13]—one must ask whether there are compelling reasons of public policy to support the omission.

One must begin with the tragic wreck we are making of too many of our schools. In America, unfortunately, the market in educational services has created a multitiered system, in which parents with the funds to purchase the top educations for their children point their progeny down the road to success with far more confidence than parents who cannot. We as a nation should be ashamed at how little we really do to ensure the access of every child to the best possible education. Even the most casual perusal of Jonathan Kozol's excellent book, *Savage Inequalities*, will illustrate what a joke we have made of the ideal of equality of educational opportunity.[14]

Many parents respond to what they perceive as troubles in the public schools by opting out, as my wife and I have. Approximately 12 percent of American children attend private schools, (the number as of 1991 hovered somewhere above 5 million) and, of those, 85 percent attend religious schools, just over half of them Catholic schools. The remaining 15 percent attend "independent" schools—private schools without religious affiliation.[15]

A majority of American parents say they would send their children to private rather than public schools if they could afford it, which is the sentiment to which politicians play when they talk of creating a voucher system to help defray the cost. Parents cite a variety of reasons: smaller classes, better discipline, more parental involvement. (The only field in which parents rank public schools higher than private schools is the quality of sports programs.)[16] Most parents also say that private schools do a better job than public schools of educating children, and that is where the sharp debates occur. If one compares the test scores of public school students against those of *independent* school students, this is usually, and dramatically, true. If, however, one compares the test scores of public school students against those of religious schools, the story the numbers tell is much more complex.

Since the pioneering work of the sociologist James Coleman in the 1980s, it has been widely accepted that the Catholic schools offer at least as good an education as the public schools—in particular, that they do better with many poor and minority children who would, in the public schools, be at risk. Coleman argued that the Catholic schools are more successful in part because they are structured to provide the "social capital"—in particular, a substitute family structure—that many poor children lack and that other work has demonstrated to be important to academic success.[17] If Coleman is correct, then the move across the country to close many Catholic schools because of budget cuts will fall with special violence on the children who need them most.

However, the proposition that the Catholic schools in fact do a better overall job has recently been under fire. Well-known data show that students in Catholic schools are higher achievers on average than students in public schools. Actually, the facts are more subtle, and whether the students in Catholic schools do significantly better depends on the question one sets out to ask.

For example, in 1986, the National Assessment of Educational Progress (NAEP) tested children in grades 3, 7, and 11 in mathematics and science and found that the median Catholic school scores were higher than the median public school scores at every grade level, with the greatest differences—14.7 points (out of 500) in mathematics and 15.7 points in science—coming in grade 7. (The defenders of the public schools put an interesting spin on the numbers, suggesting that the difference was "only" 15 points—which is a bit like saying that a student with a grade point average of 3.60 has not really done better than one with a grade point average of 3.45, a difference of "only" 15 percentage points, although one is an A– and the other a B+.) The data also show that "the math-science gender gap is wider in Catholic schools," although "Catholic school girls still score higher than public school boys." However, the NAEP numbers also show that the median public and Catholic school scores are much lower than those of students in independent schools. Moreover, when the comparison is made not between Catholic schools and public schools but between religious schools generally and public schools, most of the differences vanish. For example, in 1991, students at public schools achieved median Scholastic Aptitude Test scores of 419 verbal and 473 mathematics (of a possible 800), while students at religious schools had median scores of 437 verbal and 472 math.[18]

Besides, even when it is clear that students in Catholic schools do better, critics press the sensible argument that the public schools have to take everyone and the Catholic schools do not. Defenders of the Catholic schools usually shoot back that most Catholic schools do not have selective admission policies, and, if the old New England prep schools of the "St. Grottlesex" tradition are excluded, those religious schools that are selective tend to be selective mostly along denominational lines. The Catholic schools, advocates point out, also tend to reflect their communities demographically. In 1991, for example, 63.7 percent of the children in the Catholic schools of Washington, D.C., were black, a proportion just slightly lower than that for the city as a whole.[19]

My concern here, however, is not with the empirical evidence on the relative success of religious schools in teaching subjects that the public schools offer as well. After all, no matter what the data—even if the data showed that the religious schools were *worse* than the public schools—many parents would choose the schools anyway. My concern, therefore, is with what the religious schools offer that the public schools do not—the aspects of the schools that make many parents want a religious education for their children so badly that they are willing to pay after-tax dollars in order to get it, even as their taxes go to support the public schools that they do not use.

Parents who seek a religious education for their children are often more interested in the inculcation of strong values— and, in particular, the school's reinforcement of the values they teach at home—than they are in the religious aspects.[20] Their image of public schools, accurate or not, is of a place where values are destroyed instead of reinforced. The battles over such issues as sex education and condom distribution provide examples of just what many parents fear most about the public schools: that they will, because experts distrusted by the parents say so, shoulder aside values that the parents cherish most.

Still, one cannot brush aside the constitutional problems by painting the religious schools as simply independent schools with a healthy dose of ethics thrown in. There is no escaping the fact that religious schools provide religious education, and whether parents choose them because of this aspect or in spite of it, the fact of the religious nature remains. So although millions of parents choose religious schools for their children, and millions more would if they could, the question remains whether a government otherwise inclined to aid the parents in their quest for better education for their children can aid the particular choice that most private school parents make.

Notwithstanding its explicit 1983 endorsement of at least some forms of tax relief for parents who choose religious schools, the Supreme Court has caused a tremendous mess with its jurisprudence about state aid to religious schools. In particular, the question of direct rather than indirect assistance remains open. One might suppose that freedom of religion means that the state cannot penalize parents for choosing to send their children to schools organized by and for religious communities, but according to the Court, one would be wrong. Not only *can* the states increase the burdens on parents who choose religious as against other private schools for their children—the implication of a number of Supreme Court cases is that the states *must* do so.

Many of the contradictions and confusions are notorious. For example, according to the Supreme Court, the public schools may release religious students for special instruction while requiring other students to remain in school—but the program is permitted only if the special instruction is held away from the public school grounds.[21] The state can provide religious schools with textbooks but not maps;[22] if on the other hand religious schools purchase their own textbooks, the state cannot reimburse them.[23] But, again, a system of tuition tax credits available to all parents on an equal basis—including parents with children at parochial schools—has been sustained.

The doctrinal confusion has resulted from a sense that if religious education benefits from public funds, the forbidden

wall of separation is breached, competing with a sense that it is
wrong to penalize the religions for not being secular. Many
thoughtful scholars and judges have taken the position that the
wall is so high that the state cannot take any steps to ease the
burdens on those parents who choose to send their children to
private religious schools. This does not seem a defensible rule. It
has the effect of penalizing the choice of a religious school (as
against another, nonreligious private school), and, therefore,
treats religion as worse than other grounds on which to choose
an education. This approach does not cherish the freedom to
choose a religion—it cherishes the freedom to choose a religion
if you are wealthy enough to afford one.

The idea that religious schools should be ineligible for government assistance of any kind places the schools in an awkward and even humiliating constitutional tradition. In 1925, the
Court held that the Constitution protects "the liberty of parents
and guardians to direct the upbringing and education of children
under their control."[24] Half a century later, striking down state
assistance to private segregation academies, the Court warned
that the right to send children to a private school does not entail
a requirement of state subsidy.[25] The very next year, the Justices
emphasized the point, ruling that the Constitution does not allow
government activities that enhance "the attractiveness of segregated private schools."[26]

The rule against enhancing the "attractiveness" of schools
that engage in racial discrimination is easy to understand,
because segregation is a constitutional anathema and a moral
evil. The rulings that limit the ability of the state to assist students
in private religious schools, which seem to place private religious
schools in the same category as private segregation academies,
are harder to understand, because religion, unlike racial segregation, is a value that both the society and the Constitution is supposed to cherish. As the Supreme Court wrote in 1946, the First
Amendment "requires that the state be a neutral in its relations
with groups of religious believers and non-believers; it does not

require the state to be their adversary. State power is no more to be used so as to handicap religions than it is to favor them."[27]

The proposition that government should not be the adversary of the religions is sufficient to resolve the matter. If neutrality means that the government cannot take steps to treat religious schools better than other schools, it surely means as well that the government cannot take steps to treat religious schools worse. As I said at the outset, the policy conundrum surrounding vouchers cannot be resolved here, but a small but controversial corner of it can be. Should a voucher program ever be established—and I am by no means saying that it should be— parents who choose to send their children to religious schools should be eligible alongside parents who send their children elsewhere. In a technical sense, this does indeed constitute government support for religion, for a voucher is nothing but a direct subsidy from government revenues. But it is support without discrimination—all religious schools would be equally eligible, and none would have any advantage over nonreligious schools. For the government to subsidize some private schools but refuse to subsidize the religious ones would make religious schools more costly and would thus constitute a government-created disincentive to use them. In other areas of constitutional law, we do not call such disincentives "neutrality"; we call them "discrimination."[28]

THE TEACHING OF VALUES

If one is repelled by the image of government-aided flight of religious children to the private schools, one can try to solve the problem the other way around, by working to make the public schools more responsive to the concerns of religious parents. Nowhere are those concerns more sharply exposed than in the bitter battles over the teaching of values in the classroom.

Not so very long ago, the inculcation of civic values—the aspects of ethical character that were thought to make one a good citizen—was seen as an important purpose, and perhaps the principal one, for the establishment of public schools and, in particular, for making attendance mandatory. Even John Dewey, for all the contempt he lavished upon religion, believed that the transmittal of strong social values was what the public school classroom was *for*.[29] Nowadays, the idea that the government might sponsor the teaching of values is usually met with the cynical question, *Whose?*—for we have moved sharply into a morally relativistic age, and the public schools have certainly felt the sting.

Consider the stir created in the summer of 1992 when the New York City Board of Education voted 4 to 3 to require that all groups providing AIDS education in public school classrooms agree to spend more time stressing abstinence than safe sex. The AIDS educators were outraged, arguing that sexually active children were not likely to listen to the message of abstinence, so that the safe sex message would be lost and many might die.[30] Perhaps this is so, and I generally would defer to the judgments of professionals on such matters. Still, from the tone of many of the comments, it is difficult to resist the impression that some educators simply feel uncomfortable with stating a clear and simple value—they seem to believe that in some way, by telling students what they *should* do (instead of telling them how to do what they want to do), they are engaging in a form of pedagogy best avoided. One is put in mind of the disturbing example, mentioned by Betty Mensch and Alan Freeman in a sensitive article in *Tikkun,* of the preschool workers who chose not to tell one child that it was "wrong" to hit another, fearing the consequences of such interventionist techniques.[31]

But if students cannot be told that abstinence is a good and desirable thing—if that simple societal value cannot be stated in the classroom without causing an uproar—then what hope is there that we can convince children that bigotry and avarice, for example, are wrong? After all, one might reasonably argue that if sexually active children will not pay attention to strong suggestions of abstinence, then children leaning toward racism may not pay attention to suggestions of tolerance and respect either. But if the message is a good one, a right one, the danger that children will tune it out is hardly sufficient reason not to try. That, I think, is why many advocates of the teaching of abstinence believe that those who object to stressing it do not really consider it a value worth stressing. Probably, this criticism is unfair; but if we continue to be reluctant to teach values, little ammunition will be available with which to refute it.

As a religious parent, I would not dream of sending my children to a school that felt itself constrained not to reinforce the message of abstinence that my wife and I teach, but, instead, offered "safe sex" instruction without the repeated caveat that adolescent sexual activity is wrong. I am not much interested in whether psychologists have reached resolution on whether it is harmful to the child or not—I think sexual activity is a bad thing for kids to undertake before they are emotionally mature. I do not deny that many and perhaps most do, and mine might. That does not mean, in my judgment as a parent, that they should not be discouraged. There are only two plausible responses to my concern, and both are deeply offensive. First, I could be told, "We know how to reach your kids and you don't"; second, the message might be, "Because we need to do it this way to reach other kids, yours will just have to suffer."

Such arguments, I suspect, are what many religious parents hear in the official responses to their objections to various aspects of sex education—especially sex education unaccompanied by moral exhortation—that I discussed in chapter 9. The sense that no one cares about their concerns helps explain why so many religious parents choose to leave the public schools. It also explains why they are furious that they have to pay for schools they feel they *cannot* use (because of the moral messages conveyed by the curriculum), and yet cannot receive government aid when they establish schools of their own.

The sociologist Robert Wuthnow has tied the sudden upsurge in the number of private Roman Catholic and Jewish schools around the end of the Second World War to a broad perception of the importance of religion as a force in people's lives and a widely felt need to do a better job of teaching values, especially religious values, to children.[32] Protestants, interestingly, relied on the public schools, perhaps out of a faith that those schools already reflected their dominant values. This last point bears emphasis. Many Catholics and Jews fled the public schools for just that reason—that a dominant *sectarian* ethos was, in their judgment, being taught to their kids. Now many Protestants are fleeing as well, which is evidence, perhaps, that the old ethos is no longer the dominant one. The angry squabbling about "secular humanism" is an effort to give a name to what many parents believe has replaced it.

Toothpaste cannot be squeezed back into its tube. It may be that the relativistic ethic of our age has doomed forever the project of having the public schools engage in what was once called "civic education"—turning out adults who would be fully prepared for civic life, another term one rarely hears any longer. There is little agreement today on what the values *are* that citizens ought to learn, or at least the lack of agreement is often put forth as a reason for not teaching values. Actually, however, there are some broad values on which vast majorities of Americans tend to agree, and the importance of sexual abstinence during adolescence may be one of them.[33]

Unfortunately, it is not only the grade schools that are failing to train young people for citizenship. The colleges, as many depressing reports confirm, are not doing much to pick up the slack. Philosopher Bernard Murchland, who has spent time informally polling his own students on their visions of the good citizen, found much talk about rights or about solving the nation's problems, little about responsibilities to the larger polity.[34]

Yet, in a way, all of this argument is silly. Nobody really imagines that the education of children can proceed without the inculcation of values *any* values, even if indirectly. Few people think that it should. On the contrary, the idea that children *should* be taught the values they need to be productive citizens was a principal motivation in the move for mandatory schooling. The writings of John Dewey, the great secular philosopher of education, are full of a sense that without public education in fundamental values, a democracy will wither and die. (As it happens, Dewey was also vehemently antireligion, but that is a different problem.)

The need for teaching values is palpable. Most Americans, when they think about the need to inculcate positive values in the young, probably think about the complex of problems besetting the urban poor, especially (but not uniquely) in communities of color. But as Ben Wildavsky has pointed out, the need to learn something about the difference between right and wrong is just as great in the mighty suburban schools that are the pride of the American public education system as it is in any inner-city classroom.[35]

Sometimes, when I do public speaking, I like to tell a story that I call "The Most Dangerous Children in America." I tell of the time that my daughter (then five) and I were caught in a crossfire between two rival drug gangs in Queens. I describe my terror because we were separated, and I could not go to her until the shooting stopped. (She was not alone, but with her uncle and her grandmother.) None of the shooters looked to be beyond the teen years. I grow quite emotional as I fill in the details, and the audience usually gasps in horror and clucks in sympathy, right on cue.

Then I tell another story, about the days when I used to ride the commuter train from Stamford to New Haven, Connecticut. In the morning, the train would also pick up teenaged boys and girls for delivery to private schools along its route. One day I happened to overhear a conversation between a few of the girls, who were arguing, it seems, over which was a more exclusive community—Westport or Fairfield. (Both are Connecticut shore towns within commuting distance to New York City.) The girls bandied the names of wealthy celebrities who lived in this town or that one. Then, finally, the little girl from Westport came up with what she thought was the topper. She announced that D.— a famous entertainer—lived in Westport. The girl from Fairfield came right back with what should have been the winning shot: No, D. did not actually live in Westport, she was only visiting a friend who did. She knew it, the Fairfield girl said, because she had actually *met* D., at her father's store.

But this did not quite end the argument. The girl from Westport reared up and inquired frostily, "Your father has a *store?*" And, as the girl from Fairfield cringed in shame, the other pressed the attack relentlessly home: "What does he sell there— *hardware?*"

End of discussion.

I then remind my audience that relatively few of the people who die in drug-related violence are actually bystanders, as little consolation as this is to the families of those few, or the families of those who are involved, willingly or not, in the drug trade. More to the point, I note, the teenaged drug dealers in whose crossfire my daughter and I were caught will be dead or in prison in a few years. Those girls on the train, however, likely will grow up to attend the best schools and move on to professional careers. And, one day, many of them will be making decisions that affect the lives of millions of Americans.

Now which, I ask, is the more dangerous group of children?

Usually, my audience stays with the drug dealers. I don't really blame them. In all but my most sober moments, I do too. But the threat to security that they represent is only one danger that children can pose. The threat of powerful adults without any sense of generosity toward other people, the sort of people who decide that poverty is mainly the fault of people who are poor and that nobody is discriminated against—that is a threat to the future. Probably, if they see a threat at all, the audience thinks that it will be resolved by the values the children will learn as they become young adults. Perhaps so; but a solution that posits a change in values also has to posit a source for the new ones— and, as I look around our popular culture, I am at a loss to think what source the audience imagines will repair the damage. How much better if children were to learn the right values from the beginning; and how much better were the schools to play a role in the teaching.

True, we have sharp divisions over values in America. But that does not mean that no values are better than others. We have sharp divisions, too, on whether human beings evolved over millions of years from lower forms of life, or whether humans were specially created just a few hundred decades ago. But we still manage to make a choice that scientific creationism should not be taught in the schools. Is it really so great a leap to teach our children that theft, excess, and bigotry are wrong, or that respecting the persons, property, and privacy of others is right? If the leap really is so great that it cannot be made, then those teenaged girls on the commuter train, and not the drug dealers in Queens, represent the most dangerous children in America.

TEACHING ABOUT RELIGION

What *should* the public schools say about religion generally? One problem with the public school curriculum—a problem, happily, that has lately had much attention—is that the concern to avoid even a hint of forbidden *endorsement* of religion has led to a climate in which teachers are loath to *mention* religion. A number of studies have concluded that the public school curriculum is actually biased against religion.[36] But one need not go that far in order to appreciate the importance of teaching children about the role of religion at crucial junctures in the nation's his-

tory, from the openly religious rhetoric of the Founding Generation, through the religious justifications for the abolition of slavery, the "social gospel" movement to reform American society
and industry, or even the civil rights movement of the 1950s and
1960s. (Of course, children should study the negative side as
well: from the religion-based prohibition movement that culmi-
nated in the Eighteenth Amendment and the Volstead Act to the
destruction of many Native American religious traditions to what
the historian Jon Butler has called the "African spiritual holocaust"—that is, the willed destruction during the nineteenth century of the African religious traditions that the slaves brought
with them and tried to preserve.[37])

The movement to teach about religions in the public
schools is not, as some might imagine, a smokescreen for infiltra-
tion of the education system by the religious right. On the contrary, John Buchanan of People for the American Way—a liberal
organization that normally exists in a relationship of mutual
antipathy with the right—agrees that there is a problem. Says
Buchanan: "You can't have an accurate portrayal of history and
leave out religion."[38]

Both supporters and opponents of teaching about religion in
the classroom have worried about the constitutional status of
such instruction. But there is nothing to worry about, and,
indeed, it would be bizarre if the command of the Establishment
Clause turned out to be that religion may never be mentioned in
the classroom, even when it is historically relevant. Nothing in the
Supreme Court's decisions on school prayer or school curriculum
is inconsistent with the idea that public schools can teach about
religion, or even that the schools can use religious materials and
texts in doing so. On the contrary, the Court, with one exception,
always has taken pains to explain the way in which the challenged practice endorses or even coerces religious belief.

That single exception is the Supreme Court's 1980 decision
in *Stone v. Graham,* which struck down a Kentucky statute
requiring that the Ten Commandments be posted on classroom

walls. *Stone* stands on a shaky footing, because the Justices seemed to assume that the only reason the Commandments could possibly be there was to advance a religious doctrine. As the dissent pointed out, however, the Kentucky statute requiring that the Commandments be posted cited not a religious purpose, but their "significant secular impact on the development of the secular legal codes of the Western World."[39] This might have been a smokescreen, but it was odd—and not consistent with precedent—for the Court to indulge a presumption that the use of religious materials must have a religious purpose.

Justice Lewis Powell, agreeing with the Court's 1987 conclusion that a statute requiring "equal time" for scientific creationism was unconstitutional, surely got the answer right in his separate opinion, in which Justice Sandra Day O'Connor joined:

> School children can and should properly be informed of all aspects of this Nation's religious heritage. I would see no constitutional problem if school children were taught the nature of the Founding Fathers' religious beliefs and how these beliefs affected the attitudes of the times and the structure of our government. . . . [A] familiarity with the nature of religious beliefs is necessary to understand many historical as well as contemporary events. . . . [The Establishment Clause] is properly understood to prohibit the use of the Bible and other religious documents in public school education only when the purpose of the use is to advance a particular religious belief.[40]

Of course!—there is nothing complicated about it. One cannot pretend that the nation's history was different than it was, and one cannot make sense of large chunks of that history without understanding the religious traditions that helped create it.

It ought to be embarrassing, in this age of celebration of America's diversity, that the schools have been so slow to move toward teaching about our nation's diverse religious traditions. But matters are beginning to change. In 1988, a gathering of business, political, and religious leaders produced the Williamsburg

Charter, which calls for greater attention to the role of religion in American life, including the establishment of a public school curriculum on the history of religions. That same year, a diverse group of religious and education organizations joined to issue a set of guidelines for teaching "about" religion without indoctrination.[41] And all across the country, public schools are working to incorporate into their curricula a more sensitive understanding of the role of religion in American history and culture.[42] In 1991, schools across the country began using new primary school textbooks developed by Houghton Mifflin Company (in response to pressure from California, the largest market for school texts). The new books emphasize the contributions of Christianity, Judaism, and many of the nation's other religious traditions.

Still, the new goal of teaching about religion is not without its problems—especially if the goal remains, as advocates insist it does, to teach about religion "objectively." Richard Baer of Cornell University has warned that although teaching respect for all religions "has a nice democratic ring to it," it could, if taken literally, lead to "intolerable consequences for those persons who take seriously the truth claims of the Christian gospel." Baer worries that a requirement of "objectivity" would make it illegitimate for teachers to criticize any religions, including Satanism, fanatical apocalypticism, or snake handling.[43]

There is, moreover, the tricky problem of what to do when children begin to ask the hard questions. After all, if the material is well taught, many children will surely be intrigued by what will be for many their first exposure to religious traditions different than their own—or, in some instances, to any religious traditions at all. Sooner or later, teachers using the new books and other programs will be asked questions like, "But is it true?" or "What happens when we die?" or "Who made God?" The only safe answers will be those that so frustrate school children searching for certainty: "Well, many people believe that . . . and on the other hand, many others think. . . ." Few teachers are likely to enjoy picking their way through this particular minefield, but keeping the nation's religious heritage out of the classroom is not the answer. As one observer has put it, "The challenge will be finding consensus on an educational approach that describes religious doctrine without indoctrinating. But the option, denying children a piece of their culture and past, is more dangerous."[44]

III

THE CLOTHED
PUBLIC SQUARE

11

(Dis)Believing
in Faith

ONE reason that education is so bitter a battleground in the struggle over the role of religion in American society is that knowledge is seen as the key to power. The preliminary question, however, is what constitutes the key to knowledge. Scientific creationism sharply poses this problem with respect to the justification of factual claims. The claim that racial discrimination is wrong poses this problem with respect to the justification of moral claims.

In this chapter, returning to a theme discussed in chapter 3, I once more consider the arguments raised by some contemporary philosophers for keeping religious discourse out of the public square. This time around, however, I have a different focus: the ways in which religious ways of knowing are relegated to inferior status in the justification of moral and factual claims, and what that relegation suggests about the way contemporary philosophy views religion. After an examination of the way in which the modern attitude toward religion in the public square would have crippled the civil rights movement, I propose instead the image of a public square that does not restrict its access to citizens willing to speak in a purely secular language, but instead is equally open to religious and nonreligious argument. In chapter 12, I illustrate this approach through a discussion of situations in which the state is forced to define either human life or human death.

THE PROBLEM OF JUSTIFICATION

It is useful to begin by considering a question raised by the philosopher Jeffrey Stout in the introduction to his very fine book on justification after the Enlightenment: "Do we, then, have any knowledge?" he asks.[1] Stout's concern is whether, in a post-Enlightenment world, a world in which the authority of God is no longer available as a justification for truth claims, we can be sufficiently sure of anything to be able to say that we know it. The requirement of justification simply means that a hypothesis—whether about the natural or moral world—must comport with certain rules before it will be accepted.

For example, the hypothesis that dropped objects tend to fall to earth is a hypothesis about the natural world. If one wants to test it according to the rules of natural science, one would try to set up an experiment that would yield one result if the hypothesis were false, another if the hypothesis were true—dropping lots of objects, say, and seeing whether they all fall to earth. By contrast, the hypothesis pressed by Patrick Buchanan at the 1992 Republican Convention—that homosexuality is morally wrong—is an example of a claim of moral knowledge. And the trouble with claims about moral knowledge is that even today,

more than two centuries after the Enlightenment, we have no
settled rules by which to try to determine their truth.

Once upon a time, all over the Western world, the rule was
simple: a false hypothesis (whether about the physical or the
moral world) was one not in accord with God's word. Even the
Enlightenment at first altered this only a little bit. Sir Isaac Newton, for example, believed that he was glorifying God (and vali-
dating God's word) through his observations of the physical universe. (Indeed, although often seen as enemies of the
Enlightenment, the scientific creationists discussed in chapter 9
criticize evolutionists in part on the ground that their scientific
method is un-Newtonian.) However, the principal contribution of
the Enlightenment was to introduce rationalism to philosophy, to
press the case that human reason, by observing and deducing,
could resolve both moral and factual propositions without the
need for resort to divine authority. Without the rationalism of the
Enlightenment, one might seriously ask how much longer it
would have taken to develop modern science, the modern ideal
of democracy, or the modern concept of rights.

But rationalism has its problems and contradictions, and the
real question Jeffrey Stout poses is whether the many critics of
Western philosophy (and of history and science and everything
else) have been so successful that not only is God unavailable as
a justification for knowledge, nothing else is either. After all, a
rule for how knowledge is justified is knowledge too, and it, too,
must be justified—as must its justification, and so on. Thus, Stout
is worried about the possibility of an infinite regress of justifications needing justification, an epistemology that finally swallows
itself.

Today's theorists of the liberal tradition have rejected even
the slender connection to Christian theology that the original
Enlightenment theorists preserved, proposing in its place an
often bewildering variety of approaches to the problem of determining the validity of moral claims. The most famous of these
remains John Rawls's problematic but justly famous idea of plac-

ing us all in the "original position"—asking what moral propositions each of us would accept if forced to stand behind a
metaphorical "veil of ignorance," where we would lack knowledge of such characteristics as our gender, race, wealth, and education.[2] A number of other theorists, as recounted in chapter 3,
have tried to craft rules to govern dialogue in the public square,
rules, generally, that force religious citizens to restructure their
arguments in purely secular terms before they can be presented.

I have already explained why this approach might strike
many religious people as unsatisfying and even demeaning to
them in their struggles to find within their faith communities
answers to questions about the ultimate. Proceeding once more
by way of example, I next explore the implications of the exclusion of the religious way of knowing from debates about factual
and moral truth. By so doing, I illustrate some of the fears about
the nature of religion and the religious that underlie contemporary liberal philosophy—and why the fears are misplaced.

RELIGIOUS CLAIMS OF
FACTUAL TRUTH

All of this leaves an intriguing question: just what is it that liberal
philosophy finds so objectionable about religious ways of knowing the world? One might begin to understand the answer by
returning briefly to the discussion in chapter 9 of the claims by
scientific creationists for balanced classroom treatment of their
theories whenever the theory of evolution is discussed. The
reader will recall that in the world view of the creationists, evolution theory is not simply contrary to religious teachings; it is
false. Nor is it false in some intuitive or metaphysical sense.
Based on the interpretive tool of literal biblical inerrancy, evolution theory is *demonstrably* false.

One liberal response to is to offer a careful argument that

the tools of science have proved to be superior for understanding the natural world, a proposition that scientists are quite prepared to demonstrate, and one that might, as John Ziman has suggested, provide an alternative to the usual liberal dismissal of the creationists as religious fanatics.[3] There is, however, a more fundamental liberal difficulty with the creationist claims: in the world of post-Enlightenment liberalism, science deals with *knowledge* about the natural world, whereas religion is simply a system of *belief,* based on faith. The creationists might (to their surprise) cast their lot with Wittgenstein, who observed, "But I might also say: It has been revealed to me by God that it is so. God has taught me that this is my foot. And therefore if anything happened that seemed to conflict with this knowledge I should have to regard *that* as deception."[4] This, of course, is precisely the logic that motivates many Christian fundamentalists to oppose the teaching of evolution or support the teaching of creationism. They are informed by God's revelation; no artifice of mortal man can contradict that; and any "evidence" that the revelation is false must be either erroneous or deceptive.

Because of this approach, members of religious traditions that teach their followers "truths" about the world are suspect in the liberal world view when they speak those truths in the public square. After all, the public square relies on dialogue as the tool for discovering truth, and individuals who will dismiss as deceptive all evidence against their views can hardly be viewed as welcoming dialogue. On the contrary, liberal theory accuses them of violating two important rules of a shared dialogue: they begin at inaccessible starting points and they reason through inaccessible methodologies—inaccessibility, in both cases, meaning that those who do not share the religious tradition will not agree.

Of course, in our public dialogues over many divisive issues, such as abortion and war, partisans on either side begin from starting points so radically distinct that there is little hope of finding commonality. For this reason, critics of liberalism, Reinhold Niebuhr very much to the fore, have suggested that *all* deeply held commitments should be treated as religious—a notion that also fires the assaults by the religious right on the "religion" of "secular humanism." But I think that Cushing Strout has provided an adequate response to this argument: "[T]he result is to deny the atheist his repudiations and to sweep up so much into the category of religion that it becomes entirely unclear what possibly could be omitted if it pretended to any organization of values or depth of commitment. In this usage 'religion' then becomes simply equivalent to moral seriousness."[5]

What is often less noted, but no less true, is that just as we may not share common starting points, we may not share common reasoning methods either. For example, survey data indicate that most Americans regard a fetus as a human child. However, only a minority of the members of that majority thereby conclude that abortion should be banned in all circumstances; others, in varying degrees, support a variety of restrictions on abortion.[6] Plainly, the question of how to balance fetal humanity against the needs of the pregnant woman is a divisive one. Evidently, not all Americans strike the balance in the same way, although dialogue may still be possible—since 38 percent say that they wonder whether their position on abortion is correct.[7]

When one moves from moral knowledge to factual knowledge, the results are not different. Most Americans believe, in the virtual absence of any evidence at all, that Earth has been visited by beings from other planets, and no amount of scientific argument to the contrary seems to shake them. A plurality, and sometimes a majority, of Americans admit to holding a variety of unpleasant racial stereotypes.[8] In short, the idea that we share either common starting points or common forms of reasoning from our starting points may be no more than a pleasant fantasy. Nevertheless, with all the different reasoning methods that people use, it is only the forms that are dictated by religious traditions that liberalism rules out of bounds. So, for example, whereas the black parents discussed in chapter 9 are free to offer proof that the racist history their children learn in school is false, the "proofs" offered by the creationist parents are treated as irrational, which is to say, crazy.

The psychology of liberalism probably makes this diagnosis inevitable, because liberal theory distinguishes sharply between facts and values in a way that many religious traditions do not. The liberal celebration of the freedom of individuals to pursue their desires rests on the presumption that they first agree on the characteristics of the world in which they live, and only subsequently decide how to value them. As Roberto Unger has put the point, "Wherever liberal psychology prevails, the distinction between describing things in the world and evaluating them will be accepted as the premise of all clear thought." However, writes Unger, "The contrast of understanding and evaluation is foreign to the religious consciousness, for its beliefs about the world are simultaneously descriptions and ideals."[9] Liberalism rests critically on that contrast, and no simple call upon a principle of neutrality toward religion can hide the implicit tension.

Think back on the problem, introduced in chapter 1, of the Jehovah's Witnesses, who believe that accepting a blood transfusion violates God's law against ingesting blood. The Jehovah's Witnesses do not necessarily desire death, but they do not want to preserve life through means that violate their reading of Scripture. In this sense, they are acting consistently with the traditional Christian understanding that life is a basic good but not an absolute one, exemplified by Jesus' admonition, "No one has greater love than this, to lay down one's life for one's friends" (John 15:13).[10] What we know from the cases is roughly as follows. If a mature, conscious Jehovah's Witness refuses a blood transfusion that might save her (corporeal) life, a court *probably will not* order it. If a mature, conscious Jehovah's Witness refuses a blood transfusion that might save her (corporeal) life and then lapses into unconsciousness, a court *might well* order it. If a mature Jehovah's Witness arrives at the hospital already unconscious, and her family refuses permission for a blood transfusion that might save her (corporeal) life, a court *will* order it. And if a

Jehovah's Witness parent refuses a blood transfusion that might save the (corporeal) life of a minor child, the court will temporarily suspend parental custody and appoint a guardian, who will invariably grant permission for the transfusion.[11]

In none of these cases does the court give much weight to the proposition that accepting a transfusion will lead to eternal damnation. But that is hardly surprising, because no notion of the free exercise of religion is needed to explain any of these decisions. The right of a Jehovah's Witness to refuse a blood transfusion for herself or for a family member seems, as a legal matter, to be of precisely the same scope as the right of any individual to refuse live-saving medical treatment for herself or for a member of the family. Among those whose objections are not of a religious nature, mature adults may indeed refuse treatments that might save their lives, but they may only rarely refuse those treatments on behalf of unconscious relatives—generally, only in cases involving "heroic" measures—and they may never refuse those treatments on behalf of minor children.* Among those whose objections are of a religious nature, the scope of discretion is precisely the same; religion adds nothing to the mix.

What sort of statement does this make about the response of the legal culture to the underlying religious belief? The usual answer is to say that the legal system's refusal to take account of the religious claim that the transfusion must lead to perdition is a statement not that the claim is false, but that it is irrelevant. There is, however, a logical sense in which the refusal to take account of the claim *is* to treat it as false. For if the claim is true, life eternal would seem plainly to trump the transient life available on earth. Put otherwise, if the claim is true, the Witness is

---

* Parents may sometimes refuse *life-extending* treatments of seriously ill children, as in the *Baby Jane Doe* case. (*Weber v. Stony Brook Hospital*, 60 N.Y.2d 208, 456 N.E.2d 1186 (1983), *cert. denied*, 464 U.S. 1026 [1983].) That case upheld parental discretion to withhold treatment when the child would die in any case, but would simply live longer, and not well. The result would certainly have been different had it been likely that the infant would, with treatment, have recovered fully.

better off dead—dead, that is, in the ordinary language, materialistic sense of the word. That is precisely why the transfusion is refused—because the Witness has reached that very conclusion. By forcing the Witness to live and be damned rather than permitting her to die and be saved, the state is necessarily treating her religious claim not as irrelevant, but as false.

There is more than a mere semantic distinction between acting neutrally toward a religious belief—refusing to consider it as either true or false—and acting as though it is false. Take, for example, the case of a religious worship practice that runs afoul of a law of general application, such as a law against drug use or animal abuse. One might argue that the state is only neutral if it enforces the law against the religion in question. However, enforcement of the law constitutes neutrality *only from the point of view of the state.* From the point of view of the religion, matters are quite different. By punishing adherents of the religion for doing what their faith demands of them, the state is not—in their eyes—acting with neutrality toward the truth or falsity of the belief in the religious demand. On the contrary, by presuming to punish members of the faith who follow its dictates, the state is necessarily treating their beliefs as false—for if the beliefs were true, there would be no reason for the state to outlaw the practices that the beliefs demand.

Part of the trouble with contemporary liberal epistemology is that it is not capable of treating as a factual inquiry a question like "Can the Jehovah's Witness achieve salvation after receiving a blood transfusion?"—or, for that matter, a question like "Is there life after death?" These questions, to liberal theory, involve matters of belief, not of fact. Indeed, they inquire into matters of private conscience, which liberalism holds sacred and inviolable.

All of this is very well—except that it is wrong. Consider the way the last question is worded: "Is there life after death?" The question is whether something exists or not; it is a question designed to discover a fact. Calling a fact a belief cannot quite get around that central point. After all, whatever else might be said about life after death, one thing seems sure: either there is one or there is not.

Walter Murphy illustrates this epistemological point nicely in his epic novel *The Vicar of Christ*. The novel incudes a scene in which the Pope—Murphy's protagonist—has invited to dinner a group of seminarians and overhears two of them in heated argument over the nature of the Holy Trinity. (The Roman Catholic Church teaches that the Holy Spirit proceeds from the Father and the Son, whereas the Greek Orthodox Church insists that the Holy Spirit proceeds from the Father alone—a difference of opinion over which people have died.) Tiring at last of the debate between the two seminarians, the Pope leans over the table and asks, "What are the data?" When the seminarians seem confused, he adds an explanation: "[Y]ou have been talking about a factual problem, not one of logical relationships. Either the Holy Spirit proceeds one way or He proceeds the other. Either is perfectly justifiable in logic. What are the data on which we can determine which is correct?"[12]

Now, that might not be good Catholic theology, but it does make the point. Like the question of whether there is a life after death, the question of the procession of the Holy Spirit can be stated in a way that does not seem to offend any principle of liberal dialogue. There is no reason, then, to laugh at the claim that either question demands a factual answer. There is, however, one difficulty common to both inquiries: although stated as material propositions, they are not readily and directly testable by any material means. That is not—please note!—the same as saying that they are not testable at all. True, the questions generate no hypotheses testable against observation of the natural world. The hypotheses the questions generate are testable only against God's word. But as earlier noted in the discussion of scientific creationism (chapter 9), the issue of testability ultimately turns on what counts as evidence, which is another way of saying that the question is epistemological.

With this background in mind, it is possible to return to the question of the Jehovah's Witnesses who refuse blood transfusions. We asked at the outset whether the ground of the objection, that accepting the transfusion would mean ingesting blood and would therefore deny them eternal salvation, is a claim about fact or a claim about value. What the foregoing analysis indicates is that the very question—fact or value—has meaning only in a particular epistemology that considers as factual only those propositions that are testable against the material world, and considers a proposition falsified when the evidence of the material world runs against it. For many devoutly religious people, however, the distinction between moral truth and empirical truth is not a clean one. Many Christians, for example, might take the view of the theologian Karl Rahner, who argues that our existence as moral beings is grounded in our experience of "[t]he difference between what we simply in fact are and what we should be" according to God's will, and that "this difference is always found as something concrete, not as something abstract."[13] Like God's will itself, the difference is seen as *real:* no metaphysics, just the *fact* of God, the *fact* of divine command, and the *fact* of difference. In opening his Gifford Lectures nearly a century ago, William James complained that "many religious persons ... do not yet made a working use of the distinction" between facts and values.[14] But James, so wise in other matters, missed the point here. The point is that for many believers, the fact/value distinction, in the existential sense that James had in mind, is irrelevant.

It is in this sense that the religious are often seen by their secular critics as being closed-minded, for believers frequently refuse to make the evidentiary distinctions that the culture demands. Thus, for example, in deciding whether scientific creationism is a plausible account of the origin of the earth and of humanity (I remind the reader that I do not believe that it is), the only evidence that counts is the evidence of natural science, evidence that is empirical in the sense of being both measurable and testable. The evidence on the basis of which the creationist might have decided on a world view—Scripture itself—is out of bounds.

So, too, with the Jehovah's Witnesses. Even if the question of eternal salvation and the ingesting of blood is admitted *arguendo* to be one of fact, it leads to no hypotheses testable against the natural world: one cannot, by setting up an experiment in which some people receive transfusions and some do not, learn to a scientific certainty which people achieve eternal salvation, if, indeed, any do. The hypotheses generated by the Witnesses' claim about the blood transfusions, like the relevant hypotheses generated by the creationists' claim about the origin of life and the universe, are testable only against the relevant version of God's word.

RELIGIOUS CLAIMS OF
MORAL TRUTH

The lack of hypotheses testable against the material world helps explain why, as a matter of liberal political theory, the state cannot take account of the competing epistemologies of the Jehovah's Witnesses and the scientific creationists. However, that deficiency cannot explain the hostility of liberal theory toward *moral* premises that are generated by religious tradition. Even if many religions deny the fact-value distinction central to liberal epistemology—the distinction that turns the claims of the creationists into fact-claims and therefore rejects them—the various religious epistemologies do generate some claims that liberalism must treat as moral rather than factual in nature. For example, when the Roman Catholic bishops, drawing upon Scripture, call for a more equitable division of the nation's resources, the claim, in liberal terms, reduces to the proposition that the nation's resources *should* be more fairly distributed—and that is a classic moral claim.[15]

Moral claims, unlike factual claims, do not rely for their validity on the generation of testable hypotheses. A question that has bedeviled Western philosophy since the Enlightenment is just what moral claims *do* rely on for validity. Much of the answer has long been given by two secular constructs: the metaphor of a social contract and the deduction of a set of natural rights. Each has had its ebbs and flows. Social contract theory, with its image of citizens agreeing to join society and exchange freedoms for a set of rights, was dominant in the eighteenth century, whereas today's liberal philosophers, although in a sense they formally remain contractarians, like to reason directly to a set of rights that all individuals share. But the battles over starting points, correct methods of reasoning, and the results of application of the reasoning to the selected starting points are often cacaphonous.

A large part of the trouble, of course, is that not everyone agrees that the Enlightenment project of replacing divine moral authority with the moral authority of human reason was a good idea. Alasdair MacIntyre suggests that the Enlightenment failed because the post-Enlightenment philosophers proceeded from a set of historically contingent and utterly incoherent assumptions.[16] But he may be wrong. Perhaps the Enlightenment failed because of a psychological problem. Perhaps most people are upset with the idea that morality is itself contingent, that ethical debates have no right answers. (Survey data indicate that 79 percent of American adults believe that "there are clear guidelines about what's good and evil that apply to everyone regardless of the situation.") And, for many, it is no doubt particularly troubling to be told that there is no extrahuman Judge to say which answers are the right ones. (Survey data indicate that respondents split evenly on whether human experience or traditional religious values should serve as the basis for moral and ethical judgments.)[17]

Indeed, it is not even clear that all the philosophers of the Enlightenment believed that it was as simple as today's neo-Kantians do to dispense with the notion of the divine in moral debate. The British deists, for example, believed that reason would support the biblical claims of truth, including moral truth. Newton thought that he was proving God's word by showing God's work. Kant himself hinted at the importance of God to his emphasis on individual freedom. And, as the historian Robert Nisbet has pointed out, "Even Mill, apparent atheist through much of his life, came in his final years to declare the indispensability of Christianity to both progress and order." Nisbet adds, "The Renaissance humanists detested much of the ecclesiastical structure of Christianity in their day, but they were profoundly concerned with Christian creed. True atheists were few and far between in the Enlightenment, though this takes nothing away from the philosophes' assault on Christianity as a power in society."[18]

What was true then may be true now. No matter how upset many of us are at the idea that the religious right, as presented, for example, at the 1992 Republican Convention, might come to run things, that anger does not necessarily translate into a critique of religious knowledge as a source of moral truth. For many and perhaps most of us, the idea of moral authority itself implies the existence of an arbiter, a proposition that would help explain why a morally pluralistic nation like ours is willing to let a *court*, of all things, settle many of our toughest moral dilemmas. Perhaps no other agency of settlement seems to be available.

Except that, for vast numbers of Americans, another agency of settlement for moral dilemmas—another authority—*is* available: divine command. Liberal theory might scoff at the idea that God's will is relevant to moral decisions in the liberal state, but the citizen whose public self is guided by religious faith might reasonably ask why the will of any of the brilliant philosophers of the liberal tradition, or, for that matter, the will of the Supreme Court of the United States is more relevant to moral decisions than the will of God. So far, liberal theory has not presented an adequate answer.

THE DILEMMA OF THE
CIVIL RIGHTS MOVEMENT

Finally, liberal philosophy's distaste for explicit religious argument in the public square cannot accommodate the openly and
unashamedly religious rhetoric of the nonviolent civil rights
movement of the 1950s and 1960s. To be sure, liberalism has had
no trouble subsuming the *goals* of the movement under the
umbrella of secular argument. But justifying the results, after the
fact, as a matter of liberal dialogue does not alter the plain historical truth that the movement itself represented a massive infusion
of religious rhetoric into the public square.

The battle for the fundaments of racial equality—what the
historian Clayborne Carson has called the black freedom struggle—was a mass movement, fought on a number of fronts, including the political, the legal, and the spiritual. It had no central axis,
that is, there was no joint leadership committee allocating so much
energy to litigation and so much energy to protest. And yet, the
movement's support base, for much of its existence, was in the
church. The NAACP Legal Defense Fund raised substantial
amounts of money for their legal battles in the black churches.
The leaders of the mass-protest wing were drawn from the black
clergy, which continues to supply much of the civil rights leadership. The movement's public appeals were openly and frankly
religious, and many of the nation's political leaders joined in these
appeals, and even echoed them in supporting legislation.*

Consider, for example, Martin Luther King's famous "I Have a
Dream" speech, delivered on the steps of the Lincoln Memorial.

---

* One might argue, of course, that religion was simply a camouflage in the civil
rights movement, cloaking an egalitarian secular ideology. Although I have no
doubt that another rhetorical choice might have been available (and might
have been used, had the separation of church and self that I describe in part I
then existed), it goes too far to treat the movement's religiosity as window
dressing. On the contrary, there is every reason to think that its religious roots
were crucial to its dynamism—and there is little reason to doubt that the religious appeals were both sincere and, to adherents, quite compelling.

One of the great political speeches of our era, it was really a sermon, replete with references to "God's children." It could have
been delivered from the pulpit without a single change, for it drew
upon long-established themes in the black church tradition. The
concluding tag line, "Free at last, free at last; thank God Almighty,
we are free at last," was, as King himself said, taken from "the
words of the old Negro spiritual."[19] Or take King's "Letter from
Birmingham City Jail," which is often extolled as an outstanding
work of justification for civil disobedience, but which is an overtly
and unapologetically religious document. The letter's explicit
appeal to a higher authority was an appeal to King's own conception of God: "A just law is a man-made code that squares with the
moral law or the law of God."[20] This is classic natural law theology, and could have been lifted, word for word, from the more
recent pastoral letter of the Roman Catholic bishops on abortion.
In chapter 3 I pointed out the religious character of King's call for
the use of the ballot in his "God is Marching On" speech in Montgomery.[21] But the religious appeals were not limited to the Southern *Christian* Leadership Conference. In 1960, the Student Nonviolent Coordinating Committee which would ultimately become a
symbol of a more confrontational attitude, adopted a statement
reading in part: "The presupposition of our faith and the manner
of our action, nonviolence as it grows from the Judaeo-Christian
traditions, seeks a social order of justice permeated by love."[22]

Moreover, religious organizations were among the strongest
supporters of the Civil Rights Act of 1964, which outlawed discrimination in employment and public accommodations. They
testified in support of it. They made public appeals for it. And,
once again, only the segregations complained. Senator Richard
Russell of Georgia charged that those who made religious arguments in favor of the legislation did not understand "the proper
place of religious leaders in our national life," adding that the religions should not "make a moral question of a political issue."[23]

Indeed, there is little about the civil rights movement, other
than the vital distinction in the ends that it sought, that makes it

very different from the right-wing religious movements of the present day. In chapter 3, I mentioned Archbishop Joseph Rummel's threats to excommunicate Catholic legislators who supported prosegregation legislation. The leaders of the civil rights movement spoke openly of the commands of God as a crucial basis for their public activism. They made no effort to disguise their true intention: to impose their religious morality on others, on the dissenters who would rather segregate their hotels or lunch counters, or on those who did not accept a crucial epistemological premise of the movement—that black people are human beings. When King was challenged on just that point, he answered that "the law could not make people love their neighbors, but it could stop their lynching them."[24]

However, the fact that the ends sought were different seems to me potentially crucial, if only liberal theory will allow it to be so. The point I made in chapters 3 and 4 is the point that liberalism, if it is to survive, will have to accept: what was wrong with the 1992 Republican Convention was *not* the effort to link the name of God to secular political ends. What was wrong was the choice of secular ends to which the name of God was linked. Thus, Patrick Buchanan's world view might be objectionable to the secular liberal, but it should not be more objectionable because he offered a religious justification for it. And the world view of the civil rights movement should not have been less welcomed because it was justified in religious terms.

Unfortunately, liberal political theory so far has been unable to make this move. Rather than envisioning a public square in which all are welcome, the contemporary liberal philosophers insist on finding a set of conversational rules that require the individual whose religious tradition makes demands on his or her moral conscience to reformulate that conscience—to destroy a vital aspect of the self—in order to gain the right to participate in the dialogue alongside other citizens. And such a requirement is possible only in a liberal world that regards religious knowledge as being of a decidedly inferior sort.

BELIEVING IN FAITH

Thus liberalism, as a theory of politics, is moving in an unsettling direction. According to the philosopher Richard Rorty, "[l]ogical positivism got a bad name by calling religion and metaphysics 'nonsense' and by seeming to dismiss the Age of Faith as a matter of incautious use of language."[25] Liberal dialogue seems to be headed down the same road, and in a nation where so many citizens are centrally moved by religious conviction, the consequences for liberal theory are likely to prove disastrous—unless there is a change of course.

Such theorists as Kent Greenawalt and Robert Audi have struggled to produce theories that would admit moral propositions based on religious conviction into the public debate but would require their justification in secular terms.[26] Such theorists as Bruce Ackerman and John Rawls, although religion is not their central concern, also appear to be indifferent as to the *source* of a moral position, as long as it is *justified* in particular terms before the state can act upon it.[27] I am not sure that these rejustification theories are quite coherent, and they certainly do not answer Michael Perry's objection (discussed in chapter 3), that religious citizens are forced to split off vital components of their personalities, but at least they are the work of thoughtful scholars who are trying to cope with the dilemma that confronts the liberal theory of politics.

The ultimate solution, however, lies in another direction. What is needed is not a requirement that the religiously devout choose a form of dialogue that liberalism accepts, but that liberalism develop a politics that accepts whatever form of dialogue a member of the public offers. Epistemic diversity, like diversity of other kinds, should be cherished, not ignored, and certainly not abolished. What is needed, then, is a willingness to *listen,* not because the speaker has *the right voice* but because the speaker has *the right to speak.* Moreover, the willingness to listen must hold out the possibility that the speaker is saying something worth listening to; to do less is to trivialize the forces that shape the moral convictions of tens of millions of Americans.

There is an economy about religious belief—an economy and a tendency toward evolution. Over the centuries, the religious traditions, like traditions of other kinds, tend to abandon what is useless and preserve what it useful. The religions may not measure utility in the same terms that secular society does; but, as many sociologists have suggested, religious traditions that lack any relevance to the human experience are very likely, over time, to wither.[28] This evolution matters because it suggests that a religion that has survived must include some kernel of moral truth that resonates with broader human understandings, whether or not most people share the epistemic premises of the religion itself.

Sometimes these resonances may seem trivial or circular—for instance, most established religious traditions in America preach against extramarital sex, and Americans overwhelmingly agree that extramarital sex is wrong[29]—and sometimes, as the sociologist Peter Berger has argued, it may be that churches select their moral teachings *because* they resonate with what parishioners already believe.[30] Often, however, the religious traditions connect more deeply with aspects of the human experience. For example, in the case of abortion, which many different religious traditions teach to be wrong, a majority of Americans, while favoring many restrictions on abortion, reject the idea that the government should ban it. (So do I.) At the same time, most Americans endorse a key point in the antiabortion argument of the religions—namely, that the fetus is a human being.

Thus we see an important role of religious argument in public debate: even when most members of the public reject the religious tradition itself, many and sometimes most will be moved by the moral claims that religious conviction causes members of a faith to make—*even when the religious and the nonreligious disagree on the basis of the moral claims*. Indeed, in many cases—and the humanity of the fetus is surely one—the basis of the moral (or one might say factual) claim is probably one that most Americans would debate only uneasily, and then with difficulty. Often the moral claim seems almost instinctual, not argued for, and yet it nevertheless becomes the subject of further inquiry—and the foundation for political action.

Because of this ability of the religions to fire the human imagination, and often the conscience, even of nonbelievers—as, for instance, the civil rights movement did—the religions should not be forced to disguise or remake themselves before they can legitimately be involved in secular political argument. As one who believes deeply in the importance of both religious tradition and liberal dialogue, I consider it vital that this accommodation be made. If it is not, secular political disaster may ensue as more and more religiously devout Americans turn their backs on the intellectual traditions that have built and preserved our free institutions. For unless liberal theory and liberal law develop ways to welcome the religiously devout into public moral debate without demanding that they first deny their religious selves, the caricature of liberalism offered by the radical right will more and more become the truth, for liberalism will continue its slide from a pluralistic theory of politics to a narrow, elitist theory of right results.

In the next chapter, I explore the implications of carrying on a political dialogue that does not exclude arguments from religious tradition, but rather welcomes them, as it welcomes every useful, thoughtful voice, not because their epistemological suppositions are universally shared, but because even those with very different epistemologies might learn—or teach. I undertake this exploration by examining one of our most searing questions, the problem of the definition of human life and the justification for human death. In so doing, I tackle three secular moral problems on which a number of different religious traditions have tried to bear witness: euthanasia, abortion, and capital punishment.

12

Matters of Life
and Death

IN liberal political theory, rights attach to individuals—that is, to persons. Nowadays, we tend to take the definition of the human person as a given: we know who we are talking about when we talk about who possesses rights. But matters are not always that simple. One popular justification for the African slave trade—including by leading clergy—was that the black Africans were subhuman or even nonhuman. This view made it quite simple for many of the Founders of the Republic to maintain what today is seen as racist hypocrisy—to affirm in the Declaration of Independence that all men are created equal, while at the same time keeping in thrall substantial numbers of "kidnapped Africans" (as the antebellum Supreme Court, in a rare moment of candor, described Africans taken for import).[1] Indeed, a principal task of the mid-nineteenth-century abolitionist literature was to demonstrate that the slaves were human beings.

Today, liberal politics largely relegates those who argue over what is human to the extremes: racists who continue to press the case that black people are not fully human (a thesis supported by a vast if imbecilic underground literature), and pro-life zealots who insist that the fetus (or, properly, the conceptus) is human from the moment of conception or a time shortly thereafter. We are, in our politics, smugly certain that we know who is human and who is not.

As should be apparent by this point in the argument, I share the liberal revulsion for the racists, but not for the pro-life religionists, even though I do not share their theology. (Like the majority of Americans, I am moderately pro-choice.) Although only a small minority of respondents tell pollsters that *Roe v. Wade*[2] should be overturned, a strong majority also describe abortion as "the same as" or "as bad as" the murder of a child—which suggests that the pro-lifers who argue that the fetus is human should not be relegated too quickly to the lunatic fringe.[3] Unfortunately, one need not look far in liberal theory—or in the words of very thoughtful jurists—to find the baldly stated proposition that the definition of human life is an irreducibly religious one, and, thus, one in which the state cannot engage.[4]

But this is wrong. The government, from necessity, is constantly in the business of deciding when life begins, when it ends, and what is human. For many people, the question might indeed be a religious one. But that does not free the state from the obligation to define life, and regularly. In the absence of a definition of life, including its beginning and its end, the state could neither take a census nor prosecute murder. Laws on such diverse subjects as inheritance, torts, and taxes could not be enforced in the absence of an acceptance that the state can and sometimes must define life. Indeed, because in liberal theory rights attach to individuals, liberalism itself requires a definition of the human. If, however, the question is irreducibly religious, and if that religious character places the answer beyond the purview of the secular state, then liberalism becomes an impermissible theory of justice.

That result seems wrong. The better result, surely, is to accept the need to define life, and, if the question partakes of an irreducibly religious dimension, then to accept that as well. To accept those premises does not say how society must answer the question—it only suggests that those whose answers are grounded in religious faith have no special obligation to stay out of the argument.

In this chapter, I illustrate this proposition by defending the presence of the religious voice in three searing contemporary political arguments over the boundaries of human life. I discuss the controversy over the point at which life ends, by looking at euthanasia; the controversy over the point at which life begins, by considering abortion; and the controversy over when the state can take a life, by analyzing the death penalty.

WHEN LIFE ENDS: EUTHANASIA

In the fall of 1991, James W. Wall, editor of *The Christian Century,* argued that the growing popularity of suicide (as exemplified by the popularity of Derek Humphry's best-selling "suicide manual," *Final Exit)* represented the ultimate triumph of all that is worst and most selfish about individualism.[5] A tidy thesis, that, and one consistent with the traditional Christian teaching that death, like life, is a gift from God, whose will no human being should oppose. But of course, as one correspondent shot back, "[h]anging onto life by every means at hand can also be ultimately selfish"—a point difficult to dispute when one considers the percentage of health-care dollars used to postpone death for terminally ill patients.[6] Argued another letter writer, the thesis that suicide interposes the will of the individual before the will of God "is equally applicable to a medical intervention to save a life."[7]

The last point is well understood in Christian theology. Pope Pius XII wrote, "It is unnatural to prevent death in instances where there is no hope of recovery. When nature is calling for death, there is no question that one can remove the life-support systems."[8] Thus, "[a]lthough profoundly loving human life and defending its sacredness, traditional Catholic medical moral thought still manages to reject a moral extremism which asserts that human life must be prolonged even at the cost of imposing unimaginable and futile sufferings on patients and their families."[9]

The death of a loved one always involves suffering and anguish. The debate over euthanasia (from the Greek for "easy death") concerns questions that are specially agonizing, and not only for the families who must make the difficult choices. One is talking, now, about declining to use the weapons of our technology that can perpetuate lives; and, sometimes, about enlisting those weapons in ending them.

One must distinguish the distressingly dispassionate terms in which the debate is conducted—*active* versus *passive* euthanasia. Passive euthanasia occurs when life-support mechanisms are disconnected, and while some religious groups oppose it, the societal consensus seems to be that it should, in many cases, be acceptable. Active euthanasia, which is understandably much more controversial, involves not *letting* the patient die, but *making* the patient die—as, for example, through administering a lethal injection. Both problems present tragic choices, and both present unique opportunities for religious witness—but they are not the same problem at all.

PASSIVE EUTHANASIA:
THE *CRUZAN* CASE

Both the American Medical Association and the American Bar Association have endorsed the right of comatose patients who have no hope of recovery, or their families acting for them in some cases, to cease feeding through gastrostomy tubes, so that the patient will die, as it is said, with dignity. According to surveys, a majority of the American public feels the same way, a sharp change from the mid-1970s. This right would be limited to patients in what is called a persistent vegetative state (PVS), in which higher brain function is lost, probably forever, but the brainstem continues to function, so that blood is pumped, the lungs work, and the body continues to "live." But is there anybody in there? That is the difficult question for society to resolve, the status not of the body but of the person who once did, and perhaps still does, inhabit it.

A gastrostomy tube, it should be noted, is a thin plastic umbilical running directly into the stomach, so that, nearing the end of their lives, the patients resemble what they were in the beginning: unable to sense the world or fend for themselves, floating in darkness, nurtured by a womb. This womb, however, is metal and electronic and uncaring, rather than flesh and nerves and loving. The PVS patient's survival depends on technology, not humanity, and it is that distinction that doubtless accounts for much of the public's revulsion.

But not everyone actually finds the image of the comatose patient on life support revolting, and many pro-life groups prefer it to the alternative. The pro-life argument holds that to cease feeding through the gastrostomy tube (contrary to popular image, it is rare that the tube is actually removed, because even though food and water are no longer administered, pain medications and other substances often are) is said to be the same as allowing the patient to starve to death. Literally, this is of course true: the effect on the comatose patient of ceasing feeding and hydration (as provision of water is called in the jargon) is the same as the effect on a child refused nourishment by her parents. The individual dies. But that, of course, is the entire point— the patient is *supposed* to die. So to identify the cause of death as starvation only explains why the decision is, and should remain, an agonizing one; it does not tell us whose decision it should be.

Many, perhaps most Americans think that the final judgment should rest with the family. Efforts in many states are pressing the law in that direction. But the law is not there yet, and the continued resistance to the majority by some religious groups is a useful reminder of the reasons that we should move the law with caution. Before readily delegating to suffering families the judgment on when a comatose patient should be allowed to die, we had best take the time to consider what we as a society think precious in the human; only after deciding what it is that we value—what it is, for example, that makes us certain that we want to punish murder—can we decide when to allow some smaller unit than the society to make choices about when that precious human substance has run out.

The best way to work the problem through is to consider an actual case, and the best-known euthanasia case of recent years involved Nancy Cruzan, who was severely injured in an automobile accident and then remained for years in a persistent vegetative state. Although there was no significant possibility of recovery, Cruzan did not meet any legal definition of death. Eventually, Nancy Cruzan's family reached the agonizing decision to cease all artificial means of extending her life—to let her die, as it is said, with dignity. However, the Missouri hospital where Cruzan lay refused the family's request to have artificial life support ended, unless ordered by a court to do so.* The family therefore went to court, explaining that Nancy Cruzan had indicated in the past that she would not want life support continued in such circumstances, but they ran into a Missouri requirement that the family must prove the patient's desires by "clear and convincing evidence." This is a higher legal standard than the usual "preponderance of the evidence" rule that gov-

---

* Hospitals that refuse to terminate life support are often, and popularly, accused of callousness toward the family. In many instances, however, hospitals are fearful of liability for wrongful death or malpractice.

erns civil cases,* and it is usually imposed when vitally important personal interests are at stake. It is not an easy standard to
meet, and Missouri, by imposing it, rendered it extraordinarily
difficult for the Cruzan family to have life support removed.

The *Cruzan* case eventually reached the Supreme Court,
which, by a vote of 6 to 3, upheld the power of the state of Missouri to impose a heightened burden of proof. The Justices
decided that what was really before them was the question of
which error is worse—keeping alive a patient who would rather
die, or removing life support from a patient who would rather
live. The Court concluded that a state "may permissibly place an
increased risk of an erroneous decision on those seeking to terminate an incompetent individual's life-sustaining treatment." In
an opinion by Chief Justice William Rehnquist, the Court explicitly rejected the argument that the state "must accept the 'substi-
tuted judgment' of close family members even in the absence of
substantial proof that their views reflect the views of the patient."
The trouble, wrote Rehnquist, is that "there is no automatic
assurance that the view of close family members will necessarily
be the same as the patient's would have been had she been confronted with the prospect of her situation while competent."[10]

The case was presented to the public as a question of
whether the Constitution protects a right to die, even though the
court majority did not treat it that way. The question is one that
has divided legal scholars, as all tough and some easy questions
do. The Court in the *Cruzan* case tapdanced around it. Justice
Scalia, in a separate concurring opinion, thundered against it. But
it was Michael Kinsley, writing in the *New Republic* even before
the decision was handed down, who administered what could
have been the coup de grace: "[J]ust because it's sensible doesn't
mean it's in the Constitution."[11]

---

* Criminal cases are governed by a higher standard still, that the facts constitut-
ing each element of the offense be proved "beyond a reasonable doubt."

On the other hand, just because it's sensible doesn't mean it isn't in the Constitution, either. Justice William Brennan's dissent came close to asserting, but did not quite conclude, that the Due Process Clause of the Fourteenth Amendment does in fact protect an individual's right to die. Justice John Paul Stevens, in a separate dissent, seemed to see implications here for abortion: he warned that the heart of the state's policy was "an effort to define life's meaning" rather than "an attempt to preserve its sanctity." Rather than allowing the state to enforce its definition, he argued, Nancy Cruzan's life should be "defined by reference to her own interests." But what the state of Missouri did, Brennan concluded, was impermissible: "It is not within the province of secular government to circumscribe the liberties of the people by regulations designed wholly for the purposes of establishing a sectarian definition of life."[12]

The implication of Stevens's opinion is that it is not possible to define life without partaking of what he describes as "theological or philosophical conjecture." As I explained at the outset, this cannot be so—or, if it is so, it cannot fairly be made an objection to the definition of life, for if life cannot be defined except in impermissibly "sectarian" terms, the state is essentially unable to act.

If the state must define life, is there any reason that a religiously motivated definition should be prohibited? One answer is that the Establishment Clause does not allow it. Of course, that answer is already an evasion. Surveys, as we have seen, show that the great majority of legislators consult their religious consciences before voting. There are, moreover, countless statutes in force that had their clear origins in religious understanding.[13] Indeed, much of the common law may be described this way, which is why the courts used to say that "Christianity is part of the common law." It is to avoid the pitfalls of attempting to screen for motivation that the Supreme Court developed the much-maligned *Lemon* test (discussed in chapter 6), which asks whether the legislation, no matter what motivated it, possesses a secular purpose.

This is where the definition of life—or of death—takes on the greatest analytical difficulty. Defining life as starting at point A or ending at point B is obviously secular, in the sense that without the definitions, the state cannot act. (If we do not know when life ends, we cannot tell whether someone has been killed or not.) The problem then becomes deciding what sources the state may draw upon in making that determination. But if the question is about the legitimate sources of authority, one risks—again—looking into the motivation for the law rather than its purpose in the world.

The practical difficulty is that when one encounters the big questions—questions, literally, of life and death—one may well ask the impossible when one asks citizens not to consult the entirety of their moral convictions. It is not easy to imagine a religious self coping with the question of what life is through a relentlessly secular analysis. In other words, part of what Stevens says may be right—a determination of the boundaries of life may indeed include an irreducibly religious dimension. But, if that is true, it is necessarily an irrelevant objection, for the state, as we have seen, has no choice but to define life.

That is not to say that the state may not, in particular cases, cede control to others, in effect changing the locus of the decision from the larger society to a smaller unit. When the state allows abortion, it is not so much denying the possibility of fetal life as declaring that the decision will be made by another entity—the pregnant woman. Similarly, when the state allows the cessation of feeding and hydration, it is not saying that the patient is not alive, or that the patient should not continue to live—it is placing that decision in a different societal unit, the family. As a matter of politics, it makes sense to say that the state is free to alter the decisional locus in this manner; but it also makes sense to say that the state can move the decisional locus back to the larger society if it so chooses, by restricting the availability of abortion or euthanasia.

In the case of Nancy Cruzan, the state of Missouri was willing to move the decisional locus to the family, but only if the family was able to meet a very high standard to show that it was acting in the way that the patient, if conscious, would have wished—a sensible, if controversial, compromise. A state probate judge eventually ruled that the family had met the enhanced "clear and convincing evidence" standard that the Supreme Court had permitted the state to impose. The hospital ceased feeding and hydration and, after twelve days, she died.

Before Nancy Cruzan died, pro-life demonstrators went to the hospital with the apparent purpose of trying to "reconnect" the gastrostomy tube (which was, of course, never removed). They protested outside in a kind of deathwatch, sometimes raucous, but at othertimes not unlike the candlelight vigils one often sees outside prison walls on the eve of an execution. In short, they ensured that their voices would be heard. And sometimes the voices got nasty. After Nancy Cruzan died, the Reverend Joseph Foreman, a leader of the protest, snapped, "Even a dog in Missouri cannot be starved to death."[14] Asked Mario Mandina of Lawyers for Life, "Where does it stop? Do we start taking chairs away from paraplegics?"[15]

Commentators understandably gave Foreman a difficult time. Typical was Fred Bruning of *Newsday,* who was moved to wonder "what diploma mill provided the good preacher his spiritual bona fides."[16] And it is likely that that the Cruzan family found the words and actions of the pro-life protesters unspeakably cruel.

Yet the fact that the demonstrators made their point badly does not mean there was no point to be made. Foreman's concern, plainly, was that the thing that is precious in the human, the thing that makes life worth protecting, does not vanish because higher brain function is lost. Consequently, the starvation that occurs when feeding and hydration cease—not the underlying injury that caused the coma—is the cause of the end of that precious human substance. And it is the family, the unit to which the state has delegated the decision, that has made the choice to cease the feeding and, thus, to destroy that precious human substance.

That is the essence of the pro-life case. This being America, of course, it is necessary to translate the argument from ethical to legal terms. Legally, it is an argument over the conditions in which it is appropriate for one human begin to bring about the death of another. The "bringing about," in this case, may be seen as passive—declining to feed—although the distinction between that which is passive and that which is active is never an easy one to draw, as we will see momentarily. But the legal and political systems, reflecting the views of the majority, have rejected the principal policy implications of the pro-life case: euthanasia in the *Cruzan* sense is widely available.

On the other hand, the essence of the pro-life case, the part that provides the religious dimension of the dialogue, remains, as it should, very much part of the national debate. We continue to grapple with the question *What is the human?* as we try to cope with the seemingly endless supply of agonizing questions that the widespread availability of passive euthanasia has generated. Can the state, in deciding whether to terminate life support, take account of the incompetent's religious views—including, for instance, her opinion on what follows death?[17] Can the state refuse permission to remove a pregnant but brain-dead woman from life support, in the interest of preserving fetal life? Does it matter if the woman was a supporter or opponent of abortion?[18] Can the state continue to supply life support to anencephalic infants, in the hope of harvesting their organs for other infants?[19]

As a society, we struggle with these questions, we agonize over them, we suffer. As a society that respects life, that is precisely what we should do. And if the pro-life religionists who oppose all euthanasia can keep us aware of the need to understand the human essence, without which none of these matters can fully be resolved, that is all the more reason to be glad that they are with us as we thrash the answers out in the public square.

ACTIVE EUTHANASIA:
THE CASE OF "DEBBIE"

And when one thinks formally of euthansia, one is not really thinking—or should not be, anyway—of the Nancy Cruzans of the world, the human husks, persistently vegetative and without hope of recovery. Those are so-called "near-death" cases: if the person on whose behalf the decision is made does not quite fit the legal definition of death, the fit is nevertheless very close. To let such a person die is, in a formal sense, euthanasia, "easy death." But it presents the easier, not the harder case.

The harder case is the individual who is conscious and fully competent, who could go on living for a very long time but prefers not to. This individual opts out of life not because of depression or neurosis or an inability to deal with the ordinary stresses of life, but because of a fear that the quality of life is in irreversible decline, that the body is dying anyway, perhaps painfully. Think, for instance of the cancer sufferer, racked with pain as the murderous little cells rush greedily from one part of the body to the next, consuming whatever they find there; the AIDS victim who slowly wastes away, watching one bodily system after another break down; or the person afflicted with Alzheimer's disease, of which Lewis Thomas has written, with his typically graceful force: "It is not in itself lethal, unmercifully; patients go on and on living, essentially brainless but otherwise healthy, into advanced age, unless lucky enough to be saved by pneumonia."[20]

For individuals in such circumstances as these, voluntary euthanasia—or, if one prefers, assisted suicide—will often seem the wiser and more comfortable choice. We are, through better technology, living longer, but at a peculiar cost: we spend a greater proportion of our longer lives in ill health than we once did.[21] Is it clear that everyone does, or should, value this trade-off—that a long but sick life is obviously better than a short but healthy one?

The January 1988 edition of the *Journal of the American Medical Association* featured an article by an anonymous physician recounting his decision to administer a lethal injection to a twenty-year-old woman he identified only as "Debbie," who lay dying of cancer in the hospital where he worked.[22] He had never met the patient before the night he helped her die. He did not have Debbie's formal permission, nor that of her family, although he claimed that she had indicated while conscious that she did not want to linger, for she said—her last words—"Let's get this over with." Wrote the anonymous physician: "I could not give her health, but I could give her rest." He did so; Debbie died within four minutes of receiving a fatal intravenous dose of morphine in the presence of a second woman whom the author does not identify.

The story of "Debbie" is horrifying, and, understandably, it created an uproar, for whether the author had permission or not, this was no *Cruzan* case. The writer did not simply remove the trappings of modern medical technology that were extending a life that his patient no longer wanted; he used modern medical technology as an affirmative tool to shorten that life, and he did it without ever consulting the attending physician or even making certain that the patient knew what he was up to. Was the anonymous physician easing pain? playing God? violating his oath? Or following it?

JAMA opened its letter columns, and the debate was on. The grounds for euthanasia in this case, wrote one correspondent, were "terribly murky."[23] The physician in question, another pointed out, had killed a patient "whom he did not know and with whom he had no relationship," an act that symbolized for the writer the transformation of medicine from "the helping profession" to "the killing profession."[24] A third argued that means short of killing could have alleviated the patient's pain.[25] And a group of ethicists concluded that the author "appears to have committed a felony: premeditated murder."[26] (Perhaps this is why one writer to *JAMA* suggested that the story had been manufactured.[27]) The anonymous physician also had his defenders among the letter writers, including one who called him "brave, caring, and progressive."[28] Another lauded the author's courage in "risk[ing] his career to relieve the suffering of another."[29]

However the anonymous author's actions might be described, his essay forced into the open what had theretofore been largely a matter of quiet academic speculation or private familial agony—the matter of when and how it is appropriate for one person to assist another in ending a life that the second wants to leave. A consensus developed: in the case of "Debbie," the physician was abusive, overstepping his bounds. The principal reason was not that the euthanasia was active instead of passive— a separate problem—but that he did not obtain clear and unequivocal permission. Indeed, it was suggested by some critics that he had acted to alleviate not the patient's suffering, but his own.[30]

The killing of "Debbie" was probably a homicide, as the ethicists concluded, which might explain why the physician chose to remain anonymous. But the assisted-suicide movement is growing, and, as more patients consent or even beg to die, the law will have to find a way to cope. One possibility is to allow physicians, in the manner of Dr. Jack Kevorkian of Michigan, to provide the means for suicide but to allow the patient to implement them—much as Brutus ran on his sword while someone else held it. However, the influential House of Delegates of the American Bar Association recently rejected a resolution that would have approved physician-assisted suicides, despite evidence that the members supported it.[31]

To try to avoid the "Debbie" situation (which it condemns), the Hemlock Society, the most prominent of the right-to-die organizations, has proposed guidelines for assisted suicide. The Society would restrict the right to terminally ill patients with no more than six months to live and would require independent confirmation of this prognosis. The guidelines also require written certification of the patient's wish, attested by two witnesses who are not relatives.[32]

The guidelines are sensible, if one plans to allow for active euthanasia in the first place, but they are a long way from covering the field. In particular, although they cover the matter of legal and perhaps ethical responsibility, they do not come to grips with the tougher moral question of compassion—and, one might add, *company*—for the patient. The problem of compassion and company was illustrated in the summer of 1992, when a nurse in a Toronto hospital was placed on trial for administering a lethal dose of potassium chloride to a patient he saw choking. The twist is that the patient, Joseph Sauder, was dying anyway, and fast. He was in an irreversible coma and had just been removed from life support at the family's request. He had received massive doses of pain killers. At the time the potassium chloride was given, Sauder was not expected to live an hour. He had been left to die—with dignity, one presumes—attended by the nurse who was later accused of killing him.

The nurse was convicted of a reduced charge and barred from the nursing profession. But, as sociologist Arthur W. Frank pointed out, something was out of kilter:

> Many physicians would have stayed with their patient until death occurred. Whatever relationship [Sauder's] physicians had with their patient, they defined their task as completed when the patient's death was imminent. No more medical decisions remained to be made, and their expertise was undoubtedly required elsewhere. Sauder was left with a nurse who had qualified 18 months earlier. Just dying isn't much of a medical event, as urban hospital practice goes.[33]

For many ethicists, especially religionists, this approach sums up the problem. Whatever the justifications for active euthanasia in particular cases, they fear that if assisting death becomes a matter of routine, respect for the value of life in general will fall. Surely one can draw some judgments about our society from how we respond to that concern.

Although doctors have assisted death for years—no, Dr. Kevorkian did not start it—the medical establishment has long been queasy about admitting the practice. One reason, of course, is fear of legal liability. But there is another reason, related to the Sauder situation, noted a few years ago by medical ethicist Lawrence J. Schneiderman:

> Today, the euthanasia debate takes place under the shadow of Nazi doctors who appropriated the term to describe the "special treatment" given first to the physically and mentally handicapped, then to the weak and elderly, and, finally, to Jews, gypsies, and other "undesirables" as part of the Final Solution—all in the name of social hygiene.[34]

Could the contemporary movement toward euthanasia lead to a similar disregard for humanness in the rush to apply technology to rid the society of whomever it considers undesirable? Some observers think so, and base their opposition to assisted death on precisely this ground. Schneiderman would like to think not, but he offers a sensible caution:

> But we are different, are we not? Not like *them*. And yet, and yet . . . didn't we American physicians commit atrocities of our own, such as allowing untreated blacks to succumb to the "natural course" of syphilis; misleading Spanish-speaking women into thinking they were obtaining contraceptives, when in fact they were receiving inactive dummy tablets to distinguish drug side-effects, resulting in unwanted pregnancies; and injecting cancer cells into unwitting elderly patients? All for the sake of medical progress . . . we can only look back and shake our heads.[35]

For Schneiderman, this is not necessarily an argument against ever assisting suicide, provided that we continue to feel anguish over every case. Says sociologist Frank, the good thing about the Toronto euthanasia case is that when the nurse saw Sauder choking, "*he himself suffered* with his patient" (which might be a defense of the anonymous author of the "Debbie" article as well, had he not gone to the trouble of telling us in print of how tired he was of these middle-of-the-night calls to treat patients who were *in extremis* anyway).[36] When we lose our sense of anguish and tragedy, says Schneiderman, we risk facing the horror, thinking of all those whose deaths the society assists as "common waste requiring special treatment rather than special cases sharing a common fate."[37]

Much of the religious opposition to euthanasia seems to rest precisely on a disbelief that humans can successfully draw this distinction. One sees echoes of this in the common pro-life complaint—common, whether or not true—that one result of transforming abortion into a right is the disappearance of a moral standpoint from which to discourage its exercise.[38] Using one's rights is said to be, in America, a positive good—which is why some in the pro-life movement insist that the very existence of abortion clinics is an invitation to choose abortion.

Given such fears, such history, and such awful possibilities, it does not seem to me to be a bad thing when religious people press for a recognition in the euthanasia debate of the humanity of the person whose life might soon be ended, as a way of ensuring that the tragic dimension is not lost. Many in the right-to-die movement point with envy to the Netherlands, where thousands of terminally ill patients are said to be assisted to death each year. Yet the transformation of the agonizing decision over leaving this life into a routine, more supported choice is not obviously a step toward placing greater value on human dignity. That does not mean it is a step toward Nazism—here Schneiderman is surely right that the analogy tends to get overdone—but we must not assume that every road leads to something wonderful simply because it does not lead to the Holocaust.

Still, I must confess a bias in the matter. I share the traditional Christian view that suicide is wrong. I further believe, with the German Jesuit theologian Karl Rahner, that "we do not die at the end, but we die throughout the whole of life"—so that the contemporary insistence on either discovering or hastening the "moment of death" can become as idolatrous as the placing of too great a value on its indefinite postponement.[39] The Christian call is to live our lives, as best we can, in the image of Jesus Christ. And that call includes the manner of our dying. Jesus, after all, accepted death as well as life as gifts from God.

It is not my desire to impose this tradition on anyone—only to relate it, for what moral guidance it might offer. And I also offer a caution: like many traditions, this one provides guidance in all cases, but does not necessarily lead to an absolute rule. One can hardly read, for example, Barbara Brack's moving account of the suicide of her mother, who suffered from Alzheimer's—a suicide that Brack knew was about to occur, fully accepted, and did nothing to prevent—without coming away certain that there is more than one side to the Christian perspective on taking one's own life.[40] Besides, one can read the Christian tradition as forbidding only arbitrary and capricious decisions to end one's own life—but the carefully thought-out choices of the terminally ill that the time has come to leave, especially when certified in accordance with strict procedural guidelines, can hardly be dismissed as mere passing whims. As one Catholic priest has put the point, "Jesus healed many people, but they all died. He did not prevent death."[41]

WHEN LIFE BEGINS: ABORTION

In 1981, a young lawyer named Stephen Galebach published an article in *Human Life Review,* explaining how, in his view, the Congress could overturn the Supreme Court's decision in *Roe v. Wade*[42] through the simple expedient of enacting a statute that would define human life as beginning at conception.[43] The thesis was a startling one; overturning constitutional interpretations of the Supreme Court is supposed to require constitutional amendment or, at the very least, the appointment of a new Justice or two. But according to Galebach, the Court itself left this invitation open by its frank confession in *Roe* that it was unable to discover any societal consensus on the point at which life begins. It was up to the legislature, Galebach argued, to fill in the holes, providing evidence of consensus where the Court had discovered none.

A Human Life Bill was duly introduced later that same year, and a Senate subcommittee held hearings. Supporters introduced data that, in their view, demonstrated a shared scientific understanding on the proposition that human life begins at or close to conception. Opponents argued that the question of when human life begins is not a scientific question at all; or, failing that, that the evidence relied on by the bill's supporters was very bad science. The subcommittee, by a 3 to 2 vote, reported favorably on the bill. Perhaps unsurprisingly, it died in the larger Judiciary Committee, which never formally took it up.[44] However, the pro-life movement's concern with fetal life hardly ended with the Human Life Bill, and the Republican platform has for years been committed to support of a constitutional amendment declaring that the fetus, from the moment of conception, enjoys the same right to life that attaches to other people.

Few scholars, it should be stipulated from the outset, find *Roe v. Wade* a glowing example of judicial reasoning at its best. Many legal scholars more identified with liberal than conservative causes have been sharply critical of the Court's opinion in *Roe,* including, for example, John Hart Ely, who is personally pro-choice but considers *Roe* bad constitutional law, if (as he doubts) it can be considered law at all.[45] Robert Burt has argued that *Roe* frustrated rather than enabled public moral dialogue, because it foreclosed a broad range of other answers even though they were not involved in the case.[46] Guido Calabresi has noted that the *Roe* Court decision in effect says to immigrants from pro-life religious traditions that their beliefs are not welcome in America.[47] And Michael Perry, who at one point was a supporter of *Roe,* has more recently come to believe that the decision is premised on the proposition that "the protection of fetal life is not a good of sufficient importance," a proposition

sufficiently contested among "people of good will and high intelligence" that reliance on it "as a basis for constitutional judgment" is "plainly imperial."[48]

Roe, as Judge Ruth Bader Ginsburg has pointed out, is one
of those opinions in which the Court went much further than it
had to in granting judgment—and, by omitting the search for
narrower ground that characterizes much that is best in Anglo-
American jurisprudence, the Justices effectively foreclosed any
possibility of compromise.[49] That does not mean that Roe is
wrong or that the Court is to blame for the society's deep divisions over the issue; it does mean that had the Justices written
more cautiously, they might have found themselves less the center of the dispute.

Moreover, even if defensible as an opinion, Roe contains one
very peculiar concession—a concession that might be seen as the
immediate progenitor of Galebach's proposal for a human life
statute. The Court correctly rejected the proposition that the fetus
is a juridical person, entitled to the protections of the Fourteenth
Amendment, which guarantees equal protection of the laws and
prohibits the deprivation of life without due process of law. What
the Court said about this proposition, however, is fascinating: "If
this suggestion of personhood is established, the [pregnant
woman's] case, of course, collapses, for the fetus' right to life
would then be guaranteed specifically by the Amendment."[50]

Now, as an initial matter, the legal scholar in me is compelled to note that the Court's assertion is false. The Fourteenth
Amendment does not guarantee a right to life—it guarantees
only that life cannot be taken by the state without due process of
law. The distinction matters. If a state chooses not to punish
murders of its citizens, it does not violate their rights to life,
unless its choice is made on the basis of a forbidden ground,
such as race. If, for instance, the state chooses to punish murders
of peace officers more severely than murders of other citizens, it
has not violated anybody's rights. Consequently, even were the
fetus deemed a person, the state still would have the power to

allow it, under some circumstances, to be killed—a point, oddly enough, made by *Roe* opponent Robert Bork in his testimony against the bill sparked by Galebach's article.[*]

But the Court's concession that the right to life of a fetus deemed human would trump the privacy right of the pregnant woman was, understandably, energizing for opponents of abortion. Had the majority written a different opinion—specifically, one in which the question of fetal personhood was less central—then the prospect of congressional legislation to fill in the blank spaces, as it were, would simply be silly. The public debate need not focus as heavily as it does on when human life begins. But it does, because the Court wrote as it did, which is why the idea of defining human life as a way of slowing down a nation that now aborts some 1.6 million pregnancies each year is so tantalizing for the pro-life side.[51]

The pro-choice side, of course, has been as quick as the pro-life side to see the threat that the debate over the humanity of the fetus poses to the continued existence of the broad abortion rights that *Roe* ushered in. Pro-choice scholars have undertaken to rewrite *Roe,* defending abortion rights on such grounds as sex equality instead of privacy.[52] (My own view is that the equality argument is by far the stronger.[53]) Scientists and theologians have responded to the pro-life argument directly, listing reasons why the fetus should not be considered human. All of this falls within the realm of fair, thoughtful, and useful public dialogue on a difficult moral question.

What is less fair and thoughtful and useful, however, is the increasingly frequent assertion that the definitions of life offered by many in the pro-life movement are out of bounds because they are drawn from religious traditions—or, indeed, that the whole question of when life begins is off limits because it is irreducibly religious in nature. Justice John Paul Stevens made this

[*] In the brutal campaign to defeat Bork's 1987 nomination to the Supreme Court, it was widely—and falsely—reported that he had *supported* the Human Life Bill, when, in fact, he testified that it was unconstitutional.

suggestion in his separate opinion in *Webster v. Reproductive Health Services,* which upheld a statute placing a number of restrictions on abortion. Justice Stevens, in his dissent, was concerned about the statute's preamble, which stated, in so many words, that human life begins at conception. In Stevens's view, the preamble necessarily adopted a particular theological approach and was therefore a violation of the Establishment Clause.[54]

But Justice Stevens is probably mistaken on both his premise and his conclusion. His empirical assumption is not accurate—there are atheists and agnostics aplenty in the pro-life movement—but that is not quite the point. More important, as we have already seen in the discussion of euthanasia, it is either incorrect or irrelevant to suggest that the definition of life is irreducibly religious, which is why his premise is wrong. Indeed, part of the problem with the reasoning of *Roe* is that the Court proscribes governmental definition of life—but it can reach the result that it does only by declining to define the fetus as human. If the act of deciding when life begins is, of necessity, a religious exercise, then the *Roe v. Wade* Court plainly engaged in one. And, as the Court is itself part of the government, then the government is doing what the government cannot—one of the many contradictions in *Roe* as written. Moreover, if the decision on whether the fetus is a person is inherently religious, the autonomy of the pregnant woman is no escape. To say that every woman should thus make the choice for herself has the style of a brisk, practical solution, and is usually the right one. But assigning the decision on fetal personhood to the woman says only that the state declines to make it, and if the state declines to make it, the state is declining to treat the fetus as a person— which is, according to the logic of Justice Stevens's position, a religious decision that the state is barred from making.

That disposes of his premise. His conclusion is also wrong, because it in effect reads the Establishment Clause to do the work that I have shown (in chapters 6 and 9) it must not be allowed to: to force the religiously devout to bracket their religious selves before they may enter into politics. Still, Stevens's approach is entirely consistent with the work of any number of theorists who consider antiabortion activities by individuals or groups whose motivations are religious to be an illiberal and thus impermissible activity in a secular democracy.

Laurence Tribe of Harvard Law School, himself ringingly pro-choice, offered this response in his book defending *Roe:* "The participation of religious groups in political dialogue has never been constitutional anathema in the United States. . . . Thus, the theological source of beliefs about the point at which human life begins should not cast a constitutional shadow across whatever laws a state might adopt to restrict abortions that occur beyond that point."[55] The Supreme Court has also understood the point. In *Harris v. McRae,* the Court held that a statute limiting the use of public funds for abortion was not unconstitutional merely because it "coincide[d] with the religious tenets of the Roman Catholic Church."[56]

But even if religion is an acceptable wellspring of secular moral activity, one might still argue, along with many of the great theorists of the liberal tradition, that it is impermissible, except to prevent harm, to impose one individual's vision of morality on another. In other words, even if the religiously devout can enter politics freely and argue in whatever terms they like, they must suffer the same restriction as everyone else in a liberal polity: they can regulate the conduct of others only to protect someone else. Laws against abortion, it is often said, simply do not meet that test and are therefore illiberal no matter what the motivation behind them.

The idea that it is wrong to impose a moral judgment on others is a commonplace of contemporary political dialogue, and it represents the present-day conception of the nineteenth-century philosopher John Stuart Mill's justly famous "harm principle," through which he sought to circumscribe government power, restricting it to the prevention of harm to others.[57] One who accepts this principle might well conclude that abortion rights must be protected because abortion may offend one's fellow citizens, but it does them no harm.

The quick theoretical answer is that abortion is the one case in which that test does not work. Since the question to be decided is whether the fetus—unquestionably harmed by abortion—is one of the persons to whom the Millian harm principle extends its protections, one can hardly begin by saying that only the pregnant woman is affected. Opponents of abortion rights argue that what they are doing is indeed justified by the harm principle, because they are preventing harm to fetuses. Supporters respond that the fetus is not a person. That might be the conclusion of the argument, but it can hardly be a premise.

The quick practical answer is that the society imposes moral judgments all the time. Perhaps most obviously, the civil rights movement certainly involved the imposition of morality on others—notably the forced integration of facilities such as lunch counters and hotels that the white owners preferred to segregate. The fact that the society was obviously correct to ignore the owners' pleas of property rights does not mean that no external moral judgment was imposed.

But what important bit of government action fails to impose one group's moral judgment on another? In the twentieth century, transferring the cost of a moral preference from the group that prefers it to someone else seems to be much of what our government is for. Taxes involve the imposition of moral judgment: you have to pay for what my conscience says the government should do, if I happen to have more votes. War imposes the moral judgment of the leaders on conscripts, and, often more important, on the enemy. Punishing theft imposes a moral judgment on others; so does punishing hate crimes or flag desecration. So do motorcycle helmet laws, or laws prohibiting discrimination on the ground of veterans' status or sexual orientation. We impose morality when we allow the owners of a business to reap profits and when we prohibit them from colluding with owners of other businesses. Affirmative action imposes moral judgment, as do "right-to-work" laws and the regulations of the Occupational Safety and Health Administration.

Besides, the considered moral judgments of citizens are often (in the case of the Congress, if we believe the surveys, *almost always*) informed by religious belief. In the particular case of the abortion debate, it should be plain that there is no escape from the imposition of morality. A pro-life statute enforces a moral regime on pregnant women; a pro-choice statute enforces a moral regime on fetuses. True, one might want to argue that fetuses do not matter, so that we need not care what is forced upon them, but that argument simply assumes what is to be proved.

Nothing is accomplished by calling one's opponents sectarian zealots. On the abortion issue, there are zealots on both sides, and not all of them are driven by religious conviction. Besides, there is a more important point, having less to do with political than with constitutional debate. Constitutional rights should be cast in positive, not negative terms. What should matter is the source of the right, not the motivation of those who want to take it away. Thus the claim that the right to privacy is broad enough to encompass abortion, if it is to be defended, should be defended on its own terms, rather than on the basis of what play of forces motivates some opponents. The argument must be pressed that the right stems from *this* clause, understood in *this* way—for if there is no preexisting right, then there is nothing available for religiously motivated opponents to take.

This is the reason, as many theorists have recognized, the right to choose abortion, if indeed it survives, must be based on an approach that allows abortion *even if the fetus is human*—instead of an approach that denies that humanity under cover of the pretense that the definition is none of the state's business. The conclusion of fetal humanity by no means ends the argument; it simply forces the striking of a balance. As the philosopher Judith Jarvis Thompson has written, "Even supposing that the embryo has a claim against the woman that she not end the pregnancy, it does not follow that she may not end the pregnancy."[58]

The literature is full of arguments for and against the notion that women should be free to choose abortion whether or not the fetus is human. This is not the place to resolve that painful and divisive argument. My point is that the only fair way around a successful legislative effort to define the fetus as human—the only option that does not deride religiously based moral judgments as inferior to secular ones—is to argue for a right to abortion despite it. And an argument of that kind does not require an attack on the religious motivations of any abortion opponents.

DECIDING WHEN THE STATE CAN KILL: CAPITAL PUNISHMENT

Taking the life of another human being is the ultimate penalty that secular society can impose. The death penalty, abandoned in most of the Western world, continues to be overwhelmingly popular in an America that seems unable to cope with the violence that has turned some inner cities into battle zones.

It is an article of faith—and a misleading one—that people who are against abortion rights tend to favor capital punishment and those who are in favor of them tend to oppose it. Many in the pro-life movement are against the death penalty as well, and some are pacifists. Many in the pro-choice movement believe in capital punishment. Forceful religious arguments are presented on either side of the death penalty issue. Still, the stereotype influences our political arguments over life and death issues.

Both choices—to allow the state to kill a murderer and to allow a pregnant woman to kill a fetus—involve, fundamentally, three sets of moral judgments. First, there is the question of what is human. Second, there is the question of when a human can be killed. Third, there is the question of who gets to decide when those conditions have been met—the decision locus.

As a political matter, all of these questions have long been settled in the death penalty debate. As a Christian, I prefer that the society be as sensitive to the agonizing questions about human essence on this matter as it is when groping toward the right answer on euthanasia or abortion, and I certainly will not cease my witness in that cause, but I also recognize that political support for the death penalty is vast and deep. That support is why the battle to end the death penalty is fought principally in the courts, not in the legislatures.

I oppose capital punishment, but I am not convinced by the arguments for its unconstitutionality, although it is plain that the death penalty can be unconstitutional in particular circumstances. For example, the framers of the Fourteenth Amendment were specially sensitive to the practice throughout most of the South of applying the criminal law less harshly for crimes against blacks than for crimes against whites—thus the amendment's famous language, "equal protection of the laws."[59] The most egregious contemporary example of this practice is the well-documented tendency of juries in capital cases to value the lives of white murder victims more highly than the lives of black murder victims, as demonstrating by the greater likelihood that the killers of whites will be sentenced to death. This statistical tendency, on its face, violates the letter, history, and spirit of the Equal Protection Clause—no advocate of originalism could ask for a cleaner case—but the the Supreme Court mysteriously rejected the constitutional claim when it came before the Court in the mid-1980s.[60]

Facial assaults on the constitutionality of the death penalty have also been unsuccessful, other than causing a brief moratorium in the mid-1970s as the states rewrote hopelessly arcane and often incoherent capital punishment statutes.[61] Because the Constitution explicitly mentions capital punishment, some theorists argue, the death penalty cannot sensibly be ruled unconstitutional. In 1980, however, the legal scholar Paul Brest hit upon a provocative hermeneutic and antihistoricist argument for holding the death penalty to be a violation of the Eighth Amendment's clause prohibiting cruel and unusual punishments. Wrote Brest:

> The adopters of the clause apparently never doubted that the death penalty was constitutional. But was death the same event for inhabitants of the American colonies in the late 18th century as it is two centuries later? Death was not only a much more routine and public phenomenon then, but the fear of death was more effectively contained within a system of religious belief. Twentieth-century Americans have a more secular cast of mind and seem less willing to accept this dreadful, forbidden, solitary, and shameful event. The [judge] must therefore determine whether we view the death penalty with the same attitude—whether of disgust or ambivalence—that the adopters viewed their core examples of cruel and unusual punishment.[62]

Brest might well have added what is also true: death as a penalty was long ago justified by the argument that God would correct the errors of mortal man. Brest is surely right to link capital punishment to concepts of the afterlife, but he is wrong on his sociology, because survey research suggests that "twentieth-century Americans" strongly believe in both.[63] So while I endorse Brest's personal repugnance at the death penalty, a penalty that strikes my religious self as sinful and my secular self as a blot on civilized society, his constitutional argument is in the end unconvincing, not in its logic, but in its factual premises.

But there is a further point here. Suppose that the nation does indeed support the death penalty by such overwhelming margins precisely because most Americans still believe that God will correct our errors. (Support for the death penalty, like support for at least some abortion rights, tends to be consistent across denominational lines.)[64] The link, of course, is not perfect; but is it sufficiently present that it might be considered a religious justification for official killing? And, if so, might we not turn Brest's point on its head and argue that the fact that Americans *do* believe in an afterlife should be taken to imply the unconstitutionality of capital punishment?

Worded that broadly, the answer surely is *No*. After all, there is scarcely a criminal statute that has been on the books more than a few decades that did not have its genesis in an effort to transform religious law into secular morality. Nevertheless, one might argue that support for the death penalty is different, for it is premised (in the hypothetical that we are pursuing) upon the supposition that there is an afterlife in which God will correct human error. So one might object that a secular legal culture can take no account of popular belief in the afterlife.

Of course, a concern about the afterlife can lead people to support very good things—antipoverty programs, for example—as well as very bad ones. Still, if the government *is* allowed to act on the basis of a belief in the afterlife, it could decree wholesale slaughter of its citizens, on the theory that God will sort it all out later. (Lots of governments have done precisely this, and some still do.) One can scarcely imagine a greater horror, but it is useful to isolate the part of it that is horrible. Since the image of a national effort to eradicate poverty because of concern over the afterlife is unlikely to evoke the same horrified response, the religious motivation cannot be the source of the revulsion that all of us feel at the image of religious slaughter. My modest suggestion is that the revulsion is mainly a reaction against wanton murder—not against particular governmental motivations for it. The fact that Stalin's reign of terror lacked a religious motivation is not a point in its favor.

One might consider in this connection another religious argument over killing: the Christian doctrine of just and unjust wars. Traditionally, a Christian may fight in a just war but not in an unjust war. However, contrary to what seems to be the popular understanding, the just war doctrine was never designed—not in words, anyway—as a means for permitting nations to enlist

Christians to fight in the right causes. On the contrary, the concept of a just war bears no relation to the concept of a just cause. The doctrine stems from the effort to answer an agonizing question: given the pacifism of the Christian tradition, can a Christian act violently to avoid harm to someone else? The answer, reached through intricate philosophical and theological argument, has been that a Christian can use violence only to prevent a greater violence. Thus, a just war is a war that is necessary to prevent a still greater slaughter—it is emphatically *not* a war fought for a good cause.

Capital punishment does not stand up well against the test of the just war doctrine. Because the evidence for the death penalty's deterrent effect is so slender, it is hard to make the point with any force that the death penalty will prevent a greater slaughter. The justification might instead be one of retribution, but the retributive power of the state is an awesome one, and should be used with care.

When the state kills, on the battlefield or in the gas chamber, it might claim to be valuing the human—an eye for an eye. Part of the problem, however, is that the sense of suffering for the human is too often missing. Politicians seem positively gleeful in their support for the death penalty; victory in war is always the occasion for grand celebrations. That is why here, as in the anguished debates over abortion and euthanasia, the role of the religionist in the public square can be to keep up a steady drumbeat of question, to try to force the society to see the human faces even of those it feels obliged to kill. We may never suffer with the murderer the way that we suffer with the murdered, but in the case of capital punishment, as in the case of euthanasia or abortion, we are a better society if the necessity to kill is the occasion for sadness, not joy.

13

Religious Fascism

ALL of us finally die. Few of us are able to control the manner of our dying, which is why thoughtful people choose instead to control the manner of their living. We make choices, both as individuals and as a corporate political entity—that is, as We, the People of the United States, in whose name the Constitution is written and by whose sufferance the government holds power.

This brings us, finally, to two questions about the future. The first, the one that has principally moved this book, is how we as a nation will, in future, treat those whose religious devotion is a major motive force in their characters when they seek to use their religious rhetoric in the public square. The second, the one around which we have but hinted, is how we as a nation plan to cope with the fact that so much of the religious rhetoric in the public square—certainly, the rhetoric that captures the attention of the media—is so often pressed in causes aimed at limiting what America and Americans might be. That so much public religious rhetoric seems to be invoked by the fringes of the American right is not a reason to fear the rhetoric; if the causes are wrong, let the causes be the enemies. And by throwing wide the doors of the public square, we might also find ourselves welcoming a majority, not a fringe; for most Americans are religious, and most religious people look to their faiths for moral guidance. There is no reason to presuppose that those who will enter will advocate positions that are inimical to American freedom. If they do so, their religiosity should not make them more to be feared.

THE RISE (AGAIN) OF THE CHRISTIAN RIGHT

In a thoughtful interview a few weeks before the 1992 presidential election, Skipp Porteous, a former fundamentalist minister who founded the Institute for First American Studies, reflected on the transformation of the Christian right from Jerry Falwell's failed Moral Majority to Pat Robertson's far more successful— and, in some ways, far more sinister—Christian Coalition. Said Porteous: "When the Moral Majority folded its tent, that fooled a lot of people. People thought it was over. But the thing has never died; it went underground, and the major shift has gone from national politics to local politics."[1]

Secular liberals have rarely appreciated and have never seemed sympathetic to what Falwell instinctively understood: the powerful sense of an America spinning out of control in ways that are, for many religious people, profoundly threatening. Dismissing these fears as racism, sexism, or homophobia does nothing to quiet them. Such insults will simply send those who express the fears rushing into the waiting arms of the next demagogue. What is needed, especially from liberals who pride themselves on a politics of inclusion, is a dialogue that takes the fears seriously, a dialogue that teaches but also tries to learn. Falwell's Moral Majority very briefly filled this dialogic vacuum that liberalism should never have allowed. All too many liberals—Bill Clinton, there is reason to hope, will be different—have cheered Moral Majority's failure rather than trying to appeal in a constructive way to the emotions Falwell tapped.

Pat Robertson, it seems, has understood both Falwell's error and Falwell's lack of vision. The error was to press at once into the maelstrom of national politics, where every utterance of every candidate that Moral Majority supported was subjected to intensive scrutiny for evidence of religious belief leaking into the public square. The result, after a while, was that Moral Majority became so controversial that its endorsement was the kiss of death. The lack of vision arose from Falwell's impatience, his desire to have Washington now rather than tomorrow, or the day after. The result was that Falwell was enticed into coalitions with national candidates who spoke the language of his movement but had little true interest in his issues. To take the most obvious example, neither President Reagan nor President Bush, for all of their courting of the Christian right in their rhetoric, ever made a serious effort to press for school prayer or a ban on abortion in all circumstances.

Robertson, learning from Falwell's mistakes, has largely turned his movement away from a serious effort to influence the immediate results of national elections. It is not that he has become invisible, but rather that his work at the national level has become a masterpiece of misdirection: he antagonized liberal and moderate voters alike (and many conservatives as well) with the viciousness of his attack on Bill Clinton (and most of liberalism) at the Republican National Convention in August of 1992, but while columnists were calling for Robertson's head, the foot soldiers of his Christian Coalition were busily, but invisibly, getting out the relatively small number of votes that one needs to elect candidates to local school boards, water districts, or city councils.

"These people are in it for the long haul," said Porteous in the 1992 interview. "They're not worried about this year or next year." He added, "All these people they're electing to water control ... and school board[s], they're in the system now, and they're going to be working their way up. In 20 years, if these people aren't stopped, they're going to run the country."[2]

The critic, of course, must be careful, for it is easy to be McCarthyite about the Christian right. The threat posed by the Christian Coalition has little to do with its religious nature, and when liberals imply otherwise, as they too often do, they stoke the flames of resentment (I feel the heat myself) among religiously devout people who are already worried about a culture that trivializes their efforts to cope with the maddening moral complexity of the modern world. But if the Christian Coalition is seen as a religious rather than a secular danger to American politics, its defeat will be anything but certain. Religious dangers are avoided, if at all, by calls upon the courts and the Establishment Clause. Secular dangers are avoided, if at all, by calls upon the legislature, through the device of the ballot.

This distinction matters, but in a nation where the fear of religion often paralyzes liberal sensibilities, it may be a difficult distinction to grasp. So let me repeat: If the Christian Coalition is wrong for America, it must be because its message is wrong on the issues, not because its message is religious. As a Christian, I may dispute Robertson's theology and what seems to me an un-Christian effort to use religion as a force for fostering division and hatred rather than one for fostering brotherhood and healing; as a student of religion, I may despair for the future of a faith that struggles so hard to merge itself with the state; but as a participant in a secular politics, I must recognize that neither of these concerns will do anything to stem the Christian Coalition's drive for power—a drive for power that I should oppose only if I oppose the particular policies for which the coalition stands. The error, as a matter of secular politics, is to suppose that it is the Christian Coalition's *religiosity* rather than its *platform* that is the enemy.

Of course, one wants to be careful of overstating the case:

even though the Christian Coalition is obviously a force to be reckoned with, liberal and libertarian fears of a new ascendancy by the religious right may be as overblown as conservative fears of a national movement toward "political correctness" in speech. After a particularly scathing sermon by a seminarian, a character in the play *Mass Appeal* complains to the priest, "I don't come to church to be preached to." In the long run, the American people are like that, too. That may be the principal reason that, in the 1990s, the fundamentalist Christian right has lost much and perhaps most of its political influence. Religiously based political movements need be no more harmful than secular ones: if the American public does not like what a movement is selling, the movement will, in the end, go out of business.

It is easy to understand why so many people worry about the religious right, with such leaders as the Reverend Pat Robertson insisting, "[W]hen the people say, 'We've had enough,' we are going to take over"[3]—especially when one bears in mind the neat riposte of John le Carré's fictional spymaster, Control: "Like everyone who's had enough, he wants more." Yet, in the end, the political market will always be our best check on potential oppressors. If Bailey Smith's religion is one that denies that God hears the prayers of Jews (see chapter 5), other religionists may criticize his theology, and everyone who cares about equality and pluralism can shun political candidates who seek the endorsement of those who share Smith's view. If, as Tip O'Neill used to say, all politics is local, then the defeat of the Christian right will not come about because smart philosophers dream up clever but naked versions of the public square, that is, it will not be an *intellectual* defeat. It will not come about because thoughtful judges engage in a fruitless effort to rule religious motivations for government activity out of bounds, which is to say, it will not be a *legal* defeat. It will not come about because concerned citizens issue comprehensive lists of all the many sins that the religious right has committed, which is to say, it will not be a *public relations* defeat. No, the defeat of the Christian right—if indeed defeat is to be—will come in precisely the arena that Tip O'Neill would doubtless say that it must: local politics. In the end, if one does not like the direction that a political movement threatens to take a democratic polity, one must convince a sufficiency of one's fellow citizens of the danger, creating a democratic counterinsurgency. And then, harder still, one must get this majority to the polls on election day.

How many voters are needed for this democratic counterinsurgency? "Our goal is to have 10 trained activists in each of America's 175,000 precincts by the end of the decade," says the executive director of the Christian Coalition. "That would be 1.75 million trained activists in the country."[4] The number is daunting indeed, for it means, in simple terms, that the opponents of the Christian Coalition must get at least 1.75 million plus one.

Opponents of the new Christian right who see this as too much work—*Why can't we just litigate? Won't a press conference do just as much?*—simply are less serious than the Christian Coalition itself about winning. More often than not, in this democracy, the side that is better organized, works harder, and rings more doorbells is the side that is likely to win. It does no good, afterward, to wave press clippings or public opinion polls as evidence that the victors were undeserving.

THE LAW

At the same time, even as we gird to defeat in political battle those who press upon us programs that would be destructive of American values, we must not make the mistake of regarding the idea of religion itself as destructive of those values. Despite all the wrongs that are done in its name, religion at its best will tend to strengthen, not weaken, the values most Americans hold dear. We must recognize, however, that our essentially instrumentalist conception of the state—the conception that asks of every goal *how* it can best be done rather than *why* it should be done—is, potentially, quite destructive of religious comunities. This instrumental vision plainly underlies the Supreme Court's opinions in such cases as *Employment Division v. Smith*[5] and *Lyng v. Northwest Indian Cemetery Protective Association*,[6] in both of which the religious practices of Native Americans were forced to yield to the government's vision of good policy. (Both cases are discussed in chapter 7.) It underlies as well the judicial decisions to authorize blood transfusions for unconscious Jehovah's Witnesses who had, while conscious, refused them (see chapter 11) and to treat as insignificant the belief of a Jewish Air Force officer that he is required to wear a yarmulke or the choice of a Christian lawyer to attend court on Ash Wednesday with ashes on his forehead (both discussed in chapter 1). In every case, the religious practice is treated as a hobby—something sufficiently trivial that competing state interests can readily override it.

The Religious Freedom Restoration Act, which, at this writing, was virtually assured of congressional passage and presidential signature, would change at least some of these cases, even if it would not alter our society's essentially instrumental vision. The RFRA would require a state to show a compelling interest before it would be able to apply a neutral law in a way that interefered with a central aspect of a religious practice, which is a very good idea. A diverse coalition of religious organizations, unable to agree on almost anything else, has supported the bill. What is more interesting is the coalition that has opposed it. For example, some pro-life groups have expressed fears that the RFRA would allow religious exemptions from antiabortion laws. The act's sponsors have tried to make clear that this is not so, but the concession is a peculiar one. If the issue of religious freedom is large enough to require federal protection, there is no reason that those whose religious traditions approve of or even encourage abortion in certain circumstances should not share in that protection.

Serious questions about the Act were also raised by the Federal Bureau of Prisons, which warned that without an exception for correctional facilities, the RFRA might cause havoc.[7] The concern is far from implausible when one recognizes the vast number and diverse array of cases that have arisen from the denial by prison authorities of religious liberty claims. Inmates have asked for special diets, for temporary release from heightened security classifications in order to attend services elsewhere on the prison grounds, and much more. As a rule, the courts have rejected the requests, deferring—much as in the military cases—to the considered professional judgments of prison officials.[8] The Bureau of Prisons, understandably, would like to keep that deference in place.

Yet if, as I have argued, religion tends to be a positive not a negative force in people's lives, we should think it a good thing when people convicted of serious crimes turn to religion in prison. Requiring prison officials to make reasonable efforts to honor the requests of prisoners for enough freedom to pursue their religious faiths would be a positive good, unless it is our desire to discourage the religious commitment that might make a difference in whether, upon release, inmates return to the styles of living that led to their incarceration in the first place.

Perhaps there are aspects of prison discipline that are special and need exceptions from RFRA. Perhaps there are aspects of abortion that are special and need exceptions. The trouble is that nearly everyone who is committed to a cause believes it to be special; if all of them deserve exceptions, there is no point to the legislation. Religious freedom, like other liberties, is most comprehensible when painted in the broad, ringing language of the Constitution's clauses that protect individual rights. When rights become mired in the delicate negotiations over statutory drafting, they wind up looking as cramped and instrumental as anything else that government does. At that point, rights become not a precious fundament of human personality but the artificial product of one more government program. Surely religious liberty deserves a better fate.

THE FUTURE

In chapter 11, I made reference to the legal theorist Bruce Ackerman, whose account of liberal political theory, the book *Social Justice and the Liberal State,* is understandably concerned to avoid a religious domination that will destroy liberal dialogue. It is intriguing to note that Ackerman dedicates his book to Andrei Sakharov, who, in his memoirs, was quite open in his admiration of Russia's small community of Seventh-Day Adventists for their refusal to allow state policy to trump religious conscience. In particular, Sakharov remarked on the Adventists' spiritual strength in maintaining their pacifist position and therefore declining to fight in the armed forces.[9] Although nothing in Ackerman's approach forbids individuals from acting on independent religious claims (as long as they do not seek to make them the basis of state policy without further justification), the example of the Adventists involves much more than a question of individual conscience. The Adventists are a *group*—they are a community of worship, struggling together toward a better vision of the ultimate questions. The formation of conscience that causes them to be willing to serve in the military but not to fight is a by-product of this search; but it is the search itself that is most significant.

A respect for religious autonomy demands a respect for that group activity of searching. But, for liberal theories of politics, that respect constitutes a considerable risk: after all, a group that searches for ultimate meaning might find it. Having found it, the group would then place that meaning at the center of its conceptual universe. (Otherwise, the meaning is not *ultimate.*) But if that discovered ultimate meaning becomes the *center* of the group's conceptual universe, it will necessarily displace the competing claims for ultimate meaning that are made by that powerful agglomeration of individuals known as the state. Thus, the group that is free to search for meaning will almost unavoidably become, for its members, a source of sense and value—an authority—that they will, in many cases, consider superior to the authority of the state. A tension will be created between the effort by the state to impose a set of meanings on the world and the search by the religions for meanings of their own.

Consider as one example the system of chattel slavery that existed in the New World for better than two centuries. This system was supported by several meanings imposed by the state: not only the asserted inferior humanity of Africans and the claimed primitive nature of African religions and culture, but, more broadly, an essentially hierarchical view of the natural world of which society is a part, a vision of an order in which some things must be superior to (and thus be able to command) others. By combining these visions, it was possible to describe a reality in which the (hierarchically inferior) Africans were most fitted to serve the (hierarchically superior) masters.

From early on, many faith communities challenged these ascribed meanings. As a theologian noted with pride in the mid-1960s: "Those Rhode Island ministers of the eighteenth century who denounced the slave trade while some of their wealthiest members derived their incomes from that source were early links in a long chain of courageous protest on this issue. John Woolman laying the concern for freeing slaves upon the Quakers, the abolitionists during the era before the Civil War, and many Christians of this century have dared to go against the prevailing patterns of discrimination and segregation."[10] Indeed, one reason that it should not be surprising that both the nineteenth-century abolitionist movement and the twentieth-century civil rights movement had their origins in the religions is that it is precisely there, in the realm of the religions, where humans search for ultimate meaning, that one is most likely to find the powerful challenges to the meanings that the state seeks to impose. And that is what one found.

Of course, it is true that powerful religious voices were raised in support of racial oppression as well.[11] But that point is a distraction. No religion *always* challenges the state's imposed meanings, and few do it very often. Yet it is the process of the quest for meaning, the group search for sense and value that is central to the religious task as I have defined it, that is more likely than other competing sources of authority to turn up alternative meanings precisely because of religions' focus on the ultimate.

The religions, for all their arrogance and sinfulness, can often provide approaches to the consideration of ultimate questions that a world yet steeped in materialistic ideologies desperately requires. This is particularly true for religious traditions that contemplate eternity: "The expectation of an eternal issue for human life will also help to liberate a man from the ruinous illusion that the quality of the means he chooses is of less importance than the ends he seeks. It is of the essence of the eternal, as the goal of life, that method and end are always in exact and perfect harmony."[12]

The corollary, however, is ominous. The closer the religions move to the center of secular power (as against influence), the less likely they are to discover meanings that are in competition with those imposed by the state. The simple reason for this is that if the religions are able to impose their own meanings, there is no longer any distinction, and, thus, no longer important work for the triumphant religions as autonomous agencies to do. This abandonment of the role of external moral critic and alternative source of values and meaning will make sense when the Second Coming is at hand, but not before. Until that time, it is vital that the religions struggle to maintain the tension between the meanings and understanding propounded by the state and the very different set of meanings and understandings that the contemplation of the ultimate frequently suggests.

In a state that does little regulating—the state, for example, that the Founders envisioned when they wrote the First Amendment—this tension will but rarely be apparent. As the apparatus of government grows, and its control over the lives of citizens increases, the situations in which meanings are imposed become of necessity far more numerous, and conflicts between the visions imposed by the state and the visions imposed by the religions become more frequent. A pervasive, totalitarian state will of course find these conflicts threatening, which is why religious liberty is among the first freedoms to go when statist dictators take firm hold. A state that loves liberty and cherishes its diversity, however, should revel in these conflicts, welcoming them as a sign of political and spiritual health. And that is the nation that America should be.

POSTSCRIPT

S HORTLY after this manuscript was completed, the federal government's siege of the Branch Davidian compound near Waco, Texas, ended in disaster when a fire erupted after the exhausted law enforcement officers tried to force an end to the standoff by pumping tear gas into the buildings. Eighty-six members of the religious group, including seventeen children, died in the fire, which was apparently set by members of the religious group. The nation was understandably horrified, even though the mass media, for once, had difficulty allocating blame, offering as candidates the agents on the scene, the Attorney General, even the President, before settling, sensibly, on the Davidians themselves.

All the talk about blame—about who should have guessed that who would do what when—misses the more important point. People to whom religion truly matters, people who believe they have found the answers to the ultimate questions, or are very close to finding them, will often respond to incentives other than those that motivate more secularized citizens. In particular, the threat of death—the end of mortal existence—will mean less to some religionists, which is why, for example, Buddhist monks were willing to immolate themselves to protest American policies in Southeast Asia. Americans were as fascinated and horrified by those suicides as by the events in Waco. But why the surprise? The lesson of history is that the very religious, when threatened by overwhelming secular force, will often prefer suicide to surrender. When 900 Jewish defenders committed suicide at Masada rather than give in to the Romans, when the early Christian martyrs chose to face the lions rather than recant, the societies of their times probably thought them fanatical, and gazed at the results of that "fanaticism" with the same stupefied mystification as the news media and most of our politicians show as they contemplate the events in Waco. Our inability to understand the choice to die, even to take one's own life, rather than yield is a mark of how firmly the mask of secularism has fallen over our society. Our insistence that only a fanatic would make the choice is evidence of how little we wish to be confronted with—still less to understand—the deeply religious personality. For many religious people, the shadow of death is simply less terrifying and mysterious than it is to the more secular among us; for this material realm is not all that is.

Perhaps the Davidians were indeed as crazy as the news media has chosen to paint them. Certainly they broke secular laws, were violent people, and may have abused children. The secular state had no choice but to try to punish them, especially after they murdered four law enforcement agents. In short, much about their theology and their practices seems to represent moral evil. As a Christian, I might call it sin; and as a secular citizen, I would agree that their actions, if proved, merited punishment under criminal laws. But even if we judge them harshly, we must not make the mistake of confusing their sinfulness with their religiosity; all the sins they may have committed are also committed by people who are not adherents of minority religions. In other words, we must not assume that it is *the fact of believing deeply* that made the Davidians dangerous, even if it is true that *what they believed deeply* made them dangerous. This is the principal distinction I have defended in this book: we must be able, in our secular society, to distinguish a critique of the content of a belief from a critique of its source. Otherwise, the putative "fanaticism" of the Davidians becomes virtually indistinguishable from the "fanaticism" of Martin Luther King, Jr.—for both were willing to risk the wrath of secular society for what they believed. We often try to avoid making that distinction, by pretending that King was moved by secular rather than religious concerns. Far better, surely, to conclude that King's religion moved him to act as hero and the Davidians' religion moved them to act as very much the opposite, but that in neither case was *the fact that the motivation was a religious one* reason for censure.

King, of course, was finally murdered for his activism, as he always knew he might be—which is why we must not compound the initial analytical mistake by supposing that only a crazed fanatic can believe sincerely enough that he or she will prefer an instant reunion with God to a humiliating surrender to more powerful human beings.

NOTES

A note on citation style: When judicial decisions are cited in these notes, they are cited in accordance with the special rules for legal writing, which readers unfamiliar with the genre may find confusing. But the rules are actually quite simple. In the notes to chapter 9, for example, the following citation appears: "*Ware v. Valley Stream High School,* 75 N.Y.2d 114, 550 N.E.2d 420 (N.Y. 1989)." This means that the case, decided by New York's highest court in 1989, can be found on page 114 of volume 75 of the second series of New York Reports (an official series of reports of decisions in the New York appellate courts) as well as on page 420 of volume 550 of the second series of the Northeastern Reporter (an unofficial series of reports of decisions from the courts of a number of states).

CHAPTER 1

1. "Talking to God," *Newsweek,* Jan. 6, 1992, p. 38; Letter to the Editor, *Newsweek,* Jan. 27, 1992, p. 10. The letter called the article a "theocratic text masquerading as a news article."
2. "Talking to God," p. 39. The most recent Gallup data indicate that 96 percent of Americans say they believe in God, including 82 percent who describe themselves as Christians (56 percent Protestant, 25 percent Roman Catholic) and 2 percent who describe themselves as Jewish. (No other faith accounted for as much as 1 percent.) See Ari L. Goldman, "Religion Notes, "*New York Times,* Feb. 27, 1993, p. 9.
3. See, for example, Jon Butler, *Awash in a Sea of Faith* (Cambridge: Harvard University Press, 1990).
4. Collum, "The Kingdom and the Power," *Sojourners,* Nov. 1986, p.

4. Some 82 percent of Americans believe that God performs miracles today. George Gallup, Jr., and Jim Castelli, *The People's Religion: American Faith in the '90s* (New York: Macmillan, 1989), p. 58.

5. Madeline Kochen, "Constitutional Implications of New York's 'Get' Statute," *New York Law Journal,* Oct. 27, 1983, p. 32.

6. *Estate of Thornton v. Caldor, Inc.,* 472 U.S. 703, 711 (1985) (Justice Sandra Day O'Connor, concurring).

7. Michael W. McConnell, "Religious Freedom at a Crossroads," *University of Chicago Law Review* 59 (1992):115.

8. Robert G. Kaiser, "Hypocrisy: This Puffed-Up Piety Is Perfectly Preposterous," *Washington Post,* March 18, 1984, p. C1.

9. Tom Stoppard, *Jumpers,* quoted in Jeffrey Stout, *The Flight from Authority: Religion, Morality and the Quest for Autonomy* (South Bend, Indiana: University of Notre Dame Press, 1981), p. 150.

10. Ibid.

11. Stephen Arterburn and Jack Felton, *Toxic Faith: Understanding and Overcoming Religious Addiction* (Nashville, Tenn.: Oliver-Nelson Books, 1991).

12. Martin E. Marty, "Reformed America and America Reformed," *Reformed Journal* (March 1989): 8, 10.

13. *Employment Division, Department of Human Resources v. Smith,* 494 U.S. 872 (1990).

14. *International Society for Krishna Consciousness v. Lee,* 112 S. Ct. 2701 (1992).

15. *Lyng v. Northwest Indian Cemetery Protective Association,* 485 U.S. 439 (1988).

16. *Roberts v. Madigan,* 921 F. 2d 1047 (10th Cir. 1990).

17. *Goldman v. Weinberger,* 475 U.S. 503 (1986).

18. 45 U.S.C. 774, as amended by Pub. L. No. 100–80, Dec. 4, 1987.

19. Alan M. Dershowitz, *Chutzpah* (Boston: Little, Brown, 1991), pp. 329–30.

20. See Ruth Macklin, "The Inner Workings of an Ethics Committe: Latest Battle over Jehovah's Witnesses," *Hastings Center Report* 18 (February/March 1988): 15.

21. For sensitive discussions of the tension between meaning as discerned by the faithful and meaning as imposed by the state, see David Tracy, *The Analogical Imagination: Christian Theology and the Culture of Pluralism* (New York: Crossroad, 1981); Michael Perry, *Love and Power: The Role of Religion and Morality in American Politics* (New York: Oxford University Press, 1991); Elizabeth Mensch and Alan Freeman, *The Politics of Virtue: Is Abortion Debatable?* (Durham, N.C.: Duke University Press, 1993); and

Robert M. Cover, "The Supreme Court, 1982 Term—Foreword: *Nomos* and Narrative," *Harvard Law Review* 97 (1983): 4.

22. William James, *The Varieties of Religious Experience* (New American Library, 1958), p. 42, quoted in A. James Reichley, *Religion in American Public Life* (Washington, D.C.: Brookings Institution, 1985), p. 22; and Emile Durkheim, *The Elementary Forms of Religious Life* (London, 1915), quoted in Joan Brothers, *Religious Institutions* (London: Longman Group, 1971), p. 7. As should be obvious, I do not quite accept the famous definition of religion by the anthropologist Clifford Geertz, a definition that emphasizes religious symbols rather than the life of a faith community. See Clifford Geertz, *The Interpretation of Cultures* (New York: Basic Books, 1973).

23. Jonathan Weiss, "Privilege, Posture and Protection: 'Religion' in the Law," *Yale Law Journal* 73 (1964): 593, 604.

24. Timothy L. Hall, "Religion, Equality, and Difference," *Temple Law Review* 65 (1992): 1, 28.

25. See *Africa v. Commonwealth of Pennsylvania*, 662 F.2d 1025 (3d Cir. 1981), *cert. denied*, 456 U.S. 908 (1982).

26. Wade Clark Roof and William McKinney, *American Mainline Religion: Its Changing Shape and Future* (New Brunswick, N.J.: Rutgers University Press, 1987), p. 6.

27. Garry Wills, *Under God: Religion and American Politics* (New York: Simon & Schuster, 1990), p. 85.

28. Michael Lerner, "Can the Democrats Be Stopped from Blowing It Again in 1992?" *Tikkun* (July–Aug. 1992): 7.

29. See, for example, Robert Booth Fowler, *Unconventional Partners: Religion and Liberal Culture in the United States* (Grand Rapids, Mich.: Wm. B. Eerdmans, 1989), pp. 111–28.

30. Mark Silk, *Spiritual Politics: Religion and America Since World War II* (New York: Simon & Schuster, 1988), p. 179.

31. Paul L. Wachtel, *The Poverty of Affluence: A Psychological Portrait of the American Way of Life* (Philadelphia: New Society Publishers, 1989).

32. See for example, the data cited in Roger Finke and Rodney Stark, *The Churching of America, 1776–1990* (New Brunswick, New Jersey: Rutgers University Press, 1992).

CHAPTER 2

1. See Tom Wicker, "The Democrats as the Devil's Disciples," *New York Times,* Aug. 30, 1992, Sec. 4, p. 3. col. 1.

2. See, for example, John Putnam Demos, *Entertaining Satan: Witchcraft and the Culture of Early New England* (New York: Oxford University Press, 1982).

3. Peter Applebome, "At Oral Roberts U., Evangelist's Divine Plea Causes No Alarm," *New York Times,* Feb. 16, 1987, Sec. 1, p. 8., col. 3.

4. See Damon Darlin, "Legions of Strangers, Guided by Moon, Become Seoul Mates,"*Wall Street Journal,* Aug. 24, 1992, Sec. A, p. 1.

5. Maria Augusta Trapp, *The Story of the Trapp Family Singers* (New York: Doubleday, 1957), pp. 59–60.

6. See generally Sigmund Freud, "Obsessive Actions and Religious Practices" in James Strachey, ed., *The Standard Edition of the Complete Psychological Works of Sigmund Freud,* vol. 9 (1906–1908) (London: The Hogarth Press, 1959).

7. Robert Coles, *The Spiritual Life of Children* (Boston: Houghton Mifflin, 1990), pp. 10–21.

8. Stephen Arterburn and Jack Felton, *Toxic Faith: Understanding and Overcoming Religious Addiction* (Nashville, TN: Oliver-Nelson Books, 1991), p. 160.

9. Cushing Strout, *The New Heavens and New Earth* (New York: Harper & Row, 1974), p. 135.

10. See *Reynolds v. United States,* 98 U.S. 145 (1879).

11. Some outsider religions—for example, the Mormons, the Christian Scientists, and the Southern Baptists—have survived official or unofficial repression to become quite powerful in the contemporary world. Others, such as the Amish and the Mennonites, have survived in limited geographical enclaves. For a fascinating discussion of the role of a religion's narrative traditions in resisting state power, see Robert M. Cover, "The Supreme Court, 1982 Term— Foreword: *Nomos* and Narrative," *Harvard Law Review* 97 (1983): 4. The nation's cruel history of creating outsider religions is particularly ironic, given how many of America's early faith communities originated in efforts to escape suppression in Europe.

12. See J. Thomas Ungerleider and David K. Wellisch, "Deprogramming (Involuntary Departure), Coercion, and Cults," in Marc Galanter, ed., *Cults and New Religious Movements* (Washington, D.C.: American Psychiatric Publishing, 1989), p. 241.

13. Robert J. Lifton, "Cult Processes, Religious Totalism, and Civil Liberties," in Thomas Robbins, William C. Shepherd, and James McBride, eds., *Cults, Cultures, and the Law: Perspectives on New Religious Movements* (Chico, Calif.: Scholars Press, 1985), pp. 59, 69.

14. In addition to Lifton's own essay, cited in the previous note, the misuse of his famous book *Thought Reform and the Psychology of*

Totalism is discussed in Lee Coleman, "New Religions and 'Deprogramming': Who's Brainwashing Whom?", in Robbins, Shepherd, and McBride, *Cults, Culture, and the Law,* p. 71.

15. See, for example, Flo Conway and Jim Siegelman, *Snapping* (Philadelphia: Lippincott, 1978), in which self-described former cult members are interviewed.

16. See, for example, *Taylor v. Gilmartin,* 686 F. 2d 1346 (10th Cir. 1982); *Ward v. Connor,* 657 F. 2d 45 (4th Cir. 1981); and *Cooper v. Molko,* 512 F. Supp. 563 (N.D. Cal. 1981).

17. *New York County Board of Ancient Order of Hibernians v. Dinkins,* 1993 W.L. 54832 (S.D.N.Y.).

18. See Francis X. Clines, "First the Gay Protest, Then the Other Irish March," *New York Times,* March 16, 1993.

19. John Courtney Murray, *We Hold These Truths: Catholic Reflections on the American Proposition* (New York: Sheed and Ward, 1960), pp. ix–x. Murray added that the conclusion that no inconsistency exists is "one of the truths I hold." *Ibid.,* p. x.

20. Alexis de Tocqueville, *Democracy in America,* tr. George Lawrence (Garden City, N.Y.: Anchor Books, 1969) pp. 295, 291, 292. The Lawrence translation is based on the 12th edition, which was published in 1848.

21. Ibid., p. 292.

22. Rogers M. Smith, *Liberalism and American Constitutional Law* (Cambridge: Harvard University Press, 1985), p. 180.

23. Tocqueville, *Democracy in America,* pp. 513, 515–16.

24. David Tracy, *Plurality and Ambiguity: Hermeneutics, Religion, Hope* (Chicago: University of Chicago, 1987), p. 83.

25. Carl F. H. Henry, *The Christian Mindset in a Secular Society: Promoting Evangelical Renewal and National Righteousness* (Portland, Ore.: Multnomah Press, 1984), p. 32.

26. Harold Kushner, *Who Needs God* (New York: Summit Books, 1989), p. 27.

27. Martin Luther King, Jr., "Letter from Birmingham City Jail," in James M. Washington, ed., *A Testament of Hope: The Essential Writings of Martin Luther King, Jr.* (San Francisco: Harper & Row, 1986), pp. 289, 293.

28. See *Wisconsin v. Yoder,* 406 U.S. 205 (1972).

29. *Employment Division, Department of Human Resources v. Smith,* 494 U.S. 872 (1990).

30. Garry Wills, *Under God: Religion and American Politics* (New York: Simon & Schuster, 1990), p. 380.

31. The procedural objection arose because opponents (and some supporters) of ordination for women argued that the change should come about by amending the constitution of the church,

which would have required votes at two consecutive general conventions. (General conventions are held every three years.) Rather
than wait, the leaders of the pro-ordination movement at the 1976
general convention in Minneapolis pushed through an amendment to a canon, which required only a simple majority at single
convention. See "The Episcopal Church: Women are Winners,"
Christianity Today, Oct. 8, 1976, p. 48.

32. Some scholars argue against special constitutional treatment for
the religions on just this ground. See, for example, Mary E.
Becker, "The Politics of Women's Wrongs and the Bill of 'Rights':
A Bicentennial Perspective," *University of Chicago Law Review* 59
(1992): 453.

33. For an argument that the terms "inferior" and "superior" have no
significance within the divided nature of traditional Christian worship, see Thomas Hopko, "On the Male Character of the Priesthood," *St. Vladimir's Quarterly* 19 : 147. It is important to bear in
mind that just like "superior" and "inferior," such categories as
"sexist" are secular categories, developed for secular purposes,
such as describing the behavior of human beings in a market,
where discrimination on the basis of race or sex runs contrary to
the purposes for which we as a nation (and sensible moral
philosophers) have concluded that the market exists. To apply
them to human behavior in arenas where epistemic premises are
different is to mix apples and oranges. The fact that some members of a religious community think that the terms apply to it—
and that other members surely read God's Word according to sexist premises—does not provide any reliable standpoint from
which a non-member can make a measurement.

This point can perhaps better be understood by analogy to
another intermediate institution with which the state should but
rarely interfere—the family. If an individual decides to have children and therefore seeks a spouse of the opposite sex, there is no
intellectually interesting sense in which one can call that decision
"sexist" or "heterosexist," even if those terms might apply to an
employer's judgment to place the same restriction on those it is
willing to hire. The epistemology (or, if one prefers in this context, the ideology) of the market simply does not fit comfortably
into the family, which demands, as the religions do, an epistemology of its own.

34. On tensions in the pro-life movement between Operation Rescue
and the more traditional groups, see Faye Ginsburg, "Saving
America's Souls: Operation Rescue's Crusade Against Abortion," in
Martin E. Marty and R. Scott Appleby, eds., *Fundamentalisms and
the State* (Chicago: University of Chicago Press, 1993), p. 557.

35. Mark V. Tushnet, *Red, White and Blue: A Critical Analysis of Constitutional Law* (Cambridge: Harvard University Press, 1988), pp. 269–76.

36. Tracy, *Plurality and Ambiguity*, p. 84.

37. See E. J. Dionne, Jr., *Why Americans Hate Politics* (New York: Simon & Schuster, 1991), pp. 209–210.

38. Tushnet, *Red, White and Blue*, p. 248.

39. Owen M. Fiss, "The Irrespressibility of Reason," *Yale Journal of Criticism* 5: (1992). 213, 218.

CHAPTER 3

1. "State of the Union: Transcript of President Bush's Address on the State of the Union," *New York Times,* Jan. 29, 1992, p. A16.

2. For example, Representative Newt Gingrich of Georgia said that unlike the Democrats, the Republicans stood for values based on "6,000 years of written historical experience in the Judeo-Christian tradition." Quoted in Charles M. Madigan, "GOP sounds the attack," *Chicago Tribune*, Aug. 19, 1992, p. 1. President Bush said that unlike the Democratic platform, the Republican platform rested on "our country's Judeo-Christian heritage unrivaled in the world." Quoted in Michael Hirsley, "Religious Right finds it still has might," *Chicago Tribune*, Aug. 30, 1992, Perspective Section, p. 1. The platform itself explicitly celebrated the "Judeo-Christian heritage that informs our culture."

   I should note that I recognize and value deeply my own, and the nation's, spiritual and moral inheritance from the Biblical tradition. But it is not un-American to celebrate a competing religious tradition or to dispute the Republican platform's version of precisely what a thoughtful respect for the Biblical tradition requires of secular politics.

3. Sanford Levinson, *Constitutional Faith* (Princeton, NJ: Princeton University Press, 1988), p. 105.

4. For the quote from President Bush, see David S. Broder and Ruth Marcus, "Bush Charges Democratic Platform Ignores God," *Washington Post,* Aug. 23, 1992, p. A14. For the quote from Pat Robertson, see "Excerpts from Speech by Pat Robertson," *New York Times,* Aug. 20, 1992, p. A22.

5. Don Noel, "Will the Religious Right Still Dominate the GOP in 1996?" *Hartford Courant,* Aug. 20, 1992, p. C13.

6. See Tom Wicker, "The Democrats as the Devil's Disciples," *New York Times,* Aug. 30, 1992, Sec. 4, p. 3.

7. "Using God as a Cudgel," *New York Times,* Sept. 1, 1992, p. A16.

8. William Safire, "God Bless Us," *New York Times,* Aug. 27, 1992, p. A23.

9. Martin Luther King, Jr., "Our God Is Marching On!" in James M. Washington, ed., *A Testament of Hope: The Essential Writings of Martin Luther King, Jr.* (San Francisco: Harper & Row, 1986), pp. 227, 229.

10. Quoted in "The 1992 Campaign," *New York Times,* Aug. 30, 1992, Sec. 1, p. 31.

11. See Richard John Neuhaus, *The Naked Public Square: Religion and Democracy in America* (Grand Rapids, MI: William B. Eerdmans, 1984).

12. See, for example, Robert N. Bellah, *The Broken Covenant* (New York: Seabury, 1975).

13. Frederick M. Gedicks, "The Religious, the Secular, and the Antithetical," *Capital University Law Review* 20 (1991): 113, 122.

14. Robert Wuthnow, *The Restructuring of American Religion* (Princeton, N.J.: Princeton University Press, 1988), p. 244.

15. Theodore Y. Blumoff, "Disdain for the Lessons of History: Comments on *Love and Power,*" *Capital University Law Review* 20 (1991): 159, 186.

16. Kathleen M. Sullivan, "Religion and Liberal Democracy," *University of Chicago Law Review* 59 (1992): 195, 196. For a general attack on the critics of the hostility thesis, see Frederick Mark Gedicks, "Public Life and Hostility to Religion," *Virginia Law Review* 78 (1992): 671.

17. Sanford Levinson, "Religious Language and the Public Square," *Harvard Law Review* 105 (June 1992): 2061, 2063.

18. Stephen Holmes, "Gag Rules or the Politics of Omission," in Jon Elster and Rune Slagstad, eds., *Constitutionalism and Democracy* (New York: Cambridge University Press, 1988), pp. 19, 20–21, 45.

19. Bruce Ackerman, "Why Dialogue?" *Journal of Philosophy* 86 (1989): 5, 17–18.

20. Thomas Nagel, "Moral Conflict and Political Legitimacy," *Philosophy and Public Affairs* 16 (1987): 215, 218.

21. Even philosophers who try to see both sides of the problem often fall into this trap. For example, the legal theorist Kent Greenawalt on the one hand urges liberalism to take seriously the notion that religion can be the principal motive force for many of its citizens, and on the other hand urges the citizens to take seriously the claim of liberalism to a public square where political argument is offered in secular tems. See Kent Greenawalt, *Religious Convictions and Political Choice* (New York: Oxford University Press, 1988). For a detailed and thoughtful critique of attitudes toward religion in contemporary liberal philosophy, one expressing ideas

that in some ways anticipate my own, see Michael Perry, *Love and Power: The Role of Religion and Morality in American Politics* (New York: Oxford University Press, 1991).

22. Michael J. Perry, *Morality, Politics, and Law: A Bicentennial Essay* (New York: Oxford University Press, 1988), pp. 72–73.

23. See *Roberts v. Madigan,* 921 F. 2d 1047 (10th Cir. 1990).

24. The comment about the Supreme Court was made by Florence Kennedy, a member of the board of directors of the National Organization for Women, in connection with the nomination of Clarence Thomas to the Supreme Court, and was promptly repudiated by Patricia Ireland, the group's president. The comment typified an unsubtle anti-Catholic theme in much of the academic, intellectual, and mass media response to the Thomas nomination. I am constrained to add, lest the reader mistake my point, that I was not a supporter of Thomas's and that I believed Anita Hill's charges of sexual harassment.

25. See, for example, the discussion of the religious views of scientists and social scientists in Robert Wuthnow, *The Struggle for America's Soul: Evangelicals, Liberals, and Secularism* (Grand Rapids, MI: William B. Eerdmans, 1989), pp. 143–57.

26. *Roe v. Wade* 410 U.S. 113 (1973).

27. See E. J. Dionne, Jr., *Why Americans Hate Politics* (New York: Simon & Schuster, 1991), pp. 209–210.

28. James Davison Hunter, *Culture Wars: The Struggle to Define America* (New York: Basic Books, 1991), p. 144.

29. Garry Wills, *Under God: Religion and American Politics* (New York: Simon & Schuster, 1990), pp. 90–91.

30. Garry Wills, *Under God,* p. 63.

31. George Gallup, Jr., and Jim Castelli, *The People's Religion: American Faith in the 90's* (New York: Macmillan Publishing Co., 1989), pp. 122–23.

32. Ibid, p. 123.

33. Wade Clark Roof and William McKinney, *American Mainline Religion: Its Changing Shape and Future* (New Brunswick: Rutgers University Press, 1987), p. 123.

34. Gallup and Castelli, *The People's Religion,* p. 196.

35. Quoted in Ari L. Goldman, "O'Connor Warns Politicians Risk Excommunication Over Abortion," *New York Times,* June 15, 1990, p. A1.

36. Leslie Bennetts, "The Holy Terror of Cardinal O'Connor," quoted in Richard John Neuhaus, "The Immutable Rebels," *First Things,* Dec. 1990, p. 62.

37. Editorial, "The Cardinal Gets Tougher," *New York Times,* June 17, 1990, section 4, p. 20.

38. Cuomo, Ferraro, and Carey quoted in Frank Lynn, "The Stakes Are Raised for Catholic Politicians," *New York Times,* June 17, 1990, section 4, p. 5.

39. Quoted in Ronald Brownstein, "Catholicism a Political Issue Again," *Los Angeles Times,* June 22, 1990, p. A1.

40. "Remarks of Senator John F. Kennedy on Church and State," reprinted as Appendix C to Theodore H. White, *The Making of the President 1960* (New York: Atheneum, 1988), p. 393.

41. Quoted in Kenneth L. Woodward, "An Archbishop Rattles a Saber," *Newsweek,* June 25, 1990, p. 64.

42. Quoted in Howard Kurtz, "O'Connor's Warning on Abortion Causes Political Uproar," *Washington Post,* June 16, 1990, p. A13.

43. Mario Cuomo, "Religious Belief and Public Morality: A Catholic Governor's Perspective," *Notre Dame Journal of Law, Ethics, and Public Policy* 1 (1984): 13.

44. "Catholics Warned on School Measure," *The Times-Picayune* (New Orleans), Feb. 25, 1956, p. 1.

45. Bernard Taper, "A Reporter at Large: A Meeting in Atlanta," *The New Yorker,* Mar. 17, 1956, p. 78.

46. Quoted in "The Nation: Segregation Fronts," *New York Times,* Feb. 26, 1956, p. 2E.

47. For an account of the hasty decision to give the speech and the hasty effort to draft it, see White, *The Making of the President 1960,* pp. 259–62.

48. Quoted in Laurence I. Barrett, *Gambling with History: Ronald Reagan in the White House* (Garden City, N.Y.: Doubleday, 1983), p. 124.

CHAPTER 4

1. John Gregory Dunne, *Crooning* (New York: Simon & Schuster, 1990), p. 250.

2. Peter L. Berger, "Reflections of an Ecclesiastical Expatriate," *Christian Century,* Oct. 24, 1990, pp. 964, 965. For fuller statements of Berger's thesis, see his books *The Noise of Solemn Assemblies* (New York: Doubleday, 1961); *Facing up to Modernity: Excursions in Society, Politics and Religion* (New York: Basic Books, 1977); and *A Far Glory: The Quest for Faith in an Age of Credulity* (New York: Maxwell Macmillan International, 1992). All three books argue for the importance of a church that teaches moral truths rather than one that simply listens to the concerns of its members.

3. Falwell quoted in Alan Crawford, *Thunder on the Right: The "New Right" and the Politics of Resentment* (New York: Pantheon, 1980), p. 160.

4. "Tim F. LaHaye" (inset) in Elwood McQuaid, "What's Left for the Religious Right," *Moody's Monthly,* Feb. 1988, p. 17.

5. See Victoria A. Rebeck, "Southern Baptists Draw Line on Local Autonomy," *Christian Century,* July 1, 1992, p. 636, and David E. Sumner, "Baptists Oust Churches for Support for Homosexuals," *Christianity Today,* July 20, 1992, p. 46.

6. From a press release quoted in Russell E. Saltzman, "Meeting the Quota for Church Conservatives," *Christian Century,* Nov. 1, 1989, p. 975.

7. A useful collection of scholarly essays on the hermeneutics of biblical interpretation is Donald K. McKim, ed., *A Guide to Contemporary Hermeneutics: Major Trends in Biblical Interpretation* (Grand Rapids, MI: W. B. Eerdsmans, 1986).

8. See generally the discussion in Paul V. Marshall, *Preaching for the Church Today* (New York: Church Hymnal Corporation, 1990), especially chap. 2 and 3.

9. For a discussion of the growth of religiously based "special agenda" groups, see James Davison Hunter, *Culture Wars: The Struggle to Define America* (New York: Basic Books, 1991), pp. 89–95.

10. As Sydney Ahlstrom has pointed out, the American Protestant idea of a church totally freed from tradition and hierarchy led to the development of the "farmer-preacher," who answered God's call without formal theological education, and, in turn, to the rapid growth of "Separate Baptist" churches, which rejected the efforts of the New Engand churches to impose hierarchy on them. See Sydney E. Ahlstrom, *A Religious History of the American People* (New Haven: Yale University Press, 1972), pp. 320–24. Many of the great dissenting preachers of the late eighteenth and early nineteenth centuries, especially Jonathan Edwards (sometimes described as a Neoplatonist), might be heroes to contemporary liberals, if not for the liberal distrust of religion as an epistemological category.

11. The church traditions that feminists describe as subordinating women clearly have Biblical roots, in the sense that many who adhere to them cite Scripture as their authority. Supporters of strong distinctions between the sexes often argue, for example, that God created Adam before Eve, that Eve was created to help him, and that after the Fall, Adam was explicitly granted dominion over Eve.

　　Feminist theology has exploded the myth that such famous Genesis accounts as these have single, obvious interpretations—or that the interpretations provided by tradition are the more probably correct ones. Adam was created before Eve, which some traditions have taken as evidence of her subservience to him. But why not, feminist scholars sensibly ask, read this as evidence that Eve was the culmination of God's work? God said that Eve would be made as a "helper" of Adam (Gen 1:18). But why not, feminists inquire, read the word "helper" as it is used elsewhere in the Old Testament, as implying working in concert rather than working for? After Adam and Eve ate of the tree of life, woman was told "your desire shall be for your husband, and he shall rule over you" (Gen. 3:16), which was traditionally read as a divine instruction. But why not, feminists ask, see the dominion of man over woman as a characteristic of *fallen* man, which would imply that learning to live a sinless, Godlike life means learning to yield the dominion that a sinful world makes possible? (For discussions of the passages mentioned in this paragraph, as well as others, see Phyllis Trible, "Depatriarchalizing in Biblical Interpretation," *Journal of the American Academy of Religion*, 41 [March 1973]: 36.) The point is that there is plainly broad choice of interpretation, and it is quite plausible to suppose that God's judgment upon Christians will be based in part on which choices we make.

On the other hand, reinterpretation of some scriptural language has proven more difficult. Consider the following rather explicit instruction from Paul's First Letter to the Corinthians, which even the sexism-conscious translators of the New Revised Standard Version of the Bible were unable to find a way to tone down:

> As in all the churches of the saints, women should be silent in the churches. For they are not permitted to speak, but should be subordinate, as the law also says. If there is anything they desire to know, let them ask their husbands at home. For it is shameful for a woman to speak in church. (I Cor. 14:33b–35.)

Is this an instruction that Christians of the contemporary era are bound to follow? Many argue not, but the question is why. To call Paul a prisoner of the sexual mores of his era is not a helpful answer for Christians who consider Scripture the Word of God and thus their guide, for arguments of that kind would negate the utility of the entire Bible. (Although, to be sure, there are clever theologians, not all of them deconstructionists, who argue in precisely this fashion.) To call Paul a misogynist might be cathartic, but it yields no assistance in interpretation; besides, since many Christians (including this one) believe that Paul was divinely inspired, it is difficult to treat such secular epithets with the seriousness they no doubt deserve.

The more thoughtful answer is that contemporary readers

must distinguish between Paul's statements of doctrine and Paul's statements of advice. See, for example, Thomas R. W. Longstaff, "The Ordination of Women: A Biblical Perspective," *Anglican Theological Review* 57 (July 1975): 316. Obviously, this is no simple distinction, especially when the interpreter begins with the desire for a particular interpretive result; but that difficulty merely restates the more general point that readers who seek to do God's will must struggle with their own political predilections, as, no doubt, Paul himself was forced to do. Besides, no one ever promised that understanding God's will would be either easy or painless.

For a lively discussion of conflicts over these matters in the early Christian Church, see Elaine Pagels, *Adam, Eve, and the Serpent* (New York: Random House, 1988).

12. "From Sisterhood to Priesthood," *Newsweek,* Aug. 12, 1974, p. 52.

13. Quotes are from "The Women's Rebellion," *Time,* Aug. 12, 1974, p. 60, and the resignation letter of Charles V. Willie as vice president of the House of Deputies of the Episcopal Church, quoted in Malcolm Boyd, "Who's Afraid of Women Priests?" *Ms.,* Dec. 1974, p. 47.

14. Michael J. Perry, *Morality, Politics, and Law: A Bicentennial Essay* (New York: Oxford University Press, 1988), pp. 183–184.

15. "A Case of Woman Trouble: Female Priests Divide a Denomination," *Time,* Oct. 17, 1977, p. 80.

16. Malachi B. Martin, "On Toying with Desecration," *National Review,* Oct. 10, 1975, p. 1118.

17. Marjorie Hyer, "Episcopalians Elect First Female Bishop," *Washington Post,* Sept. 24, 1988, p. A1.

18. Albert O. Hirschman, *Exit, Voice, and Loyalty* (Cambridge: Harvard University Press, 1970).

19. Quoted in Joseph Carey, "A Denominational Gender Gap," *U.S. News and World Report,* June 19, 1989, p. 56.

20. Quoted in Julia Dunn, "Episcopal Conservatives Form New Synod," *Christianity Today,* July 14, 1989, p. 52.

21. At the time of the initial ordinations of women as priests, there was considerable question about whether Episcopal bishops would refuse to respect those ordinations. For a thoughtful (although, I think, incorrect) argument that women ordained priests but forbidden by bishops to serve should have recourse to the courts, see Frank Patton, Jr., "Women's Ordination: Should Church Disputes Go Civil?", *Christianity and Crisis,* Sept. 29, 1975, p. 214.

22. See, for example, Kathleen Sullivan, "Religion and Liberal Democracy," *University of Chicago Law Review* 59 (1992): 195.

23. James Bryce [Viscount Bryce], *Modern Democracies*, 2 vols. (New York: Macmillan, 1921), 1:90.

CHAPTER 5

1. See Forrest G. Wood, *The Arrogance of Faith: Christianity and Race in America from the Colonial Era to the Twentieth Century* (New York: Alfred A. Knopf, 1990).
2. James A. Haught, *Holy Horrors: An Illustrated History of Religious Murders and Madness* (Buffalo, N.Y.: Prometheus Books, 1990), p. 138.
3. Ibid., pp. 109–15, 29–30, 224.
4. See Richard L. Berke, "With a Crackle, Religion Enters G.O.P. Meeting," *New York Times*, Nov. 18, 1992. For the proportion of adults identifying themselves as Christians, see George Gallup, Jr., and Jim Castelli, *The People's Religion: American Faith in the 90's* (New York: Macmillan, 1989), pp. 23–26.
5. Henry Abbott, a representative to the 1788 North Carolina ratification convention, reported this fear. He was answered by James Iredell, who first talked glowingly about the need for religious freedom and then added that there was no reason to worry because "it is never to be supposed that the people of America will trust their dearest rights to persons who have no religion at all, or a religion materially different from their own." Both are quoted in Jonathan Elliott, ed., *The Debates in the Several State Conventions on the Adoption of the Federal Constitution* (5 vols.), vol. 4 (New York: Burt Franklin, 1888), pp. 192–94.
6. See James E. Wood, Jr., E. Bruce Thompson, and Robert T. Miller, *Church and State in Scripture History and Constitutional Law* (Waco, TX: Baylor University Press, 1958).
7. See Mark Silk, *Spiritual Politics: Religion and America Since World War II* (New York: Simon & Schuster, 1988), pp. 99–100.
8. *Church of the Holy Trinity v. United States*, 143 U.S. 457, 471 (1892). Justice David J. Brewer, the author of the opinion, later wrote a book entitled *The United States as a Christian Nation*. See Robert T. Handy, *Undermined Establishment: Church-State Relations in America, 1880–1920* (Princeton, N.J.: Princeton University Press, 1991), p. 13, *n* 11. Justice William Brennan, almost a century later, would refer to the Supreme Court's willingness to allow public funds to pay for a crèche as "a long step backwards" toward Brewer's "arrogant" opinion. *Lynch v. Donnelly*, 465 U.S. 668 (1984) (Justice William Brennan, dissenting). Apparently, the troubling language of *Church of the Holy Trinity* has never been explicitly rejected by the Court.

9. Professor Jacob Neusner, quoted in "Losing Our Moral Umbrella," *Newsweek,* Dec. 7, 1992, p. 60. As the Jesuit theologian John Courtney Murray put it, "pluralism may be a fact of history, but it is against the will of God." Quoted in Betty Mensch and Alan Freeman, "Losing Faith in Public Schools," *Tikkun* 7 (1992): 31, 36.

10. For a discussion of this historical effort, see, for example, Robert Wuthnow, *The Restructuring of American Religion: Society and Faith Since World War II* (Princeton, N.J.: Princeton University Press, 1988), pp. 76–77.

11. Professor John Murray Cuddihy, quoted in "Losing Our Moral Umbrella," p. 60.

12. Gallup and Castelli, *The People's Religion,* pp. 194–95.

13. Ibid., p. 174.

14. Richard John Neuhaus, *The Naked Public Square: Religion and Democracy in America* (Grand Rapids, Mich.: William B. Eerdman's Publishing Co., 1984), pp. 144–45.

15. Silk, *Spiritual Politics,* p. 160.

16. Robert A. Goldwin, "Why Blacks, Women, and Jews Are Not Mentioned in the Constitution," in *Why Blacks, Women, and Jews Are Not Mentioned in the Constitution, and Other Unorthodox Views* (Washington, D.C.: AEI Press, 1990), pp. 9, 20.

17. Susa L. Uttal, Letter to the Editor, *Biblical Archaeology Review,* Nov.–Dec. 1991, p. 8.

18. See, for example, *Lynch v. Donnelly,* 465 U.S. 668 (1984).

19. See Stephen L. Carter, "Loving the Messenger," *Yale Journal of Law and the Humanities* 1 (1989): 317.

20. William F. Buckley, Jr., *In Search of Anti-Semitism* (Continuum, 1993).

21. The text is necessarily impressionistic. During Ronald Reagan's eight years as President, explicit religious references appeared in approximately one-tenth of his speeches. William Ker Muir, *The Bully Pulpit* (San Francisco: ICS Press, 1992), p. 132. As I have seen no similar analysis for other presidents, I have no way to make a firm comparison.

22. See, for example, Laurence I. Barrett, *Gambling with History: Ronald Reagan in the White House* (Garden City, N.Y.: Doubleday, 1983), pp. 17–18, 415–19.

23. Richard Cohen, "Religion: Reagan's Divider," *Washington Post,* Sept. 5, 1984, p. A19.

24. Data are from A. James Reichley, *Religion in Public Life* (Washington, D.C.: Brookings Institution, 1985), p. 275.

25. Anne Rowthorn, *The Liberation of the Laity* (Wilton, Conn.: Morehouse-Barlow, 1986), p. 64.

26. See, for example, E. J. Dionne, Jr., *Why Americans Hate Politics* (New York: Simon & Schuster, 1991), pp. 238–39.

27. Charles Fried, *Order and Law: Arguing the Reagan Revolution—A Firsthand Account* (New York: Simon & Schuster, 1991), pp. 29–30.

28. Jaroslav Pelikan, *Jesus Through the Centuries* (New Haven: Yale University Press, 1985), p. 184.

29. See A. James Reichley, *Religion in American Public Life* (Washington, D.C.: Brookings Institution, 1985), pp. 102–3.

30. *The Messages and Papers of Woodrow Wilson,* 2 vols. (New York: George H. Doran, 1917), Vol. 1, p. 436.

31. Quoted in Max Kleiman, ed., *Franklin Delano Roosevelt: The Tribute of the Synagogue* (New York: Bloch, 1946), pp. 255–56.

32. Quoted in Wuthnow, *The Restructuring of American Religion,* p. 67.

33. George E. Mowry, *The Era of Theodore Roosevelt and the Birth of Modern America* (New York: Harper & Row, 1958), p. 111.

34. "Sympathetic Lying," *Atlantic Monthly* 12 (1863): 732, 739.

35. See Harold Hyman, *To Try Men's Souls: Loyalty Tests in American History* (Berkeley: University of California Press, 1959), pp. 167–98.

36. See Jon Butler, *Awash in a Sea of Faith* (Cambridge: Harvard University Press, 1990) and Cushing Strout, *The New Heavens and New Earth: Political Religion in America* (New York: Harper & Row, 1974).

CHAPTER 6

1. Thomas Jefferson, "Freedom of Religion at the University of Virginia," in Saul K. Padover, ed., *The Complete Jefferson* (New York: Duell, Sloan & Pierce, 1943), p. 958.

2. The quoted language is from *Lemon v. Kurtzman,* 403 U.S. 602 (1971), discussed later in this chapter.

3. For a thoughtful discussion of the reasons that the Establishment Clause applies to the states, see Justice William Brennan's concurring opinion in *Abington School District v. Schempp,* 374 U.S. 203 (1963). The application of the Establishment Clause to the states has its critics, including, implicitly, two members of the Supreme Court, but for a variety of reasons, most of them linked to the arcana of constitutional interpretation, I am not among them. To put matters most simply, I ally myself with those who believe that many of the rights that American citizens possess against the federal government through the First Amendment became effective

against the states with the adoption of the Fourteenth Amendment after the Civil War.

4. Philip Schaff, *Church and State in the United States* (New York: Putnam, 1888), pp. 22–23; quoted in Robert T. Handy, *Undermined Establishment: Church-State Relations in America, 1880–1920* (Princeton, N.J.: Princeton University Press, 1991), p. 20.

5. The decisions of the Supreme Court collectively known as the "school prayer cases" include: *Engel v. Vitale,* 370 U.S. 421 (1962) (no state-drafted prayer in public schools); *Abington School District v. Schempp,* 374 U.S. 203 (1963) (no devotional Bible readings in public schools); *Wallace v. Jaffree,* 472 U.S. 38 (1985) (no moment of silence in public schools if used as subterfuge for prayer); *Lee v. Weisman,* 112 S. Ct. 2649 (1992) (no school-sponsored spoken prayer at high school graduation).

6. *Everson v. Board of Education,* 330 U.S. 1, 18 (1947).

7. *McCollum v. Board of Education,* 333 U.S. 203, 247 (1948) (Justice Stanley Reed, dissenting).

8. Robert L. Cord, *Separation of Church and State: Historical Fact and Current Fiction* (New York: Lambeth Press, 1982), p. 49.

9. *Lemon v. Kurtzmann,* 403 U.S. 602 (1971).

10. *Bradshaw v. North Carolina Department of Transportation,* 630 F. 2d 1018 (4th Cir. 1980), *cert. denied,* 450 U.S. 965 (1981).

11. See *United Christian Scientists v. Christian Science Board of Directors,* 829 F.2d 1152 (D.C. Cir. 1987).

12. 482 U.S. 578 (1987).

13. Mario M. Cuomo, "Religious Belief and Public Morality: A Catholic Governor's Perspective," *Notre Dame Journal of Law, Ethics, and Public Policy* 1 (1984): 13, 19.

14. Robert N. Van Wyk, "Liberalism, Religion and Politics," *Public Affairs Quarterly* (July 1987): 59, 68, Franklin J. Gramwell, "Religion and Reason in American Politics," *Journal of Law and Religion* 2 (1984): 326.

15. See Michael W. McConnell, "Why 'Separation' Is Not the Key to Church-State Relations," *Christian Century,* 1989, p. 43.

16. See Richard Fox, *Reinhold Niebuhr: A Biography* (San Francisco: Harper & Row, 1985), pp. 62–192. For a discussion of the "social gospel" movement among liberal Protestants, a movement Niebuhr largely disdained, see Robert T. Handy, *Undermined Establishment: Church-State Relations in America* (Princeton, NJ: Princeton University Press, 1991), pp. 58–67, 104–125. For an argument that the theology underlying the liberal social gospel movement was closely linked to the theology underlying that of Christian imperialism, see William R. Hutchison, *Errand to the*

World: American Protestant Thought and Foreign Missions (Chicago: University of Chicago Press, 1987).

17. Jesse Choper, "Church, State and the Supreme Court: Current Controversy," *Arizona Law Review* 29 (1987): 551, 552.

18. Dean M. Kelley, *Why Churches Should Not Pay Taxes* (New York: Harper & Row, 1977), p. 143.

19. *Lynch v. Donnelly,* 465 U.S. 668 (1984).

20. *Marsh v. Chambers,* 463 U.S. 783 (1983).

21. For a useful discussion of the Court's failures on this issue, see Alan M. Dershowitz, *Chutzpah* (Boston: Little, Brown, 1991), pp. 331–34.

22. See Michael W. McConnell, "Coercion: The Lost Element of Establishment," *William and Mary Law Review* 27 (1986): 933.

23. See Douglas Laycock, "'Noncoercive' Support for Religion: Another False Claim about the Establishment Clause," *Virginia Law Review* 26 (1991): 37.

24. See *Lynch v. Donnelly,* 465 U.S. 668, 688 (1984) (Justice Sandra Day O'Connor, concurring).

25. See Mark Tushnet, *Red, White, and Blue: A Critical Analysis of Constitutional Law* (Cambridge, MA: Harvard University Press, 1988), pp. 256–57, *n* 31.

26. Steven D. Smith, "Separation and the 'Secular': Reconstructing the Disestablishment Decision," *Texas Law Review* 67 (1989): 955.

27. Kathleen M. Sullivan, "Religion and Liberal Democracy," *University of Chicago Law Review* 59 (1992): 195.

28. See, for example, Arlin M. Adams and Charles J. Emmerich, *A Nation Dedicated to Religious Liberty* (Philadelphia: University of Pennsylvania Press, 1990); Cord, *Separation of Church and State;* Mark DeWolfe Howe, *The Garden and the Wilderness* (Chicago: University of Chicago Press, 1965); Leonard Levy, *The Establishment Clause: Religion and the First Amendment* (New York: Macmillan, 1986); Anson Phelps Stokes and Leo Pfeffer, *Church and State in the United States,* rev. ed. (New York: Harper & Row, 1964).

29. Quoted in Adams and Emmerich, *A Nation Dedicated to Religious Liberty,* p. 6. For a general discussion, see Howe, *The Garden and the Wilderness.* Some historians insist that for all the focus in legal scholarship on such well-known religious pluralists as Thomas Jefferson and James Madison, both the Establishment Clause and the separation of church and state owe much more to such dissenters as Williams, who pressed for a separation solely as an aid to belief. This is the view of Adams and Emmereich, as well as of Mark DeWolfe Howe in *The Garden and the Wilderness,* pp. 1–31. For a similar argument by a legal scholar, see Timothy L. Hall, "Roger Williams and the Foundations of Religious Liberty,"

Boston University Law Review 71 (1991): 455. For a contrary view, see, for example, Anthony Champagne, "Religion as a Political Interest Group," in W. Lawson Taitte, ed., *Religion and Politics* (Austin: University of Texas Press, 1989), p. 111. As will become clear, nothing in my argument turns on whether Jefferson or Williams was the more influential.

30. James Madison, *Memorial and Remonstrance Against Religious Assessments* (1785), reprinted in Adams and Emmerich, *A Nation Dedicated to Religious Liberty*, p. 104.

31. The source for this quote is given in note 1. Jefferson's relationship to religion was far more complex than is sometimes assumed. His famous *Bill for Establishing Religious Freedom* was justified, in its own preamble, on the ground that coercion of belief was not in accord with God's plan. See Thomas Jefferson, *A Bill for Establishing Religious Freedom* (1785), reprinted in Adams and Emmerich, *A Nation Dedicated to Religious Liberty*, p. 110. For a detailed listing of Jefferson's many official entanglements with religion as governor and president, see Cord, *Separation of Church and State*, pp. 36–46.

    And when, after his presidency, Jefferson realized his dream with the establishment of the state-supported University of Virginia, he proposed that all students be required to study as a matter of ethics (not, he was emphatic, theology) "[t]he proofs of the being of a God, the creator, preserver, and supreme ruler of the universe, the author of all relations within morality, and of the laws and obligations these infer." Quoted in Herbert B. Adams, *Thomas Jefferson and the University of Virginia* (Washington, D.C.: Government Printing Office, 1888), p. 91.

    However, Jefferson's contempt for organized religion—indeed, for the existing religious faiths—is legendary. In one searing letter written late in his life he wrote of Judaism that "[t]he fumes of the most disordered imaginations were recorded in their religious code" and dismissed the teachings of institutional Christianity about Jesus as "the follies, the falsehoods, and the charlatanisms which His biographers father on Him." Thomas Jefferson to William Short, Aug. 4, 1820, in William B. Parker, ed., *Letters and Addresses of Thomas Jefferson* (Buffalo, N.Y.: National Jefferson Society, 1903).

32. Akhil Reed Amar, "The Bill of Rights as a Constitution," *Yale Law Journal* 100 (1991): 1159.

33. Quoted in Harold J. Berman, "The Religion Clauses of the First Amendment in Historical Perspective," in W. Laswon Taitte, ed., *Religion and Politics* (Dallas and Austin: University of Texas Press, 1989), pp. 49, 64.

34. James Madison's original draft of what is now the Establishment Clause, introduced in the House of Representatives on June 7, 1789, read "nor shall any national religion be established." The final Senate version, prior to conference with the House, read "Congress shall make no law establishing articles of faith or a mode of worship." All the drafts of the Clause appear as Appendix A in Edwin S. Gaustad, *Faith of Our Fathers: Religion and the New Nation* (San Francisco: Harper & Row, 1987), pp. 157–158. The legislative history leaves little doubt that the Clause, in all of its incarnations, was designed by the Founders to embody "the jurisdictional concern of federalism"—to ensure that "civil authority in religious affairs resided with the states, not the national government." Adams and Emmerich, *A Nation Dedicated to Religious Liberty*, p. 46. See also Cord, *Separation of Church and State* and Amar, "Bill of Rights." Perhaps the best evidence of this original understanding is the fact that the established churches lingered on in the New England states long after the First Amendment was adopted. The last state to disestablish its church was apparently Massachusetts, in 1803. The historian Leonard Levy has argued with some force that the late eighteenth-century establishments should be considered non-preferential, because all Christian churches (or at least all Protestant churches) were eligible for state support. Levy, *The Establishment Clause*, pp. 25–62. Thus, he contends, non-preferential aid to religion (aid for which all religions are eligible) violates the Founders' understanding of the Establishment Clause. But his explanation for the absence of state support for Catholicism or Judaism—that the numbers of citizens were too small—is only one of many possibilities. Another possibility is that the establishments were indeed preferential, in the sense that they excluded minority religions, and designedly so.

35. Amar, "Bill of Rights," p. 1131, 1158, 1159.

36. Berman, "Religious Clauses,"p. 68.

37. For reasons I will not trouble to labor here, I tend to be a supporter of constitutional jurisprudence that is guided by the original understanding, although I do not endorse the contemporary political trend of using that approach as a prop for decisions to fit ideological programs on the left or on the right. I briefly discuss the relevance of the original understanding to the particular problems of the First Amendment in Stephen L. Carter, "Originalism and the Bill of Rights," *Harvard Journal of Law and Public Policy* 15 (1992): 141.

38. "[T]he colonists and Founders lived in a more homogeneous society where religion was understood in a Judeo-Christian framework and where government contact with religion was arguably

less extensive." Adams and Emmerich, *A Nation Dedicated to Religious Liberty*, p. 90. On the development of a more religiously pluralistic America in the second half of the twentieth century, see Robert Wuthnow, *The Restructuring of American Religion*, (Princeton, N.J.: Princeton University Press, 1988).

39. See H. Frank Way, "The Death of the Christian Nation: The Judiciary and Church-State Relations," *Journal of Church and State* 29 (1987):509.

40. On the proposition that Americans are less likely than in the past to follow hierarchical commands of their religions, see, for example, Robert Wuthnow, *The Restructuring of American Religion*. On the importance of religion to moral decisions, see, for example, George Gallup, Jr., and Jim Castelli, *The People's Religion: American Faith in the 90's* (New York: Macmillan, 1989), pp. 35–38.

41. Berman, "Religious Clauses," p. 72.

42. The Establishment Clause should be read to bar *mandatory* assignment of individuals convicted of driving under the influence of alcohol to treatment programs that include prayer and other religious aspects. See *Granberg v. Ashland County*, 590 F. Supp. 1005 (W. D. Wis. 1984). But courts have held (correctly) that the mandatory assignment to 12-step programs modeled on Alcoholics Anonymous is constitutional, because the programs, despite references to a "Higher Power," are not necessarily religious. See *Stafford v. Harrison*, 766 F. Supp. 1014 (D. Kan. 1991).

43. See *United States Catholic Conference v. Abortion Rights Mobilization, Inc.*, 487 U.S. 72 (1988) (dismissing contempt citation against United States Catholic Conference and National Conference of Catholic Bishops, which failed to respond to a subpoena); *In re United States Catholic Conference*, 885 F.2d 1020 (2d Cir. 1989) (dismissing the action on grounds that plaintiffs lack standing to sue).

CHAPTER 7

1. Oddly, there is controversy over this terminology. One of the leading scholarly treatments of the accommodation issue uses the term *accommodation* to refer only to those exemptions that the state chooses to grant although not constitutionally compelled to do so. See Ira C. Lupu, "Reconstructing the Establishment Clause: The Case Against Discretionary Accommodation of Religion," *University of Pennsylvania Law Review* 140 (1991): 555. Another, expressly criticizing Professor Lupu, uses the term to cover both those exemptions that the constitution requires and those that the

state grants voluntarily. See Michael W. McConnell, "Accommodation of Religion: An Update and a Response to the Critics," *George
Washington Law Review* 60 (1992): 685. At the risk of provoking
the ire of Professors Lupu and McConnell, both of whom I much
admire, my use of the word does not follow either of theirs. My
textual reference is only to constitutionally required accommodations. Although I certainly appreciate the force of Neutralist arguments such as Professor Lupu's for restricting government discretion to grant religious exemptions from general laws, I remain
unconvinced that the offer of an accommodation that is not constitutionally required raises any serious questions under the Establishment Clause, any more than the government's explicit use of
race in an affirmative action program—also a kind of exemption
from a general law—raises any serious questions under the Equal
Protection Clause.

2. For arguments against accommodation, see, for example, Philip
Kurland, "Of Church and State and the Supreme Court," *University
of Chicago Law Review* 29 (1961): 1; Ira C. Lupu, "Reconstructing
the Establishment Clause.

3. *Employment Division v. Smith,* 494 U.S. 872 (1990).

4. Ibid.

5. Kathleen M. Sullivan, "Religion and Liberal Democracy," *University of Chicago Law Review* 59 (1992): 195, 216.

6. See Douglas Laycock, "A Survey of Religious Liberty in the United
States," *Ohio State Law Journal* 47 (1986): 409.

7. 494 U.S. at 890 .

8. Frederick Mark Gedicks, "Public Life and Hostility to Religion,"
Virginia Law Review 78 (1992): 671, 690.

9. *Cantwell v. Connecticut,* 310 U.S. 296 (1940).

10. *Kunz v. New York,* 340 U.S. 290 (1951); *Murdock v. Pennsylvania,*
319 U.S. 105 (1943).

11. *Widmar v. Vincent,* 454 U.S. 263 (1981) (meeting on a college
campus).

12. *McDaniel v. Paty,* 435 U.S. 618, 641 (1978) (Justice William Brennan, concurring).

13. Mark Tushnet, *Red, White, and Blue: A Critical Analysis of Constitutional Law* (Cambridge: Harvard University Press, 1988), p.
257.

14. 406 U.S. 205 (1972).

15. *Sherbert v. Verner,* 374 U.S. 398 (1963).

16. *Frazee v. Illinois Department of Employment Security,* 489 U.S.
829, 835 (1989).

17. *Lyng v. Northwest Indian Cemetery Protective Association,* 485 U.S.
439 (1988).

18. For effective criticism of *Lyng,* see Michael W. McConnell, "Religious Freedom at a Crossroads," *University of Chicago Law Review* 59 (1992): 115.

19. Michael W. McConnell, "Accommodation of Religion: An Update and a Response to the Critics," *George Washington Law Review* 60 (March 1992): 685, 689.

20. *Employment Division v. Smith,* 494 U.S. at 890.

CHAPTER 8

1. The 82 percent figure, the most recent one I found, is drawn from James Patterson and Peter Kim, *The Day America Told the Truth* (New York: Prentice Hall, 1991), p. 204. A 1981 Gallup Poll, probably more scientific, put the number at 53 percent. See George Gallup, Jr., and Sarah Jones, *100 Questions and Answers: Religion in America* (Princeton, NJ: Princeton Religious Research Center, 1989).

2. The case is discussed in R. Gustav Niebuhr, "California Top Court to Wrestle With 'Sin' vs. Tenants' Rights," *Wall Street Journal,* Aug. 25, 1992, p. B1.

3. See *Donahue v. Fair Employment and Housing Commission,* 13 Cal. App. 4th 350, 2 Cal. Rptr. 2d 32 (Ct. App. 1991). The California Supreme Court agreed in February of 1992 to review the decision. See 1992 Cal. LEXIS 2093.

4. *National Labor Relations Board v. Catholic Bishop,* 440 U.S. 490 (1979).

5. *Tony & Susan Alamo Foundation v. Secretary of Labor,* 471 U.S. 290 (1985). Lower courts have held that religious organizations, at least in some of their activities, are subject to the prohibitions on employment discrimination contained in Title VII of the Civil Rights Act of 1964 (see *EEOC v. Pacific Press Publishing Association,* 676 F.2d 1271 (9th Cir. 1982)) and the requirements that employers make contributions to state workers' compensation funds (see *South Ridge Baptist Church v. Industrial Commission,* 676 F. Supp. 799 (S.D. Ohio 1987).

6. *Corporation of Presiding Bishop of the Church of Jesus Christ of Latter-Day Saints v. Amos,* 483 U.S. 327 (1987).

7. Kathleen M. Sullivan, "Religion and Liberal Democracy," *University of Chicago Law Review* 59 (1992): 195, 220.

8. Ibid., pp. 221–22.

9. See Michael W. McConnell, "Free Exercise Revisionism and the *Smith* Decision," *University of Chicago Law Review* 57 (1990): 1109

10. *Corporation of Presiding Bishop v. Amos,* 483 U.S. at 342.

11. Ibid., pp. 342–43.
12. Ibid., p. 343.
13. Robert Cover, "The Supreme Court, 1982 Term—Foreword: *Nomos* and Narrative," *Harvard Law Review* 97 (1983): 4, 50–51.
14. For a discussion of whether tax exemptions for religious organizations should be considered state support, see Boris I. Bittker, "Churches, Taxes and the Constitution," *Yale Law Journal* 78 (1969): 1285. Bittker argues that even tax-exempt churches pay their "fair share" of the government's budget in other ways. For a similar argument, see Dean M. Kelley, *Why Churches Should Not Pay Taxes* (New York: Harper & Row, 1977).
15. See *New York County Board of Ancient Order of Hibernians v. Dinkins,* 1993 W.L. 54832 (S.D.N.Y.).
16. One controversy concerned charges that the Roman Catholic Church's theology interfered with its administration of care for AIDS patients, care for which the Church receives state funding. As is usually the case when the church in question is part of the mainline, compromise was finally reached. See Catherine Woodward, "Cuomo Defends Archdiocese on AIDS Care," *Newsday,* Jan. 10, 1990, News Section, p. 6; Bruce Lambert, "A Church-State Conflict Arises Over AIDS Care," *New York Times,* Feb. 23, 1990, p. B2; Bruce Lambert, "Tentative Approval for Church-Run AIDS Homes," *New York Times,* Feb. 24, 1990, Sec. 1, p. 29.
17. *Bob Jones University v. United States,* 461 U.S. 574 (1983).
18. Quoted in Laurence I. Barrett, *Gambling with History: Reagan in the White House* (Garden City, NY: Doubleday, 1983), p. 418.
19. *McCulloch v. Maryland,* 17 U.S. (4 Wheat.) 316 (1819).
20. The Supreme Court has held that religious organizations do not have a constitutional right to tax exemption. *Jimmy Swaggart Ministries v. Board of Equalization,* 493 U.S. 378 (1990). The Court has also rejected a claim that compliance with tax laws should not be required when it would violate with the tenets of a religion. *Hernandez v. Commissioner,* 490 U.S. 680 (1989).
21. The AALS power to review member schools blossomed into public view in 1989, when the Association's Executive Committee warned Boalt Hall, the law school of the University of California at Berkeley and one of the nations's most distinguished, that it needed to pay closer attention to issues of hiring and retaining a racially and sexually diverse faculty. The Executive Committee letter, which followed charges (never finally adjudicated) that the school had engaged in sex discrimination in its decisions on promotion to tenure, sparked a firestorm of controversy perhaps not merited by the fairly mild tone of the letter itself. For a sample of the commentary, compare Paul Carrington, "The Boalt Affair,"

Journal of Legal Education 41 (1991): 363 (the Executive Committee went too far); Betsy Levin, "The AALS Accreditation Process and Berkeley"; ibid., p. 373 (the Executive Committee followed established procedures); and Marjorie M. Shultz, "Debating P.C. on 'PC'"; ibid., p. 387 (Berkeley applied lower standards to promotions of men than promotions of women).

22. Cover *"Nomos* and Narrative," pp. 62–67.

23. Perhaps unsurprisingly, there has been litigation on this proposition. See *Gay Rights Coalition of Georgetown University Law Center v. Georgetown University,* 536 A.2d 1 (D.C. 1987), in which the court struggled to weigh the competing interests as it applied the provisions of the District of Columbia Human Rights Act banning discrimination on the basis of sexual orientation to Georgetown, a Catholic school.

CHAPTER 9

1. For a readable account of this history, see Sydney E. Ahlstrom, *A Religious History of the American People* (New Haven: Yale University Press, 1972), pp. 763–72.

2. Quoted in Terry Spencer, "Parents Protest Reprimand of Teacher over Creationism," *Los Angeles Times,* Apr. 2, 1991, p. B8, col. 1.

3. Ibid.

4. See *Epperson v. Arkansas,* 393 U.S. 97 (1968).

5. See *Edwards v. Aguillard,* 482 U.S. 578 (1987).

6. See *Scopes v. State,* 154 Tenn. 105, 289 S.W. 363 (1927).

7. Quoted in Lily Eng, "Anti-Evolutionist Teacher Sues School District," *Los Angeles Times,* Oct. 1, 1991, p. A3, col. 1.

8. Quoted in Dana Parsons, "A Threat to 'The Survival of Rationality' Is Evolving Here," *Los Angeles Times,* Oct. 2, 1991, p. B1, col. 2.

9. Kathleen Stein, "Censoring Science," *Omni* (Feb. 1987): 42.

10. Harold Bloom, *The American Religion: The Emergence of the Post-Christian Nation* (New York: Simon & Schuster, 1992), p. 56.

11. Quoted in untitled article, Proprietary to UPI, Feb. 13, 1989, Regional News section [NEXIS].

12. Jim Corbett, "Deviating from the Curriculum Guide Is Wrong," *Los Angeles Times,* May 21, 1991, p. B11, col. 1.

13. The figures are calculated from a table in George Gallup, Jr., and Sarah Jones, *100 Questions and Answers: Religion in America* (Princeton, NJ: Princeton Religious Research Center, 1989), p. 26. A 1991 survey found more impressive numbers. See Jim Dawson, "Evolution Fight Has New Form, But Emotions Have Endured," *Star Tribune* [Minneapolis], June 22, 1992, p. 1A (47 percent agree

that "God created man in his present form at one time within the past 10,000 years"; 40 percent agree that "humans developed over millions of years, but God guided the process"; only 9 percent say "man evolved without God"). A widely criticized 1982 survey found that 76 percent of respondents believed that evolution and creation should both be taught in public schools. For a sample of the criticism, which was probably misdirected, see "What Faulty Questions on Creationism Beget," Letter to the Editor, *New York Times*, Feb. 17, 1982, p. A22.

14. Jon Butler, *Awash in a Sea of Faith: Christianizing the American People* (Cambridge, MA: Harvard University Press, 1990).

15. Murray Gell-Mann, "First Word" [regular feature], *Omni* (Feb. 1987): 8.

16. See Petr Beckmann, *A Brief History of Pi* (Boulder, Col.: Golem Press, 1971).

17. *McLean v. Arkansas Board of Education,* 529 F. Supp. 1255, 1266 (E.D. Ark. 1982), *aff'd,* 723 F.2d 45 (8th Cir. 1983).

18. Robert Nisbet, *History of the Idea of Progress* (New York: Basic Books, 1980), pp. 128–9. The controversial thesis that Western religion in general, and Puritanism in particular, were largely responsible for the rise of modern science is developed in Robert K. Merton, *Science, Technology and Society in Seventeenth-Century England* (New York: Harper & Row, 1970). For discussion of this thesis, see I. Bernard Cohen, ed., *Puritanism and the Rise of Modern Science: The Merton Thesis* (New Brunswick, N.J.: Rutgers University Press, 1990).

19. For discussions of this proposition, see, for example, Nisbet, *A History of the Idea of Progress;* Richard John Neuhaus, *The Naked Public Square* (Grand Rapids, MI: William B. Eerdmans, 1984).

20. Polling data are discussed in Robert Wuthnow, *The Struggle for America's Soul: Evangelicals, Liberals, and Secularism* (Grand Rapids, MI: William B. Eerdmans, 1989), pp. 148–49.

21. *Scopes v. State,* 154 Tenn. 105, 117–18, 289 S.W. 363, 366 (1927).

22. Garry Wills, *Under God: Religion and American Politics* (New York: Simon & Schuster, 1990).

23. Quoted in Spencer, "Parents Protest."

24. Gell-Mann, "First Word," p. 8.

25. *Edwards v. Aguillard,* 482 U.S. 578 (1987).

26. See, for example, Duane T. Gish, *Evolution? The Fossils Say No!* (San Diego: Creation-Life Publishers, 1979); Henry Morris, ed., *Scientific Creationism* (San Diego: Creation-Life Publishers, 1974). For a more thoughtful critique of evolution by a critic of creationism, see Phillip E. Johnson, *Darwin on Trial* (Washington D.C.: Regnery Gateway, 1991).

27. For discussions of the MACOS battle, see Dorothy Nelkin, *The Creation Controversy: Science or Scripture in the Schools* (New York: Norton, 1982). Wills, *Under God,* pp. 118–20.

28. See Dorothy Nelkin, "The Science-Textbook Controversies," *Scientific American* (April 1976): pp. 92, 97.

29. David C. C. Watson, *The Great Brain Robbery* (Chicago: Moody Press, 1976), p. 46.

30. "The Chicago Statement on Biblical Hermeneutics," reprinted in Donald K. McKim, ed., *A Guide to Contemporary Hermeneutics: Major Trends in Biblical Interpretation* (Grand Rapids, MI: William B. Eerdmans, 1986), pp. 21, 22–25.

31. Loren R. Graham, *Between Science and Values* (New York: Columbia University Press., 1981), pp. 312–14.

32. Harvey Cox, *Religion in the Secular City: Toward a Postmodern Theology* (New York: Simon & Schuster, 1984), p. 54,

33. E. J. Dionne, Jr., *Why Americans Hate Politics* (New York: Simon & Schuster, 1991), p. 214.

34. Gell-Mann, "First Word," p. 8.

35. For summaries of this dispute, see "Book Series Leaves the Wrong 'Impressions,'" *Christianity Today,* Jan. 14, 1991, p. 50; Casey Banas, "'Impressions' Tempest Swirling Again," *Chicago Tribune,* Dec. 2, 1992, Du Page Section, p. 1; Retha Hill, "Frederick Schoolbook Battle Delves Into the Occult," *Washington Post,* June 5, 1992, p. D1

36. Editorial, "Condom Sense," *Commonweal* 118 (1991): 499, 500.

37. Joseph Berger, "Parents v. Condom Plan," *New York Times,* Oct. 1, 1991, p. A1, col. 5.

38. See *Webster v. Lenox School District,* 917 F.2d 1004 (7th Cir. 1990).

39. See, for example, *Mozert v. Hawkins Country Public Schools,* 579 F. Supp. 1051 (E.D. Tenn. 1984), *rev'd* 827 F.2d 1058 (6th Cir. 1987), and *Smith v. Board of School Commissioners of Mobile Country,* 655 F. Supp. 939 (S.D. Ala. 1987), *rev'd,* 827 F.2d 684 (11th Cir. 1987).

40. See *Smith v. Board of School Commissioners of Mobile Country,* 655 F. Supp. 939 (S.D. Ala. 1987), *rev'd,* 827 F.2d 684 (11th Cir. 1987).

41. See Stanley Ingber, "Religion or Ideology: A Needed Clarification of the Religion Clauses," *Stanford Law Review* 41 (1989): 233.

42. Alan Freeman and Betty Mensch, "Religion as Science/Science as Religion: Constitutional Law and the Fundamentalist Challenge," *Tikkun* 2 (1987): 64, 68.

43. See *Ware v. Valley Stream High School,* 75 N.Y.2d 114, 550 N.E.2d 420 (N.Y. 1989).

44. *Wisconsin v. Yoder,* 406 U.S. 205 (1972).

45. *Ware v. Valley Stream High School District, supra,* 75 N.Y.2d at 130, 550 N.E.2d at 430.

46. See, for example, David A. J. Richards, *Toleration and the Constitution* (New York: Oxford University Press, 1986), pp. 150–55. The same concern has motivated some scholars to challenge the right of parents to choose "home schooling"—educating their children themselves. See, for example, Ira C. Lupu, "Home Education, Religious Liberty, and the Separation of Powers," *Boston University Law Review* 67 (1987): 971.

47. *Wisconsin v. Yoder,* 406 U.S. 205, 244–45 (1972) (Douglas, J., dissenting).

48. Kent Greenawalt, *Religious Convictions and Political Choice* (New York: Oxford University Press, 1988), pp. 205–6.

49. Douglas Adams, *The Hitchhiker's Guide to the Galaxy* (New York: Pocket Books, 1981), p. 174.

50. Gary E. Crawford, "Science as an Apologetic Tool for Biblical Literalists," in Marcel C. La Follette, ed., *Creationism, Science, and the Law: The Arkansas Case* (Cambridge: MIT Press, 1983), pp. 104, 111.

CHAPTER 10

1. *Wisconsin v. Yoder,* 406 U.S. 205, 244–45 (1972) (Justice William Douglas, dissenting).

2. *Lee v. Weisman,* 112 S. Ct. 2649 (1992).

3. The first case was *Engel v. Vitale,* 370 U.S. 421 (1962). *Engel,* and the cases that followed, are discussed later in this chapter.

4. For example, a 1987 Gallup Poll indicated that two-thirds of those who were aware of a constitutional amendment to overturn the decisions supported it. See Tamara Henry, "Poll: Americans Hopeful for Education's Future," Proprietary to UPI [NEXIS], Aug. 27, 1987. In a 1992 USA Today/CNN/Gallup survey, 62 percent of voters surveyed said they were more likely to support a candidate who favored such an amendment. Richard Benedetto, "Economy Shakes American Dream," *USA Today,* Jan. 16, 1992, p. 5A.

5. *Lee v. Weisman,* 112 S. Ct. 2649 (1992).

6. *Stone v. Graham,* 449 U.S. 39 (1980).

7. *Roberts v. Madigan,* 921 F.2d 1047 (10th Cir. 1990).

8. Equal Access Act, 98 Stat. 1302, 20 U.S.C. 4071 to 4074 (1988). The constitutionality of the Act was sustained in *Westside Community Board of Education v. Mergens,* 496 U.S. 226 (1990).

9. See, for example, Ruti Teitel, "The Unconstitutionality of Equal Access Policies and Legislation Allowing Organized Student-

Initiated Religious Activities in the Public High Schools: A Proposal for a Unitary First Amendment Analysis," *Hastings Constitutional Law Quarterly* 12 (1985): 529. See also Note, " *Board of Education of Westside Community Schools v. Mergens:* Three 'R's" = Religion = *Mergens," American University Law Review* 41 (1991): 221.

10. *Wallace v. Jaffree,* 472 U.S. 38 (1985).

11. See *Muller v. Allen,* 463 U.S. 388 (1983). Many scholars argue that all state support for religion, even non-preferential assistance, is unconstitutional. The most persuasive statement of this thesis is Leonard W. Levy, *The Establishment Clause: Religion and the First Amendment* (New York: Macmillan, 1986). Levy argues that such assistance violates the original understanding of the Establishment Clause. For a forceful counterargument, that the Founders would have accepted non-preferential assistance of a variety of kinds, see Arlin M. Adams and Charles J. Emmerich, *A Nation Dedicated to Religious Liberty:The Constitutional Heritage of the Religion Clauses* (Philadelphia: University of Pennsylvania Press, 1990).

    I discuss the relevance of the original understanding to analysis of the religion clauses in chapter 6.

12. See Kenneth Eskey, "Poll says 60% would use tax cash for any school," *Houston Chronicle,* Sep. 18, 1992, p. A12 (61 percent support tax money for private and parochial schools, 70 percent support vouchers for private and parochial schools); Ari Goldman, "Religion Notes," *New York Times,* Sept. 19, 1992, p. 9.

13. See, for example, Douglas Laycock, "A Survey of Religious Liberty in the United States," *Ohio State Law Journal* 47 (1986): 409; and Michael W. McConnell, "The Selective Funding Problem: Abortions and Religious Schools," *Harvard Law Review* 104 (1991): 989. On the other side, see Jesse H. Choper, "The Establishment Clause and Aid to Parochial Schools," *California Law Review* 75 (1987): 5.

14. Jonathan Kozol, *Savage Inequalities: Children in America's Schools* (New York: Crown, 1991).

15. The 12 percent figure is from the United States Department of Education Private School Survey for 1991. See Pat Clawson, "Christian Schools Gain as Parents Give Up on Public Education," *Chicago Tribune* [Northwest section], Nov. 24, 1991, p. 1. See also "Flashcard," *New York Times,* April 8, 1990, Sec. 4, p. 8, col. 1 (12 percent figure for 1989).

16. Data discussed in Jean Merl, "Are Private Schools Better?" *Los Angeles Times,* March 29, 1992, p. A1.

17. See, for example, James S. Coleman and Thomas Hoffer, *Public and Private High Schools: The Impact of Communities* (New York: Basic Books, 1987). See also Anthony S. Bryk, *Catholic Schools*

and the Common Good (Cambridge, MA: Harvard University Press, 1993); Sam Allis Boston, "Can Catholic Schools Do It Better?", *Time*, May 27, 1991, p. 48.

18. See Joan Merls, "Are Private Schools Any Better?", *Los Angeles Times*, Mar. 29, 1992, p. A1.

19. Peter J. Daily, "Who Needs Catholic Schools?" *Washington Post*, Sep. 1, 1991, p. C1.

20. See, for example, S. R. Carroll, "Public v. Private: 1 in 7 Kids Pay for School," *Chicago Tribune*, Apr. 12, 1992, Tempo Du Page Section, p. 3. See also Clawson, "Christian Schools Gain."

21. Compare *McCollum v. Board of Education*, 333 U.S. 203 (1948) (instruction on school grounds, program unconstitutional) with *Zorach v. Clauson*, 343 U.S. 306 (1952) (instruction away from school grounds, program constitutional).

22. Compare *Board of Education v. Allen*, 392 U.S. 236 (1968) (okaying textbooks) with *Meek v. Pittenger*, 421 U.S. 349 (1975) (disallowing maps).

23. See *Lemon v. Kurtzman*, 403 U.S. 602 (1971).

24. *Pierce v. Society of Sisters*, 268 U.S. 510 (1925).

25. *Norwood v. Harrison*, 413 U.S. 455 (1973).

26. *Gilmore v. City of Montgomery*, 417 U.S. 556 (1974).

27. *Everson v. Board of Education*, 330 U.S. 1 (1946).

28. See Mark Tushnet, *Red, White, and Blue: A Critical Analysis of Constitutional Law* (Cambridge, MA: Harvard University Press, 1988), pp. 251–52.

29. See, for example, John Dewey, "The School as a Means of Developing a Social Consciousness and Social Ideas in Children," *Journal of Social Forces* 1 (1923): 513. See also Steven C. Rockefeller, *John Dewey: Religious Faith and Democratic Humanism* (New York: Columbia University Press, 1991). I am grateful to the work of Michael McConnell for bringing these sources to my attention.

30. See Melinda Henneberger, "Educators Fight New York Panel on AIDS Pledge," *New York Times*, Aug. 28, 1992, p. A1, col. 1.

31. See Betty Mensch and Alan Freeman, "Losing Faith in Public Schools," *Tikkun* 7 (1992): 31.

32. See Robert Wuthnow, *The Restructuring of American Religion: Society and Faith Since World War II* (Princeton, N.J.: Princeton University Press, 1988), pp. 67–70.

33. Compare Ted G. Jelen and Clyde Wilcox, "Religion in America: The Christian Right in the 1990s," *The Public Perspective* 3 (March–April 1993): 10. In fact, nearly half of Americans (45 percent), and more than half of American women (53 percent), believe that one should abstain from sex *prior to marriage*. See Janny Scott, "The Times Poll: Johnson Case Raises AIDS Concern if

Not Caution," *Los Angeles Times*, Nov. 28, 1991, p. A1. A strong majority (68 percent) also holds that "more sexual freedom" than currently exists would not be a good thing. George Gallup, Jr. & Sarah Jones, *100 Questions and Answers: Religion in America* (Princeton, N.J.: Princeton Religious Research Center, 1989), p. 102.

34. Bernard Murchland, "Civic Education—by Default," *Kettering Review* (Dec. 1990): 13.

35. Ben Wildavsky, "Can You *Not* Teach Morality in Public Schools?" *The Responsive Community* (Winter 1991–92): 46.

36. For citations to studies that have reached this conclusion, see Michael W. McConnell, "The Selective Funding Problem: Abortions and Religious Schools," *Harvard Law Review* 104 (1991): 989, 1012–13 n. 75.

37. Jon Butler, *Awash in a Sea of Faith: Christianizing the American People* (Cambridge, MA: Harvard University Press, 1990), p. 163.

38. Quoted in Jill Rachlin, "Putting God on the Reading List," *U.S. News & World Report*, July 4, 1988, p. 57.

39. *Stone v. Graham*, 449 U.S. 39 (1980).

40. *Edwards v. Aguillard*, 482 U.S. 578 (1987).

41. David Anderson, "Coalition produces guidelines on religion and public schools," United Press International, BC Cycle, June 3, 1988.

42. For news accounts of the move toward a curriculum that values our religious heritage, see, for example, Janet Naylor, "Religion to enter class as culture," *Washington Times*, Sep. 24, 1991, p. A1; Lisa W. Foderaro, "A Special Report: Hot Potatoes," *New York Times* (Education Life Supplement), Aug. 5, 1990, p. 23; Larry Witham, "Teachers study role of religion in history," *Washington Times*, July 27, 1990, p. F5; Don Lattin, "Ethical Illiteracy: Better Teaching of Religion Urged," *San Francisco Chronicle*, Nov. 21, 1989, p. A2.

43. Quoted in "The Textbook Reformation," *Christianity Today*, Sept. 16, 1991, pp. 47, 50.

44. Barbara Vobejda, "Why Censor Religion?" *Washington Post* [Outlook Section], April 19, 1987, p. D1.

CHAPTER 11

1. Jeffrey Stout, *The Flight from Authority: Religion, Morality and the Quest for Autonomy* (South Bend: University of Notre Dame Press, 1981), p. 8.

2. See John Rawls, *A Theory of Justice* (Cambridge, MA: Harvard Uni-

versity Press, 1971). In recent years, Rawls has modified his theory in some respects, in part to take account of the concerns of
critics who have questioned why a person of strong commitments
would ever want to step behind the veil of ignorance. In particular, Rawls has denied the proposition, often attributed to him, that
his theory is designed to yield through rational analysis a single
best set of principles of justice. See, for example, John Rawls,
"Justice as Fairness: Political not Metaphysical," *Philosophy and
Public Affairs* 14 (1985): 223; and John Rawls, "The Idea of an
Overlapping Consensus," *Oxford Journal of Legal Studies* 7 (1987):
1.

3. John Ziman, *Public Knowledge: An Essay Concerning the Social
   Dimensions of Science* (London: Cambridge University Press,
   1968), p. 21.

4. Ludwig Wittgenstein, *On Certainty,* trans. Denis Paul and G. E. M.
   Anscombe (Oxford: Blackwell, 1969), 47e, ¶ 361.

5. Cushing Strout, *The New Heavens and New Earth: Political Religion in America* (New York: Harper & Row, 1974), p. xiv.

6. For a sensitive discussion of the data, see Ronald Dworkin, *Life's
   Dominion: An Argument About Abortion, Euthanasia, and Individual Freedom* (New York: Alfred A. Knopf, 1993). Dworkin concludes that the consistent majority that tells one pollster after
   another that abortion is as bad as murdering a human child does
   not really mean it. I disagree. I do agree, however, that this majority sentiment is not dispositive of the constitutional issues in the
   abortion debate.

7. George Gallup, Jr., and Jim Castelli, *The People's Religion: American Faith in the 90's* (New York: Macmillan, 1989), pp. 168.

8. For example, the 1990 General Social Survey by the University of
   Chicago's National Opinion Research Center found that among
   white Americans, 78 percent believed that black Americans preferred living on welfare, 56 percent thought them violence-prone,
   and 53 percent considered them on average less intelligent than
   whites. According to the same survey, 74 percent thought that
   Hispanic Americans preferred living on welfare, 50 percent
   thought them violence-prone, and 55 percent considered them on
   average less intelligent. "Poll Finds Whites Use Stereotypes," *New
   York Times,* Jan. 10, 1991, p. B10.

9. Roberto Unger, *Knowledge and Politics* (New York: Free Press,
   1975), pp. 41, 157–58.

10. See, generally, Richard A. McCormick, "Theology and Bioethics,"
    Hasting Center Report, March/April 1989, p. 5. For sensitive dis-
    cussions of the background of the refusal of Jehovah's Witnesses
    to accept blood transfusion—discussions that caution against

treating the Witnesses as presumptively incompetent—see Gary R. Anderson, "Medicine vs. Religion: The Case of Jehovah's Witnesses," *Health and Social Work* 8 (Winter 1983): 31; and Gail E. Thurkauf, "Understanding the Beliefs of Jehovah's Witnesses," *Focus on Critical Care* 16 (June 1989): 199. An admittedly unscientific survey of a Jehovah's Witness congregation indicated that a strong majority of respondents would sue a medical provider who administered a transfusion against the patient's will. Larry J. Findley and Paul M. Redstone, "Blood Transfusion in Adult Jehovah's Witnesses: A Case Study of One Congregation," *Archives of Internal Medicine* 142 (March 1982): 606.

11. Not all of the children involved in these cases are young. One court ordered the transfusion of a 17-year-old Jehovah's Witness against her (and her mother's) wishes. See William Grady, "Teen's religion raises life-and-death question," *Chicago Tribune,* March 13, 1989, p. 1. For an argument that the courts have been too deferential to the wishes of Jehovah's Witnesses, and have not adequately considered the competing interests of the medical community, see David H. Bamberger, "*Mercy Hospital v. Jackson:* A Recurring Dilemma for Health Care Providers in the Treatment of Jehovah's Witnesses," *Maryland Law Review* 46 (1987): 514.

12. Walter Murphy, *The Vicar of Christ* (1979), p. 538.

13. Karl Rahner, *Foundations of Christian Faith: An Introduction to the Idea of Christianity,* trans. William V. Dych (New York: Crossroad, 1986), pp. 407–8.

14. William James, *The Varieties of Religious Experience: A Study in Human Nature* (New York: Modern Library, 1929), p. 6.

15. For a thoughtful discussion of Christian theology and wealth distribution, see Stephen Hart, *What Does the Lord Require? How American Christians Think About Economic Justice* (New York: Oxford University Press, 1992).

16. See Alasdair MacIntyre, *After Virtue: A Study in Moral Theory,* 2d ed. (South Bend, Indiana: University of Notre Dame Press, 1984), pp. 49–75. The theologian David Tracy has wittily described the Enlightenment as "a story which seemed to have no central plot." David Tracy, *The Analogical Imagination: Christian Theology and the Culture of Pluralism* (New York: Crossroad, 1981), p. 350.

17. George Gallup, Jr., and Jim Castelli, *The People's Religion: American Faith in the 90's* (New York: Macmillan, 1989), pp. 73, 71.

18. Robert Nisbet, *History of the Idea of Progress* (New York: Basic Books, 1980), p. 353. Useful discussions of the role of Christian theology in the Enlightenment may be found in Jeffrey Stout, *The Flight from Authority: Religion, Morality, and the Quest for Autonomy* (South Bend: University of Notre Dame Press, 1981); Charles

Taylor, *Sources of the Self: The Making of the Modern Identity* (Cambridge, MA: Harvard University Press, 1989); and Tracy, *The Analogical Imagination.*

19. Martin Luther King, "I Have a Dream," in James M. Washington, ed., *A Testament of Hope: The Essential Writings of Martin Luther King, Jr.* (San Francisco: Harper & Row, 1986), p. 36.

20. Martin Luther King, Jr., "Letter from Birmingham City Jail," in ibid., pp. 289, 293.

21. King, "Our God Is Marching On!" in ibid., pp. 227, 229.

22. Quoted in Charles S. McCoy, "The Churches and Protest Movements for Racial Justice," in Robert Lee and Martin E. Marty, eds., *Religion and Social Conflict* (New York: Oxford University Press, 1964), p. 37, 47.

23. For material on the role of religious groups in the passage of the Civil Rights Act, including the Russell quote, see A. James Reichley, *Religion in American Public Life* (Washington, D.C.: The Brookings Institution, 1985), pp. 246–50.

24. Roach, "War of Words on Abortion," *Origins* 20 (1990): 88, 89, quoted in Michael Perry, *Love and Power,* p. 136.

25. Richard Rorty, *Consequences of Pragmatism* (Minneapolis: University of Minnesota Press, 1982), p. 33.

26. See Kent Greenawalt, *Religious Convictions and Political Choice* (New York: Oxford University Press, 1988); Robert Audi, "The Separation of Church and State and the Obligations of Citizenship," *Philosophy and Public Affairs* 18 (1989): 259.

27. See John Rawls, *A Theory of Justice* (Cambridge, MA: Harvard University Press, 1971); Bruce Ackerman, *Social Justice in the Liberal State* (New Haven: Yale University Press, 1980).

28. For different analyses, both ending up with this conclusion, see Roger Finke and Rodney Stark, *The Churching of America, 1776–1990* (New Brunswick, NJ: Rutgers University Press, 1992), and Robert Wuthnow, *The Restructuring of American Religion,* (Princeton, NJ: Princeton University Press, 1988).

29. Despite the extravagant claims of such sex researchers as Kinsey and Hite, more scientific data collected by the General Social Survey of the University of Chicago's National Opinion Research Center indicates that 79 percent of married men and 89 percent of married women have remained faithful to their spouses throughout the marriage. See Jeff Lyons, "Keeping score: A University of Chicago research team is exploring sexual America," *Chicago Tribune* (Magazine Section), Nov. 29, 1992, p. 14. In fact, nearly half of Americans continue to believe that *pre-marital* sex is wrong; and more than half of American women think so. George Gallup, Jr., and Sarah Jones, *100 Questions and Answers: Religion in*

America (Princeton, NJ: Princeton Religious Research Center, 1989), pp. 120–21 (1987 data).

30. See Peter L. Berger, *The Noise of Solemn Assemblies* (New York: Doubleday, 1961), and *Facing Up to Modernity: Excursions in Society, Politics and Religion* (New York: Basic Books, 1977).

CHAPTER 12

1. *United States v. The Amistad,* 40 U.S. (15 Pet.) 518, 593 (1841).
2. *Roe v. Wade* 410 U.S. 113 (1973).
3. See Roger Rosenblatt, *Life Itself: Abortion in the American Mind* (New York: Random House, 1992), p. 53. For a thoughtful discussion of abortion that presupposes the humanity of the fetus, see also Frances Myrna Kamm, *Creation and Abortion: A Study in Moral and Legal Philosophy* (New York: Oxford University Press, 1992). For a historical survey of cultural attitudes, see G. R. Dunstan, ed., *The Human Embryo: Aristotle and the Arabic and European Traditions* (Exeter, Engl.: University of Exeter Press, 1990).
4. Justice John Paul Stevens, one of the wisest members of the Supreme Court, took this misstep in his separate opinion in *Webster v. Reproductive Health Services,* 492 U.S. 490 (1989). For a similar argument by a legal philosopher, see David A. J. Richards, *Toleration and the Constitution* (New York: Oxford University Press, 1986), pp. 263–64. This was formerly the view of Harvard law professor Laurence Tribe as well. See Laurence Tribe, "The Supreme Court, 1972 Term—Foreword: Toward a Model of Roles in the Due Process of Life and Law," *Harvard Law Review* 87 (1973): 1. Subsequently, he decided, correctly, that his previous view gave "too little weight to allowing religious groups freely to express their convictions in the political process." Laurence Tribe, *American Constitutional Law,* 2d ed. (Mineola, NY: Foundation Press, 198), 1350.
5. See, for example, James M. Wall, "In the Face of Death: Rights, Choices and Beliefs," *Christian Century,* Aug. 21, 1991; Derek Humphry, *Final Exit* (Eugene, OR: Hemlock Society, 1991).
6. Margaret Kelp, Letter to the Editor, *Christian Century,* Oct. 16, 1991, p. 949.
7. Edwin A. Lane, Letter to the Editor, ibid., p. 950.
8. Quoted in Henry Fehren, "Lord of Mercy and Compassion," *U.S. Catholic,* Aug. 1990, p. 39.
9. John J. Mitchell, Jr., "Knowing When to Stop: Experience, Death, & Catholic Wisdom," *Commonweal,* May 6, 1988, p. 271.

10. *Cruzan v. Director, Missouri Department of Health,* 497 U.S. 261 (1990).

11. Michael Kinsley, "To Be or Not to Be," *New Republic,* Nov. 27, 1989, p. 6.

12. 497 U.S. at 345, 350 (Justice John Paul Stevens, dissenting).

13. For a partial account, see James E. Wood, Jr., E. Bruce Thompson, and Robert T. Miller, *Church and State in Scripture History and Constitutional Law* (Waco, TX: Baylor University Press, 1958).

14. Quoted in Tamar Lewin, "Nancy Cruzan Dies, Outlived by a Debate over the Right to Die," *New York Times,* Dec. 27, 1990, p. A1.

15. Quoted in Don J. DeBenedictis, "Cruzan's Death Doesn't Still Debate," *American Bar Association Journal* (March 1991): 26.

16. Fred Bruning, "The Menace of Morality Crusaders," *MacClean's,* Jan. 21, 1991.

17. See Charlotte K. Goldberg, "Choosing Life after Death: Respecting Religious Beliefs and Moral Convictions in Near Death Decisions," *Syracuse Law Review* 39 (1988): 1197.

18. For a discussion of these and related questions, see Note, "Incubating for the State: The Precarious Autonomy of Persistently Vegetative and Brain-Dead Pregnant Women," *Georgia Law Review* 22 (1988): 1103.

19. See Beth Brandon, "Anencephalic Infants as Organ Donors: A Question of Life or Death," *Case Western Reserve Law Review* 40 (1989–1990): 781.

20. Lewis Thomas, "The Problem of Dementia," in *Late Night Thoughts on Listening to Mahler's Ninth Symphony* (New York: Viking, 1983), pp. 120–21.

21. See Arthur Barsky, *Worried Sick: Our Troubled Quest for Wellness* (New York: Little, Brown, 1988).

22. "It's Over, Debbie," *Journal of the American Medical Association,* Jan. 8, 1988, p. 272.

23. Harold Y. Vanderpool, Letter to the Editor, *Journal of the American Medical Association,* Apr. 8, 1988, p. 2094.

24. Peter A. Singer, Letter to the Editor, ibid., p. 2096.

25. Porter Storey, Letter to the Editor, ibid., p. 2095.

26. Willard Gaylin, Leon R. Kass, Edmund D. Pellegrino, and Mark Siegler, "Doctors Must Not Kill," ibid., p. 2139.

27. Bernadine Z. Paulshock, Letter to the Editor, ibid., p. 2094.

28. Eileen Moran, Letter to the Editor, ibid., p. 2098.

29. Charles B. Clark, Letter to the Editor, ibid., p. 2095.

30. Compare William D. Fiorini, Letter to the Editor, ibid., p. 2098.

31. Stephanie B. Goldberg, "Assisted Suicide Resolution Defeated," *American Bar Association Journal,* Apr. 1992, p. 107.

32. See Humphry, *Final Exit* pp. 142–43. The Hemlock Society publishes a newsletter, the *Hemlock Quarterly,* that discusses all of these issues in detail.

33. Arthur W. Frank, "Not in Pain, but Still Suffering," *Christian Century,* Oct. 7, 1992, p. 860.

34. Lawrence J. Schneiderman, "Euthanasia: Can We Keep It a Special Case?" *The Humanist* (May–June 1990): 15.

35. Ibid., p. 15.

36. Frank, "Not in Pain," pp. 861–62.

37. Schneiderman, "Euthanasia," p. 47.

38. For a criticism of the contemporary attitude that possession of a right means that exercising it is not immoral, see Mary Ann Glendon, *Rights Talk: The Impoverishment of Political Discourse* (New York: Free Press, 1991). For a suggestion, in the particular case of abortion, that the United States should follow the example of some Western European countries by permitting abortion but discouraging it, see Roger Rosenblatt, *Life Itself,* and Mary Ann Glendon, *Abortion and Divorce in Western Law* (Cambridge, MA: Harvard University Press, 1987). Glendon's Harvard Law School colleague Laurence Tribe has responded to this proposal by arguing that there is no point to having laws that aim merely at moral suasion rather than coercive effect. Laurence H. Tribe, *Abortion: The Clash of Absolutes* (New York: Norton, 1990), pp. 73–76.

39. Karl Rahner, *Foundations of Christian Faith,* trans. William Van Dych (New York: Crossroad, 1986), p. 404.

40. See Barbara Brack, "Rational Suicide: My Mother's Story," *Christian Century,* Nov. 13, 1991, p. 1054.

41. Fehren, "Lord of Mercy," pp. 40.

42. *Roe v. Wade,* 410 U.S. 113 (1973).

43. Stephen Galebach, "A Human Life Statute," *Human Life Review* 7 (1981): 3.

44. For a discussion of the procedural history of the Human Life Bill, as well as critical assessment of the constitutional arguments on both sides, see Stephen L. Carter, "The *Morgan* 'Power' and the Forced Reconsideration of Constitutional Decisions," *University of Chicago Law Review* 53 (1986): 819.

45. John Hart Ely, "The Wages of Crying Wolf: A Comment on *Roe v. Wade,*" *Yale Law Journal* 82 (1973): 920.

46. Robert Burt, "Constitutional Law and the Teaching of the Parables," *Yale Law Journal* 93 (1984): 455, 487–88 n. 106; Robert Burt, "The Constitution of the Family," *Supreme Court Review* (1979): 329, 371–73.

47. Guido Calabresi, *Ideals, Beliefs, Attitudes, and the Law* (Syracuse, NY: Syracuse University Press, 1985), pp. 95–97.

48. Michael Perry, *Morality, Politics, and Law* (New York: Oxford University Press, 1988), p. 175.

49. See "Ginsburg Laments *Roe*'s lack of Restraint," *Legal Times,* April 5, 1993, p. 10. For a powerful argument about the desirability of compromise, one that is quite sympathetic to the religious impulse in the abortion debate, see Elizabeth Mensch and Alan Freeman, *The Politics of Virtue: Is Abortion Debatable?* (Durham, N.C.: Duke University Press, 1993).

50. *Roe v. Wade,* pp. 156–157.

51. Pro-choice advocates argue that the number of abortions did not substantially after *Roe,* but that claim is quite shaky. Assertions that the nation averaged one million (mostly illegal) abortions yearly in the decade before *Roe* have practically been refuted; the more accurate number appears to be something less then 200,000 and possibly less than 100,000. See the sources cited in Samuel W. Calhoun and Andrea E. Sexton, "Is It Possible to Take Both Fetal Life and Women Seriously?" *Washington and Lee Law Review* 49 (1992): 437. On the complexities of trying to sort out the numbers, see Celeste Michelle Condit, *Decoding Abortion Rhetoric: Communicating Social Change* (Urbana: University of Illinois Press, 1990), pp. 20, 37n4.

52. For scholarly defenses of the abortion right on grounds other than privacy, see, for example, Laurence Tribe, *American Constitutional Law,* 2d ed. (Mineola, N.Y.: Foundation Press, 1988), pp. 1350 ff; Sylvia Law, "Rethinking Sex and the Constitution," *University of Pennsylvania Law Review* 132 (1984): 955; Donald Regan, "Rewriting *Roe v. Wade,*" *Michigan Law Review* 77 (1979): 1569; Judith Jarvis Thompson, "A Defense of Abortion," *Philosophy and Public Affairs* 1 (1971): 47. A more recent trend has been the defense of abortion rights as an exercise of religious freedom. See, for example, Ronald Dworkin, *Life's Dominion: An Argument About Abortion, Euthansia, and Individual Freedom* (New York: Alfred A. Knopf, 1993).

53. See Stephen L. Carter, "Abortion, Absolutism, and Compromise," *Yale Law Journal* 100 (1991): 2747. For a detailed discussion of abortion and sex discrimination, see Law, "Rethinking Sex," p. 955.

54. 492 U.S. 490 (1989).

55. Laurence H. Tribe, *Abortion,* p. 116.

56. *Harris v. McRae,* 448 U.S. 297 (1980).

57. For a contemporary philosopher's thoughtful discussion of the harm principle, see Joel Feinberg, *Harm to Others* (New York: Oxford University Press, 1984). Feinberg, unlike Mill, also believes that the government can sometimes regulate on the ground of

offensiveness rather than harm. See Joel Feinberg, *Offense to Others* (New York: Oxford University Press, 1985).

58. Judith Jarvis Thompson, *The Realm of Rights* (Cambridge, MA: Harvard University Press, 1990), p. 289.

59. For a detailed discussion of the work in this area, see Randall Kennedy, "*McCleskey v. Kemp:* Race, Capital Punishment, and the Supreme Court," *Harvard Law Review* 101 (1988): 1388.

60. See *McCleskey v. Kemp,* 481 U.S. 279 (1987). My views on the case are presented in detail in Stephen L. Carter, "When Victims Happen to Be Black," *Yale Law Journal* 97 (1988): 420.

61. The moratorium on capital punishment began when the Supreme Court decided *Furman v. Georgia,* 408 U.S. 238 (1972), and ended after the Court's decision in *Gregg v. Georgia,* 428 U.S. 153 (1976).

62. Paul Brest, "The Misconceived Quest for the Original Understanding," *Boston University Law Review* 60 (1980): 204, 220–21 (footnotes omitted). The bracketed word "judge" in the quote replaces Brest's word "interpreter" in order to clarify his meaning for the reader.

63. Some 71 percent of Americans believe in life after death, a number that, unlike many measure of religious devotion, does not show a significant decrease as education level increases. George Gallup, Jr., and Jim Castelli, *The People's Religion: American Faith in the 90's* (New York: Macmillan, 1989), pp. 58–59.

64. Andrew M. Greeley, *Religious Change in America* (Cambridge: Harvard University Press, 1989), pp. 88–89. In fact, support for capital punishment increased rapidly between the 1970s and the 1980s, also across denominational lines.

CHAPTER 13

1. Porteous quoted in Judy Lundstrom Thomas, "Religious Right Infiltrates GOP," *New Haven Register,* Sept. 27, 1992, p. A11. Thomas's syndicated article was distributed by Knight-Ridder Newspapers.

2. Quoted in ibid.

3. Quoted in E. J. Dionne, *Why Americans Hate Politics* (New York: Simon & Schuster, 1991), p. 211.

4. Quoted in Thomas, "Religious Right Infiltrates GOP."

5. 494 U.S. 872 (1990).

6. 485 U.S. 439 (1988).

7. See Jonathan Groner, "Prison Bureau Hits Religious-Freedom Bill," *Legal Times,* March 29, 1993, p. 1. The *Legal Times* story, it should be noted, was based on an internal memorandum, not intended

by the Bureau for circulation to the Congress. See "Correction," *Legal Times,* April 5, 1993, p. 1.

8. In particular, the courts have repeatedly rejected claims of prisoners who need accommodations in order to practice Islam. See, for example, *O'Lone v. Estate of Shabazz,* 482 U.S. 342 (1987).

9. See Andrei Sakharov, *Memoirs,* trans. Richard Lourie (New York: Alfred A. Knopf, 1990), pp. 493–95. See also ibid., p. 337: "Religious liberty is an important part of the human rights struggle in a totalitarian state." Ackerman's thoughtful book is *Social Justice in the Liberal State* (New Haven: Yale University Press, 1980).

10. Charles S. McCoy, "The Churches and Protest Movements for Racial Justice," in Robert Lee and Martin E. Marty, eds., *Religion and Social Conflict* (New York: Oxford University Press, 1964), p. 37, 39.

11. See Forrest G. Wood, *The Arrogance of Faith: Christianity and Race in America from the Colonial Era to the Twentieth Century* (New York: Alfred A. Knopf, 1990).

12. David F. Swenson, "The Transforming Power of Otherworldliness," in E. D. Klemke, ed., *The Meaning of Life* (New York: Oxford University Press, 1981), pp. 31, 37 (essay originally published in 1949).

INDEX